PHOTOSHOP
FOR DIGITAL VIDEO

PHOTOSHOP
FOR DIGITAL VIDEO

Creative Solutions for Professional Results

Mike Gondek

Archie Cocke

ELSEVIER

AMSTERDAM • BOSTON • HEIDELBERG • LONDON
NEW YORK • OXFORD • PARIS • SAN DIEGO
SAN FRANCISCO • SINGAPORE • SYDNEY • TOKYO

Focal Press is an imprint of Elsevier

Focal Press is an imprint of Elsevier

200 Wheeler Road, Burlington, MA 01803, USA

Linacre House, Jordan Hill, Oxford OX2 8DP, UK

 Recognizing the importance of preserving what has been written, Elsevier prints its books on acid-free paper whenever possible.

Library of Congress Cataloging-in-Publication Data
Application Submitted.

British Library Cataloguing-in-Publication Data

A catalogue record for this book is available from the British Library.
ISBN: 0240806336

For information on all Focal Press publications

visit our website at www.focalpress.com

04   05   06   07   08   09   10   9   8   7   6   5   4   3   2   1

Printed in China

CONTENTS

v

PREFACE

USING THIS BOOK

Who is this book for

This book focuses on creative & technical issues dealing with using Photoshop CS for video editing, beyond the Adobe manual. You will find useful new techniques in this book, whether you are a beginning or advanced Photoshop user. The first section prepares you to use the core Photoshop tools and commands, and is a stepping stone to the advanced techniques in the final chapters. You can skip around, and use the index or table of contents to help you find a more detailed explanation. Learn to work smarter and faster and using new techniques & tools to open up new creative possibilities for you.

You will find issues a video editor encounters and many of these issues apply to all Photoshop Users. Every Photoshop user, from beginner to advanced, will learn masking techniques which are important timeless material for anyone in web, video or print. Photoshop for Video is written for anyone who uses Photoshop!

COLOR

Bold colored text will assist you in navigating and using this book. This is helpful for instructors, students and anyone reading this book. With technical training books your eyes go back and forth from computer monitor to book. We learned from other authors, and hope they will use this feature in their books.

Blue Bold Type

Examples:

Edit >> Preferences >> File Browser [Photoshop >> Preferences >> File Browser]

Hit (**V**) to change to the move tool.

Blue type prompts you to use a keyboard shortcuts or menu command. The PC shortcut is first, followed by the Mac shortcut in brackets. Single letter keyboard shortcut are surrounded it by parenthesis to help make it more visible. The brackets are used so nobody will feel their platform was not represented in this book, and to more users become cross platform. Usually menu commands are in the same place on Mac or PC so we do not repeat ourselves in that instance (except for locating the preferences so we listed that one above). Keyboard shortcuts are faster to use than menu commands. In many cases we show you the menu command instead so you will know what action you invoked. We use menu commands in the book to help you follow the examples, but please use keyboard shortcuts when you know them.

Red Bold Type

Content on DVD

Example: Open **Chapter #/Filename.psd.**

The red type signals you to open a file which comes from the Photoshop for Video DVD. Slashes are used to separate names of folders, and help you navigate to their location quickly. This naming technique originally came from Unix, and is used in HTML and browsing the web. The name of the file will be followed by a period and a 3 letter filename extension. Red type may also tell you to load a setting file such as curves, but always means that you will be utilizing a file from the DVD.

We also use red on screenshots to point out areas of interest, or a position on an image you are to apply a tool.

DVD

Chapters

You may wish to copy the chapter folders from the DVD to your hard drive. This is recommended if you plan to follow along interactively and have enough free hard disk space. Files are in various file formats as we wish for you to find out the benefits some file formats have over others. We also use a naming convention which describes the image, and has a number afterwards. The higher the number, the closer you are to the final image. This allows you to skip parts if you are an advanced user, or to help you get back on track if you having difficulty.

Demos

Software from vendors is always in a folder with the name of the product, and inside will be 2 folders so you can choose Mac or PC. We included demos of a few choice manufacturers on the disk that you should know about. We want the focus of this to book to be on learning new techniques that will change the way you work with Photoshop.

MAC OR PC

Does not matter which platform you use, and those who work on both show the signs of craftsmanship needed to work with video. Most video design awards are won by people who work on both platforms. For being 2 different operating systems, Photoshop works similarily on Mac or PC.

Contextual Menus – You get this very useful set of menus by right clicking [**Ctrl clicking**]. We find this feature extremely useful because it is quicker than pulling down a menu or pressing keys on your keyboard. Apple does not ship a 2 button mouse, but we recommend you buy one.

Right Click [**Ctrl Command click**] on an open Photoshop file and a contextual menu shows the layer names underneath the mouse click, which you can choose to go to that layer. Enable rulers using **Ctrl R** [**Command R**], and then **Right Click** [**Ctrl Command click**] the ruler to change measurement units—we recommend using pixels for video.

Screenshots – Both Mac & PC screenshots are used throughout the book, it does not mean anything and after becoming a cross-platform person you will not even notice. The main difference between Mac & PC windows or palettes is the color, but they mostly have the same features of maximize, minimize, hide and close.

The Mac has a feature where you can command click on a finder window, and it shows you the hierarchy of where the file is located on your drive. You could

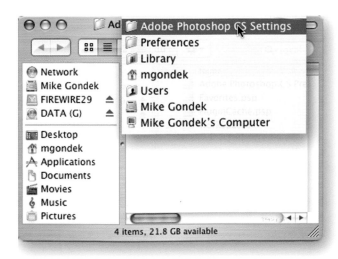

Mac contextual menu for folder navigating

release the mouse on a location you would like to navigate to. The windows explorer shows this location in the address using slashes to separate folders. You can quickly get to a location by just deleting letters after a slash and hitting return to change the window to that location.

On the PC you can right click a Photoshop file window name and get options for page setup, image size, canvas size and duplicate.

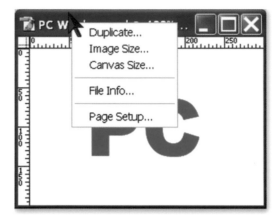

On both platforms when you have rulers enabled, you can right click on the rulers, and switch on the fly to different units measurements. For video, pixels is the recommended units to switch to. Photoshop will keep using pixels for the ruler units until you change to something else.

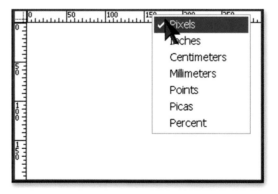

Modifier Keys – These keys are important to learning Photoshop as a professional. The differences in modifier keys between both platforms are:

PC	Ctrl	Alt	Right Click
Mac	Command	Option	Ctrl Click

Hold down all modifier keys prior to the final alphanumeric key which determines which keyboard command will be invoked. **Shift Ctrl** > makes selected type larger. The > is not a modifier key but the final stroke telling Photoshop to invoke a keyboard command.

ABOUT THE AUTHORS

Mike Gondek

An Adobe Certified Expert, first introduced to Photoshop in the form of Barneyscan Pro. Mike is a software applications trainer, graphics designer and an independent computer graphics specialist. Since 1985, he has been a Typesetter, Photo Retoucher, Color Specialist, Video Editor, Advertising Manager, Web Designer and Art Director.

As Creative Technologies Manager for a major Advertising Agency, Mike managed a Technology Research Lab and Creative Applications Phone Support. Mike also was responsible for beta testing, training and upgrading the creative software & hardware technology.

Mike worked on most major blue chip accounts including Kraft, Frito Lay, McDonalds, Amoco, Oldsmobile, Marlboro, Miller Brewing, Seagrams and has done image analysis for the US NAVY. He is also a forum leader at the www.Creativecow.net forum which is supported by the world's leading experts in video editing applications. For more information on Mike, visit his website at www.mikegondek.com.

Archie Cocke

Archie is the Chief Avid Editor for Weigel Broadcasting in Chicago, Illinois – **www.wciu.com**

And owner of iVIEW Media Services in Orland Park, Illinois – **www.iviewmediaservices.com**. Holding a Bachelor of Arts in Media Communication and a Master of Arts in Communication and Training, Archie has edited well over 150 commercials using Avid, After Effects, and of course, Photoshop. Astaunch supporter of the digital revolution, Archie has been called upon to perform the tasks of camera, audio, lighting, directing, switching, editing, and even a little bit of acting.

Archie would like to dedicate this book to Paul Schranz. Paul is a decsiple of Ansel Adams and is the man responsible for expanding Archie's horizons to include Photoshop in video projects. Paul was a mentor and friend during his higher learning.

The Authors would like to thank:

Focal Press, Adobe, Elinor Actipis, Jon Okerstrom, Home Run Inn Pizza, Visual Symbols, Cate Barr, Olivia Berdysz, George Blaise, Natalie & Bruce Bonk, Angelique Burgess, Jeff Chong, Heather Cocke, Malcolm Conyers, Gregg Deacon, John Duda, Dusty, Reneé Genova, Jeff Hinkle, Imran Mirza, Bob Karp, Christopher Kemnic, Rich Koz, Mark Las, Loki, Edie McRee, Kenny McReynolds, Christine Monahan, Peder Norrby, Renee Paczesny, Justin Palmeiro, Erika Pollard, Jennie Pozen, Rob Potter, Amedeo Rosa, Johnny Sarena, Matt & Carole Schrock, Jan Shimek, Karl Sims, Sally Shireman, Weigel Broadcasting, Fred Weintraub, Jessica Yach,

SECTION I

KNOWING PHOTOSHOP

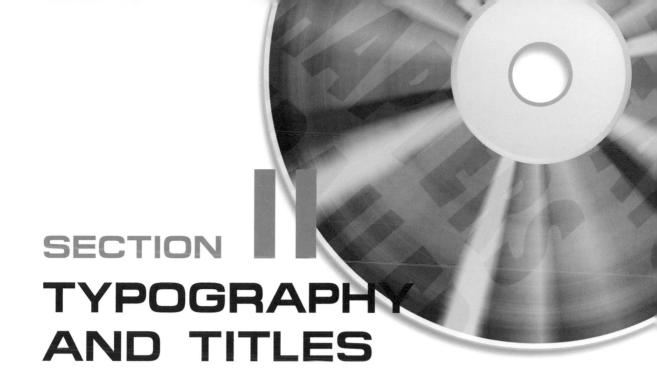

SECTION II
TYPOGRAPHY AND TITLES

SECTION III
MASKING AND TRANSFORMATIONS

SECTION IV
BETTER IMAGES

SECTION **V**

CREATIVE PROJECTS

SECTION VI
FINAL TIPS

SECTION I

KNOWING
PHOTOSHOP

1

STARTUP KIT

PREFERENCES

To reset preferences in Photoshop, depress and hold down three keys immediately after you start the program. Position your fingers over **Shift Ctrl Alt [Shift Option Command],** click to boot the application, and then depress the three keys. You will be asked whether you want to **delete your prefs** for Photoshop; choose **Yes**, so we all have the same default Adobe prefs. You will next be asked if you wish to **customize your color settings**. This is very important for how your monitor displays color, but we will configure this in the next chapter. For now, choose **No**.

Afer booting you will see the Photoshop CS welcome screen. New users of Photoshop might find the welcome window useful and want to see it each time they boot. Most Photoshop users find it annoying. To discontinue it, remove the checkmark in the box for showing this dialog at startup that appear at the bottom of the screen. Should you change your mind in the future it is easily restored by choosing **Ctrl K** [**Command K**] and clicking the **Reset All Warning Dialogs**. Most users never choose, to reset the warnings, but they are very good for new Photoshop users.

If you closed the box, you can also find it at **Edit** >> **Preferences** >> **General** [**Photoshop** >> **Preferences** >> **General**].

General

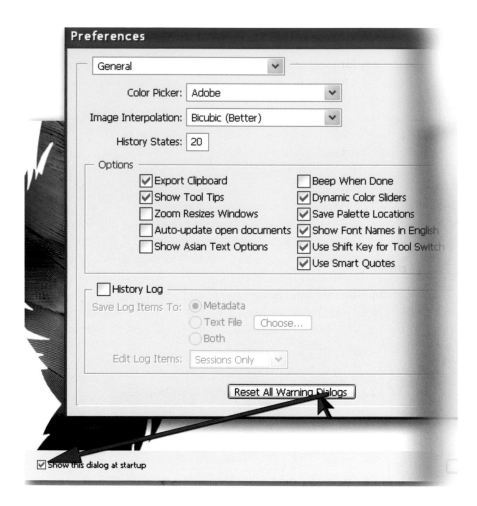

History States indicates the number of times you can use undo. Every brush stroke is one history state, and they can go fast if you don't pay attention. The default is set to 20, which is a good amount. In video the size of the files is generally smaller; you can set this amount higher if you desire to have more levels of undo. In Photoshop CS you do not have three options for setting undo, as you did in version 7 for stepping backward. The default keyboard shortcut is **Alt Ctrl Z** [**Option Command Z**], and you can change this using **Edit** >> **Keyboard Shortcuts** >> **Edit.** Adobe Image Ready, which comes with Photoshop, still prescribes to the version 7 method of having general preferences which allow you to additionally choose **Ctrl Y** [**Command Y**] for the undo key.

Change Zoom Resizes Windows is useful when you **enable it.** If enabled, when zooming using the keyboard shortcuts of **Ctrl +** [**Command +**], the window will also resize along with the image. With this disabled, your image will get cropped if you zoom in a window, unless you additionally hold down **Alt** [**Option**].

Save Palette Locations will remember the location of the palettes since the last time you quit Photoshop. Occasionally, a palette gets moved off screen and later disappears. You can fix this by resetting the preferences, as shown in the beginning of this chapter.

Use of **Shift Key** for tool switch is very useful, as you can cycle between the different swatches of a tool in the tool palette. For example, depress **Shift** (**U**) and watch the rectangle tool change into the rounded rectangle tool, into the ellipse tool, or cycle between all six swatches of that tool. **Smart Quotes** will automatically change your straight quotes to "curly" 69-shaped quotes. Click the next box to advance to the next dialog box for file handling.

File Handling

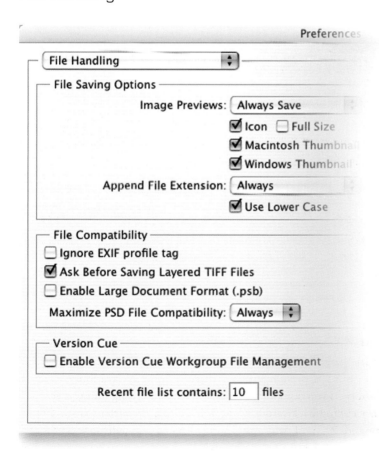

Make sure **Image Previews** are set to **Always Save**. In video, the files are small and hunting down images later can be a task. The Mac has more detailed options for Image Previews, but they basically will save an image used by the icon and a larger preview image for digital asset management software to use such as Extensis portfolio. If you choose **Never Save**, then you will not get a thumbnail in Photoshop document (PSD) format. Saving to TIF or PNG though, you will get a thumbnail automatically because it is part of the file format.

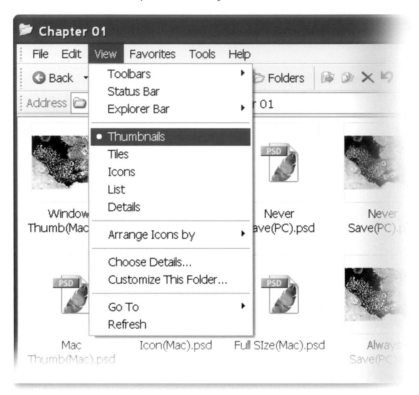

Content on DVD

Open the **Chapter 01** folder and change your view options to **Thumbnails** [**Icons**]. You will see two files inside the folder have images for icons on the PC, and three have them on the Mac. The same file was saved on both PC and Mac in all the major possibilities. The names of the files will help you make sense of this; also do a **view by Details** [**List**] and take a look at the file sizes.

	PC (Thumbnails View)	Mac (Icons View)
Icon(Mac).psd	NO Only shows icon on Mac	YES Because Mac option was on
Never Save(PC).tif	YES TIF always has icon	YES TIF always has icon
Never Save(PC).png	Yes PNG always has icon	Yes PNG always has icon
Always Save(PC).psd	NO Because PSD format	NO Because PSD format

If you wish to see thumbnails in Mac OS X, you must turn them on. In the finder, hit [**Command J**] to get the view options for the Mac OS X finder. Turn on **Show Icon Preview**, and you can make your thumbnail larger.

On the PC you will see the invisible Mac resource fork files which have a "._" prior to the name, and the icon is semi-transparent. The purpose of the resource fork is to store the creator of the file so that the Mac knows which program should open the file, along with thumbnails. These resource forks are annoying to the PC user, because they clutter up your directory. On the PC it is easy to see that the Mac data file has the larger file size at 124 K, because the bitmapped data is in there.

Error Message you do not want to see.

You will also want to turn on **Maximize PSD file compatibility**. When saving a Photoshop document, this takes all the layers and merges them into an extra layer composite. This makes the file larger, taking more time to save, but gives you the ability to place a composite of a layered file in a video editor such as Adobe After Effects. Photo Retouchers working with 300+ MB images would turn this option off so that their files save more quickly. We are working in video, and definitely want to maximize PSD file compatibility, or else an error message may appear in your video editing application. On the Mac, you can change the size of your icon preview by choosing View >> View Options, from the finder.

Important Mac view options.

Display & Cursors

Although it looks nice, seeing your individual channels in color is not as useful as seeing them in a tone of black. **Use Pixel Doubling** is another feature someone working in high resolution might utilize to speed up their machine. It basically uses a reduced resolution version of data you are working on that is displayed by your graphics card. When the computer has a chance, it will update the preview to full resolution. Leave this feature off.

You most definitely want your painting cursor to be set to Brush Size. This gives you a live preview of the brush tip size rather than a crosshair. I would also leave other cursors to standard so you can see what tool you are in. There are occasions

when you will want crosshairs to be precise in sampling or painting a pixel, and that is easily done by pressing the Caps Lock key.

Transparency & Gamut

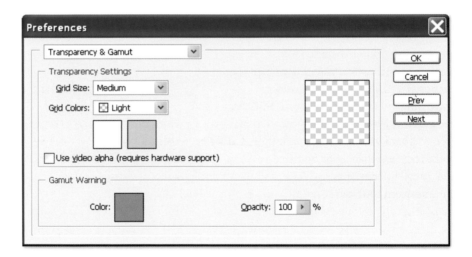

Transparency & Gamut show transparency. Photoshop by default uses a checkerboard grid of gray and white squares. This is very useful for video as we animate layers and often have to remove backgrounds. **Use video alpha** is only for the few very special one in a million people who have a graphic card which can accept Photoshop transparency information.

Units & Rulers
You are not likely to need the Units & Rulers preferences, because you can change your units of measurement by right clicking on the ruler of an open document. If designing a printed piece you will want to right click on the ruler of an open

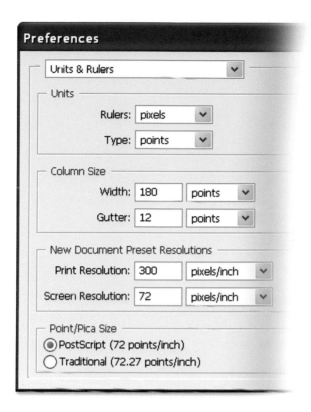

document and switch to inches or centimeters. You may also occasionally want to change your rulers to show the percentage of a document if you are working on something which needs to be sliced up symmetrically. Type is the unit of measurement used for typefaces, and luckily the world is accustomed to using the typographer's measurement of points. Changing type units to pixels is not very useful, because the size of a letter is from the ascender to the descender. Every font also has a different amount of white space built into the font. It is quicker to use the transform tool and scale the type, to get it to fit a certain height or width. The transform tool in Photoshop actually creates the bounding box from the pixels of the type. If the type you set was all caps, then the transform bounding box would surround the cap height of the text.

The Column Size is best left alone, unless you plan to crop images using image or canvas size. It is used by page layout programs. Leave the rest of the settings alone; though 72.27 is the true measurement of points to an inch; everybody uses the rounded number of 72.

Guides, Grid & Slices

You can change your guide color from the default cyan if you prefer something that shows better or if you just prefer to see a dotted line rather than the default solid. The grid can be quite useful, especially since now Photoshop CS has

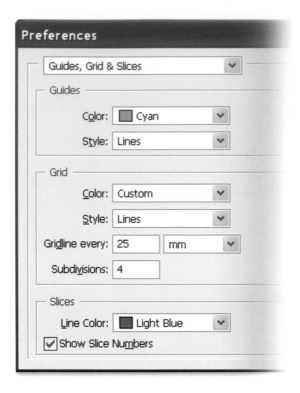

non-square pixels. Slices are used for web, and we now have an **export layers to files** script, which saves an individual file for each layer of your document.

Plug-Ins & Scratch Disks

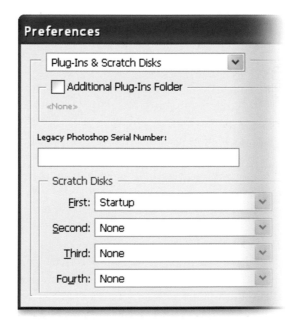

You may desire to have Photoshop CS try utilizing plug-ins from another program. Do not do this unless you are 100% sure that you want Photoshop to use that plug-in. Some people might try pointing it to your old Photoshop 7 plug-ins folder, but most will receive an error on restarting. You must also input the legacy Photoshop serial number here for older plug-ins which might require it. There are many plug-ins to extend Photoshop, but so far we found none that need this. If you try to select the After Effects plug-ins folder, when you save, you will get two different options for many file formats and possibly save in a flattened TIF accidentally.

A Scratch Disk is a hard disk in which Photoshop temporarily stores information used in various operations such as "undos." The default is set to the drive with the operating system. A much better choice to use is a raid drive and a dedicated drive for scratch disk space. Your video editing applications can also use this drive as a scratch disk. A dedicated drive will not get fragmented, as the data is removed once you quit your applications. If you do not have a dedicated raid drive, then choose a local drive with the largest amount of free space.

File Browser

Since we are working in video, set your **Do Not Process Files Larger than** to something such as 10 MB. This will skip generating new previews for files that are larger than the amount you specified. Now you might get confused after you change this and think, "Why do I still have previews for these files that are over 10 MB?" Well, if you have ever generated them before, Photoshop remembers this. Choose **Filebrowser >> File >> Purge cache** to clean out your cache and free up disk space if you need. You can also turn off high quality previews to save disk space, and most importantly, your previews will generate quicker. You can also enable **Render Vector Files**, which will generate previews for Adobe Illustrator and eps.

It will not work for freehand fh or Corel Draw cdr files, so a more proper name would be Render Illustrator Files.

TOOLS

When not using a tool that allows setting type (text tool, note tool), you can use keyboard shortcuts to select another tool. To go inside individual tools of that set and change to another version, hold down Shift and type that same letter. This is very useful for example on the dodge burn saturation tool. You can press **Shift (U)** on your keyboard and switch between the tools when fixing the color on an image. Another useful combination is to switch between (**j**) and (**s**) when you are repairing an image to go between the Clone Stamp Tool and the Healing Brush. The tools look the same between Mac and PC.

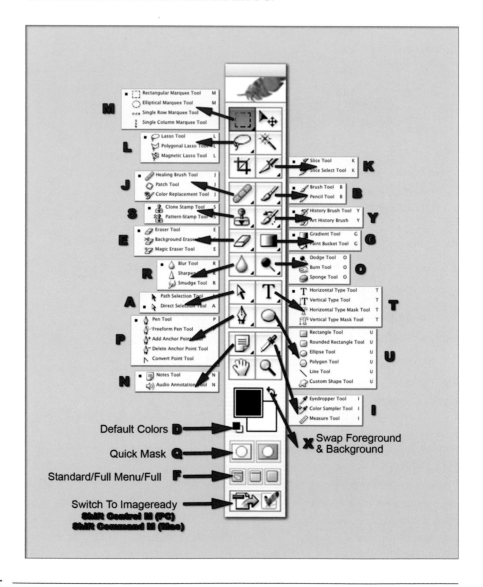

	PC	MAC
MOVE TOOL		
Move Tool	Ctrl while in any tool except hand, pen, and slice.	Command while in any tool except hand, pen, and slice.
Move item 1 pixel	Cursor key	Cursor key
Move item 10 pixels	Shift cursor key	Shift cursor key
Drag Duplicate Item	Ctrl Alt while in any tool except hand, pen, and slice.	Command option while in any tool except hand, pen, and slice.
Link/Unlink Layers	Ctrl shift click on item. Auto Select Layer is on.	Command shift click on item. Auto Select Layer is on.
Select Layer in stack	Ctrl and right click, then choose name of layer.	Ctrl and command click, then choose name of layer.
NAVIGATE SCREEN TOOL		
Hand Tool	Spacebar	Spacebar
Zoom Out Tool	Ctrl Spacebar	Command Spacebar.
Zoom Out Tool	Alt Spacebar.	Option Spacebar.
Zoom Out	Ctrl +	Command +
Zoom In	Ctrl −	Command −
PEN TOOL DRAWING		
Direct Select	Ctrl	Command
Corner Point	Alt drag last point	Option last point
Convert Point	Alt drag point in middle of path	Option point in middle of path
Add a new closed path to existing shape.	Q before you draw 2nd closed path.	Q before you draw 2nd closed path.
Switch to add to shape area	− (don't hold down Shift)	= (don't hold down Shift)
Switch to subtract area	− (don't hold down Shift)	= (don't hold down Shift)
PAINTING TOOLS (paintbrush, clone stamp, eraser, blur, dodge)		
Brush size −10 pixels	[	[
Brush size +10 pixels	]	]
Brush hardness −25%	Shift [	Shift [
Brush hardness +25%	Shift]	Shift]
Previous brush size	, (comma)	, (comma)
Next brush size	. (period)	. (period)
Brush opacity percentage	Type any 2 numbers in succession	Type any 2 numbers in succession
Previous blending mode	Shift −	Shift −
Next blending mode	Shift =	Shift =
SHAPE TOOLS		
Rounded Rectangle Tool −1 radius	[	[

Rounded Rectangle Tool +1 radius	]	]
Rounded Rectangle Tool −10 radius	Shift [	Shift [
Rounded Rectangle Tool +10 radius	Shift]	Shift]
Polygon Tool Decrease sides by 1	[	[
Polygon Tool Increase sides by 1	]	]
Polygon Tool Decrease sides by 10	Shift [	Shift [
Polygon Tool Decrease sides by 10	Shift]	Shift]
Line Tool Line weight −1 pixel	[	[
Line Tool Line weight +1 pixel	]	]
Line Tool Line weight −10 pixel	Shift [	Shift [
Line Tool Line weight +10 pixel	Shift]	Shift]
EYEDROPPER TOOL		
Temporarily switch to eyedropper tool	With paintbrush tool selected Alt	With paintbrush tool eye selected Option
Place a new color sampler	Shift Alt	Shift Option
Sample Background color	Click eyedropper in tool palette Alt	Click eyedropper in tool palette Option
DODGE BURN TOOL		
Switch dodge tool to burn	Alt	Option
Switch burn tool to dodge	Alt	Option
PAINTBUCKET TOOL		
Fill selection with foreground color	Alt Delete	Option Delete
Fill selection with background color	Ctrl Delete	Command Delete
Display Fill Dialog Box	Shift Delete	Shift Delete

These shortcuts above are essential to using Photoshop professionally for video. In order to meet the high expectations and turnaround times, you will want to learn and memorize each one. However, do not worry, as the exercises in this book will help you to learn and find the importance of these.

HARDWARE

If you are configuring a new system to be primarily a Photoshop station, most guidelines for media workstations will apply if you want optimal performance. Faster processors will speed up rendering of effects and corrections. More RAM will allow for more levels of smoothly operating undos and History Brush strokes as well as better performance with larger files. Faster hard drives with faster connections to the mother board will facilitate quicker opening and saving of larger files.

RAM

Images taken from a frame of Standard DV or D1 video are about 1 MB in size as a Photoshop image. By the time you calculate the RAM needed to run your operating system, your video editing program, Photoshop, and a single Levels adjustment, you could easily be using over 50 MB of RAM. The need for more RAM multiplies when you start working with multiple layers, layer styles, history states, etc. It is not uncommon for off-the-shelf computers from Best Buy to have 512 MB of RAM installed, and it's becoming quite common for higher end workstations to come with well over 1 GB built in. In many ways, such as working with the History Brush, History Palette, previews, and Layer Styles, more RAM can be more beneficial than more CPU speed.

For best results, make sure you match the kind of RAM, speed rating, and capacity. RAM classifies its speed as PC66, PC100, PC133, and recently we've seen PC150. These names stand for megahertz (MHz) speeds in 66 MHz, 100 MHz, 133 MHz, and 150 MHz, respectively. Faster RAM is better. Adobe recommends 256 MB or more of RAM to run the program smoothly. If you're going to be running other programs simultaneously, such as video editing and compositing applications, we recommend that you at least double that to 512 MB.

Processors

The speed game can be addicting, if not often misleading. Usually, faster processors will yield faster rendering of effects and commands. But not all processors are created equal, and some like to come in pairs. The clock speed of the newest G5 processor is many megahertz behind last year's slowest Pentium IVs. However, a dual processor G5 will eat most Pentium 3 GHz machines for breakfast.

Adobe sets their PC standard for PS CS with a Pentium III or IV. We've seen good results from higher end AMD chips. The Celeron line of processors will work, but once you get the least bit familiar with Photoshop, you will start to feel it lag. If you're starting to build or look for a computer, go with the recommendations. The choices for the Mac are simplified. You can use anything from a G3 and up.

Hard Drives

Like RAM and CPUs, speed and capacity are continually growing while the prices of the latest models remain relatively steady. If you are editing video on the same system as you will be running Photoshop, you should be familiar with the benefits of multiple hard drives. Adobe makes no requirements concerning hard drives beyond having at least 280 MB open for installing the program. What we recommend from experience is that you install a second drive (internal or external) that spins at least 7200 rpm. Using a second drive gives better performance by allowing the application and operating system to use the main drive without interrupting the second drive while you perform your Photoshop skills. Some good brands that are commonly found are from Maxtor, Seagate, Western Digital, and IBM to name just a few.

Most common computers utilize ATA drives. Like RAM, they are often classified by corresponding speed ratings for their connection to the mother board. Their speeds are usually 66 MHz, 100 MHz, and 133 MHz with respective names of ATA66, ATA100, and ATA133. Again, faster is recommended. The long-regarded professional standard in high end drives are the varieties of SCSI drives. On average, they are faster spinning, with faster transfer speeds, and until the past few years they had larger capacities. These powerhouse drives require a specific SCSI card for a motherboard to utilize them. Although they are generally known to be more stable and they offer more consistent performance when pushing their capacity limits, ATA drives have greatly narrowed the gap in terms of performance and capacity while their cost per gigabyte is currently around $1 or less!

Adobe requires Photoshop CS to run on Windows 2000 service pack 3 or XP for PC and Mac OS X v10.2 and up. So if you meet the requirement, you can format a second drive using the NTFS standard. NTFS formatting will allow unlimited file sizes, which may not be necessary when working with most still images, but can be a life saver when working with video and motion graphics.

External drives have become extremely popular in the last few years. When working in a high-volume environment with critical deadlines and large file sizes, Disk Arrays offer the best in performance and security. Disk Array—also known as RAID (Redundant Arrays of Inexpensive Disks)—includes two or more drives. Additional hardware (often a PCI card) sends data to be written to more than one drive at the same time. A disk array can either be striped, mirrored, or both. The advantage of a striped array is that a file is split between two drives, giving you faster open and save times. Data is mirrored when a file is saved simultaneously on two different drives, giving you two copies. The advantage of mirroring your data is that you have a backup which was done transparently, so if one copy goes bad you have the other. Other RAIDs include duplexing and parity, but the manufacturers are not consistent with what they call RAID 2 through 5. You can get a great RAID system from medea.com, bhphotovideo.com, and videoguys.com to mention a few.

RAID LEVEL	RAID TYPE	ADVANTAGE	DRIVES NEEDED
Raid level 0	Striped	Speed	2
Raid level 1	Mirrored	Data safety	2
Raid 0 + 1	Striped and mirrored	Speed and safety	4

The Art department at Weigel Broadcasting in Chicago uses four Mac G4 machines, with a second internal SCSI 80 GB on each computer. Each week, the four employees turn around a very demanding workload with very dependable performance. At home, our own systems use Firewire and USB 2.0 external drives.

We get excellent performance from inexpensive gear when producing DV projects of varying sizes. As High Definition continues to drop in price, the new generation Firewire 800 external drives show much potential to meet the demanding rigors of such massive data bandwidth.

Monitors

The required monitor resolution and video card set-up is 1,024 × 768 resolution with 16-bit color or greater. This is an easy requirement to meet. However, serious media professionals often use two monitors when working in Photoshop. When two monitors are used, the common setup is to have the image on one monitor and the palettes on the other. Obviously, not everyone has the luxury (or preference) of using two screens. When things get crowded and you need to maximize your screen's real estate, hide the tools and palettes by hitting **Tab.** Hit **Tab** again, and they will return in exactly the same place they were before. If you only want to hide the palettes while keeping the tools visible, hit **Shift** + **Tab** on both PC and Mac.

2
COLOR (MANAGEMENT & DESIGN)

$\mathcal{Y}$ou must follow this chapter for the DVD images to be properly displayed on your monitor. We will not be doing color corrections until Chapter 17, but we want to start you off the right way. Many people from different parts of the world will be reading this book, all with different hardware and environmental conditions. The color calibration you do here will cost you nothing but a few minutes of your time and will greatly improve your color accuracy. For video, you will want to add an NTSC or PAL monitor to your system so you see the colors as they will look on television. You cannot get every television viewer to properly adjust their own color/tint/sharpness/etc., but you can provide them with vivid, colorful, luminous images that look their best.

Calibrating your computer monitor is the first most important step to getting great images. You do not need to do the following options for professional color results. However, they will improve your results if you can afford the cost and time:

❖ Painting your room in D-50 gray paint
❖ D-50 lighting with no windows

- ❖ *A high-end monitor such as Barco*

- ❖ *Spectrophotometer to measure light emitted from your computer screen*

- ❖ *Software to input the results of your spectrophotometer*

CALIBRATE YOUR COMPUTER MONITOR

Did you calibrate your monitor? You need to calibrate for your images to look professional with a better contrast and color range. Your colors used in flat tints will also be more accurate – nobody wants their patriotic blue to go toward purple or aqua! Your monitor will drift slightly over time, and the color you see today may look different next year because of environmental or hardware conditions. How often you calibrate is up to you, but we recommend once every 2 months. This will ensure that the color you see on your monitor is close to the color another person will see. Your color will look correct and very similar to everyone else's if you calibrate – and calibrate correctly. The process is easy to remember once you have done it, but we will cover the finer points, so that you will understand how to generate a good color profile.

PC

During the PC installation of Photoshop CS, the Adobe Gamma control panel will be installed. The Adobe Gamma control panel generates a color data profile from the settings that you choose. To start generating a profile, choose **Start >> Control Panel >> Adobe Gamma**.

Before you do anything else **change the name of your description from "sRGB IEC61966-2.1" to your name and the date** (e.g.: "Jane Doe June-12-2004)." Find your button or dial for adjusting **contrast and maximize that setting**. Laptops and most LCDs don't have a contrast knob, so skip this part as you are already at the optimal contrast. Next, **adjust your monitor brightness until the gray squares in the top black bar just begin to show**. The almost black boxes in the black bar should be as close as you can get them to the black squares, but just a shade brighter. If you have dials, you can tape them in place so they do not accidentally shift until the next time you calibrate.

If you know the phosphors of your monitor, then change them. However, it is not important if you don't know – just skip to the next important setting. The two most common types of monitor are Trinitron and EBU/ITU. Remove the check in the box for View Single Gamma. You will now see three boxes which are red, green, and blue and which control the strength of each channel in your monitor. To adjust these boxes move your chair back so your eyes are about 4 feet (1.2 meters) from the monitor, and squint your eyes so that the type is out of focus.

Adjust the red slider until your solid red center box disappears against the red/black striped outer box. Do the same for green and blue slider. The sweet

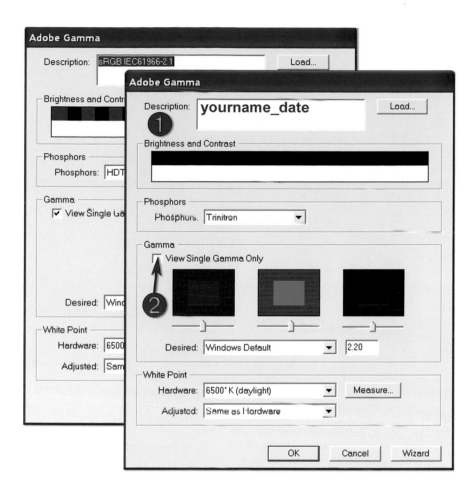

spot for the green slider is easy to find, but blue has a wider range for the inner box to disappear. Choose a point in the center of that range by remembering the left and right point where the center box disappears. Your monitor should be balanced so you are without any incorrect color casts. Amazingly, many people do not have their monitor calibrated – you can often tell this just by looking at the gray windows and black edge of a monitor. The RGB sliders are the most important settings in your Adobe Gamma control panel. They balance red, green and blue so you don't have a color cast to your image.

The surrounding colors of your environment can influence what you see on your monitor. If the room you work in is painted hot pink, or if you use a pink iMac, then your eyes will be fooled into thinking your monitor images are too cool or blue in color. This is a similar effect to when you wear white clothing, making your skin color look darker. This is why high-end monitors have a gray frame rather than saturated colors and have a hood to block out sun rays.

Finally, save your profile as an icm file, with the new description you changed earlier. Use a naming convention that describes which computer station and when

it was done. The name you use for the file can be different from the description. This is confusing, and I try to match both to eliminate that confusion. This will help let you know when you last calibrated rather than thinking you are using the sRGB profile – as have many PC users who did not change their description.

Mac

Panther (OS 10.3) updated the display color calibration and added a few more steps. It takes longer in Panther, but is more accurate in the final result. If you do not have Panther, the calibration is similar to the PC calibration and still does an excellent job.

Begin by choosing **Apple** >> **System preferences** >> **Hardware** >> **Displays** >> **Color tab**. Highlighted will be the name of the profile it is currently using.

Click Calibrate.

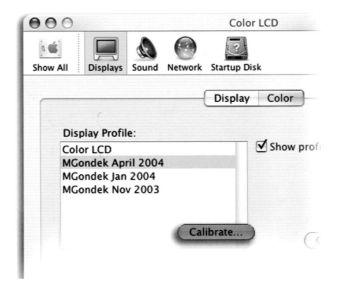

You can click on Show Profiles for this display only, which works very well to hide the others. You can change to another profile if you like, but we will be generating another one by **hitting the Calibrate button.**

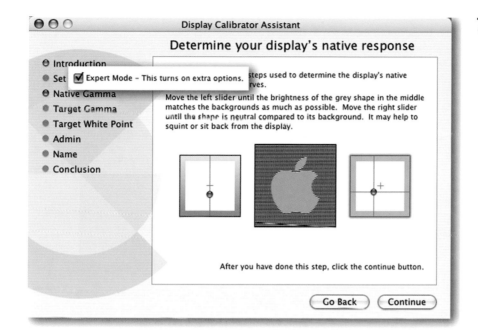

Calibrate Native Gamma.

On the introduction page click the **Expert Mode** – don't be afraid, we will *make* you an expert! Continue on to Setup, and you will actually want to defocus your eyes for the next part so that the type is actually not readable. Do this by moving your chair back so that your eyes are about 4 feet (1.2 meters) away and squint your eyes almost shut. Drag the first blue dot up or down so that the apple in the middle is the same color as the horizontal striped lines around the apple. Defocusing your eyes blurs the black and white lines, so that they actually appear gray. The next part can be tough, but this is really fine tuning. Continue with your eyes out of focus and drag the second blue dot so that the apple is even more invisible. If you drag the dot to the bottom left you will see the apple has a greenish cast, then move it toward the middle until there is no cast. Dragging the blue dot toward the edge will saturate the color toward the color of the ROYGBIV frame around it. Some people would like that frame to be more saturated, but the pastel colors are good as they won't influence your final decision. You will do this four more times in different tones to fine-tune your Native Gamma. This should go really quickly, and you will probably only be adjusting the left slider.

Good job – you are now in Target Gamma. Since you did such a great job in the previous part, you can now check the box to use your Native Gamma. Click **Continue** to go to target white point. With the great new update to 10.3, you

Use Native Gamma and set target white point.

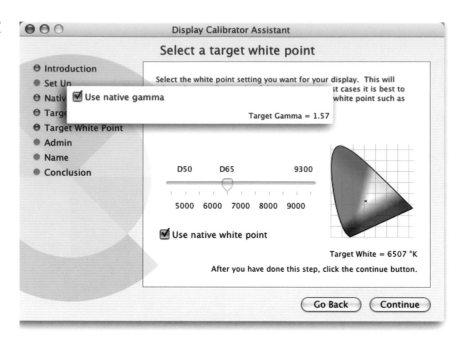

can also choose **use native white point** where in the past only CRT users checked that; then click **Continue**.

Save your profile.

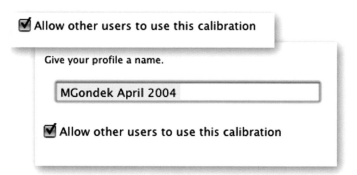

To finish, check the box to allow others to use this calibration. There is really no reason to not want to share your calibration with others, as they always have the option to not use it for their own log-in sessions. The last part is to name your profile. The best way is to use your name and the date for the profile – you will thank yourself later. Click the **Continue** and **Done** buttons, and your desktop color should now look better!

Photoshop Color Settings

The most important part is done and you should try to update your profile every 3 month, or more often if you have trouble. Premiere, After Effects, your operating system and whatever video editing application you use is now displaying your color properly. Photoshop is more advanced, as you have different output devices beside video that the file can be used for. Therefore, you have more color management options in the Photoshop application.

Let's finish up color management by choosing **edit >> color settings** [**Photoshop >> color settings**]. The settings will default depending on what national version of Photoshop you installed. Adobe assumes most people use Photoshop for print and therefore defaults to sRGB and web press. For a basic machine only used for video and nothing else, you can turn Color Management off.

We will slightly modify these settings and recommend you use these for the book and most likely your own permanent settings. There are many reasons you may want to customize these settings, and a major one is digital cameras. Most high-end digital cameras attach the Adobe RGB profile, which is a great color space with a wide color gamut. So change **RGB >> Adobe RGB (1998)**, and below it change **Color Management Policies >> Preserve Embedded Profiles**. If you want to get rid of all those nasty profile mismatch warnings, then remove the check in front of Profile Mismatches. Most people will tell you this is not recommended, and you are welcome to follow their advice. I used to do things that way, until I had a revelation. Since you are preserving embedded profiles, you are not destroying the file – just saving yourself thousands of pop-up windows for profile mismatch errors.

The advanced mode has more settings, which we would not change except for one thing. Click on **Advanced** to reveal the extra settings, and change **Conversion Options** >> **Intent** >> **Perceptual**. This just works better with a wide gamut RGB space like Adobe RGB when converting to CMYK for print. Many video professionals design DVD covers, posters and other printed material, so that is why this book also covers CMYK issues.

If you are using Adobe Illustrator, InDesign or have more computers, you will want to export your color settings for use in other apparatus or other machines. Click on **Save** and name your file – the name of your company, department and date is usually a good way to name it. For example: in Illustrator you can load the color settings you just saved from Photoshop, and your images will display the same in both programs.

COLOR SYSTEMS & SWATCHES

To pick color, you have a choice of different interfaces. You may need to match a pantone color or want to choose colors which work well together. Choose which color picker Photoshop uses in the General Preferences **Ctrl K** [**Command K**]. If you click on the foreground swatch in Photoshop, you will get one of these four interfaces.

Apple and Windows Color Pickers

Windows Color Picker.

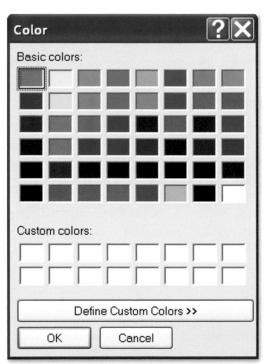

The Color Picker is set to Adobe by default on both Mac and PC, so the interface for picking colors will be the same on both platforms. You can only get the Apple Color

Picker on a Mac; and the Windows Color Picker is only on the PC. The Windows picker is not that useful, since you already have a swatches palette in Photoshop. The Apple Color Picker has five different modes that are available if you hit the unhide button highlighted in red. The five modes are:

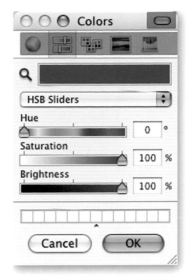

Apple Color Picker

❖ color wheel

❖ color slider

❖ color palette

❖ image palette

❖ crayola box.

In all five modes you can drag and drop colors in the common palette well of favorite colors on the bottom. You can drag the swatch locations around, and the easiest way to delete a swatch is to drag a white one on top. You drag the color from the top bar into the favorites swatches on the bottom of the palette, and that color can be picked up in Photoshop, After Effects or whatever other applications you have. For Mac users the Apple Color Picker is the way to go; for PC users we recommend the Adobe Color Picker.

Custom Colors

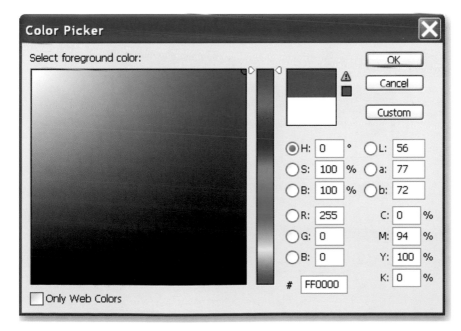

Adobe Color Picker.

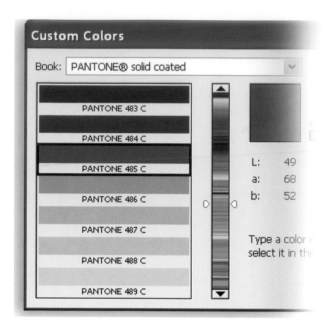

Custom Color Picker.

You can get to the Pantone color picker by **clicking on the Custom button while in the Adobe Color Picker** and **change the book option to Pantone**. If you know the Pantone number you need, just type the number and you will advance to that color. You can also use the up or down cursor keys to navigate through the Pantone colors. There are many other books you can use in this way, such as Focoltone or Toyo.

The files you create for video usage are RGB 24-bit files. Each of the three RGB channels contains 2^8 or 256 colors. So, you have a total of $256 \times 256 \times 256$ colors, which totals 16,777,216 to choose from, or 2^{24} colors. You also have an additional 8-bit alpha channel, or an image which has 16 bits per channel, which is covered in Chapter 17.

Color Palette

Color Palette flyout menu.

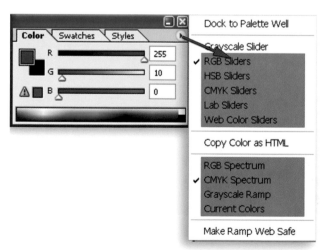

RGB

If you cannot see the color palette, choose **Window** >> **Color** to bring it to the front. You will notice that the slider's maximum value is 255. There are 256 colors in total, because 0 is considered to be a value when the Red gun on your monitor is turned off. On the top right of the palette is an arrow which will cause a wing menu to fly out of the side of the palette. Your wing menu has five slider choices and four choices for the spectrum bar. You can choose between RGB and CMYK spectrum to see the difference in how RGB is a more saturated color space. CMYK is not as vibrant as RGB, because printing inks are not as pure as light.

LAB

LAB space.

From the color palette flyout menu, you have **six different color spaces to choose from, choose LAB,** which stands for Luminance Chroma A and Chroma B. Luminance is a sliding dimmer switch which, when you slide it to the right, causes everything to become brighter. To get a perfect white, you must set A and B to the middle. To get a neutral gray you must put luminance at 50 and A and B at 0. You can now see that Chroma A is like a hue for teal green and magenta. Chroma B is your chrominance for cyan and mustard yellow. Well, all this changes if you move A and B to their maximum at 120. Don't be confused, because LAB is a great way to choose complementary colors which look good against each other. LAB is also a great place to use the unsharp mask to sharpen just the luminance channel, resulting in minimal color artifacts. Now **change the wing menu to CMYK sliders,** and your sliders will change to another color system.

CMYK

CMYK sliders are useful in video because you may have a company graphic standards guide, and it might only list the CMYK values for company colors. In video, you will most always want to work in RGB, so you must change your document using **Image** >> **Mode** >> **RGB color.** You can still use the CMYK sliders, but it will use the RGB equivalent now since you are in that color mode. Adobe Illustrator has a good trick where you can hold down **Shift** and you will move all sliders a distance proportional to each other. This method is good for mixing colors that go well with each other. To mix complimentary color you will have to double-click on your foreground swatch and move one of the values such as Luminance. You can use the **cursor keys** to make this value higher or lower.

Photoshop Swatch Palette
Choosing a color

Choose **Window >> Swatches,** to bring your swatch palette to the front. Move the cursor over an existing swatch, and your cursor will turn into an eyedropper. You will see the name of the color if you have **Show Tool Tips** enabled in your general preferences. Click and you will load that color into your foreground swatch in your tool palette. This will now be the color that your brushes will use or if you fill an area. Certain Photoshop filters and functions will also use this swatch such as color range or the halftone pattern filter.

Click Alt [Option] to add or delete swatches.

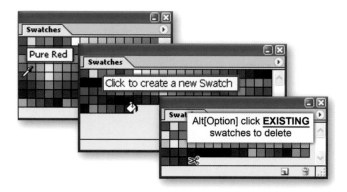

Adding swatches

Move over an open swatch, and now your cursor changes to a paint bucket. **Click when your cursor is a paintbucket and you will be prompted for a name,** and then fill that swatch with the foreground color. Hold down **Alt [Option] click to quickly add a swatch with a default name.** The default name will be Swatch 1, or the next available number, so that you do not have two swatches of the same name.

Deleting swatches

Hold down **Alt [Option] over an empty swatch** and your cursor changes to scissors. Click once while you see the scissors, and that swatch will be deleted. To delete all swatches in a palette is a little tricky. There is not a command to select and delete unused swatches as in Illustrator, but there is a trick to help. Move your cursor over the first swatch, hold down **Alt [Option]**, and keep clicking. Click until all the swatches are gone. Then create your favorite swatches, and from the **swatches wing menu >> save swatches.** If you do not save your swatches Photoshop will revert to the default colors next time you reboot.

Anytime you wish to revert to the Adobe Photoshop color swatches you can always choose **swatches wing menu >> reset swatches**. To change Photoshop from default to another set of swatches, you must choose **Edit >> Preset Manager >> Colors**. There, you can select any swatch set that you saved using the save swatches wing menu.

Color mode

CMYK is made from inks, and RGB is made from light. Printing inks are made from chemicals and natural elements and are not pure in color. Originally, printers used a CMY system, but because the inks were not pure they could not get a rich black, only a very dark muddy-looking brown by mixing cyan, magenta and yellow. They added a fourth color, black, called K so as not to confuse it with blue. CMYK is called subtractive color theory, because subtracting colors gives you white.

RGB is additive color theory, and combining red, green and blue adds up to white. You can open the files in **Chapter 02/RGB.psd & CMYK.psd** and move the layers around to see how additive and subtractive color works. In RGB, where two colors overlap you get CMY, and that is how it was decided to use those three inks to try and simulate what is created with light.

Content on DVD

A duotone is made from two inks on press, and a sepiatone is an early photographic process invented in the 1850s which used an emulsion that gave black and white images a yellowish brown tone. To make a sepiatone in Photoshop is easy. Open **Chapter 02/ZionPark_RGB.tif,** and convert the image to grayscale using **Image >> Mode >> Grayscale**. Now, you are allowed to convert it to a duotone using **Image >> Mode >> Duotone**.

Content on DVD

Click on the load button, and choose **Chapter 02/Sepiatone.ado**. You will notice that this saved Adobe duotone preset is a tritone, and there are three color swatches

Content on DVD

Original image.

Curves to apply.

used. The first color is a very dark red black, which defines much of the shape and has a curve that concentrates this color in the darkest shadows. This curve lessens the amount of the black in the middle tones. The next color is the midtone, which defines the overall base color tone of the image. The last color is for the highlights, which defines the areas of the image receiving the most light and also adds contrast to the image in the opposite direction of the shadows.

Next, you will want to compress the gamut of the image which will look more like the color range that photographs had in the 1850s Albumen process. You can open the image **Chapter 02/ZionPark_Sepiatone.psd** and double-click the levels layer to see that the highlights and shadows were compressed. We will go over levels in detail in Chapter 17. The final step is to convert the image back to RGB so you can bring it into your video editing application **Image >> Mode >> Duotone**

Content on DVD

Final sepiatone image.

COLOR PSYCHOLOGY

Different color treatments can affect the same image in different ways.

There are quite a few socially traditional color associations, such as blue for boys and pink for girls. However, if you ever received any basic training in art, you have probably heard several theories about color psychology. Countless studies have been conducted to determine which shade of yellow represents insanity and what colors will drive people to vote democratic. With so many studies done, there are as many contradicting findings. What some people might feel is an "insane" yellow, others will consider to be a soothing shade of "lazy summer." Surely, context and common sense will help drive appropriate decisions on what the "right" color is for whatever it is you are trying to communicate. At the risk of stating the obvious associations, some common color associations are in the table below.

COLOR	ASSOCIATION
RED	Anger, danger, vitality, intensity, passion, brilliance, blood.
GREEN	Coolness, refreshment, rejuvenation, nature, vegetation, Ireland.
BLUE	Water, air, service, depression, despair, melancholy.
BLACK	Negativity, darkness, opposition, mourning, death, alternative, off, solitarily, space, class.

WHITE	Light, neutrality, on, coolness, snow, cleanliness, purity, youth.
YELLOW	Sunlight, radiance, cheerfulness, celestial presence, cheer, caution, insanity.
BROWN	Earth, dirt, boredom, chocolate, caramel, neutrality.

The associations in the table mention only a few possibilities. Remember that these are rules that can be easily broken – sometimes with fantastic results. If you ever saw the Steven Soderberg film, *Traffic*, you saw a stark contrast between cool blue tones for scenes that took place in the United States and blown-out yellow tones for scenes that took place in Mexico. Aside from distinguishing between different geographic locations, one of the other cues that Soderberg left for us was the fact that blue and yellow are opposites of each other – just as the two locations were homes to where the problem starts and where the problem festers. Yellow was being used to convey the standard hot and sunny associations, but it also changed the rules by signifying negativity and corruption rather than positivity. In the context of the movie, the overstated use of color worked beautifully.

BROADCAST AND TECHNICAL ISSUES

Broadcast Safe Color

Created in 1934, the Federal Communications Commission is an independent department that serves the U.S. Congress. Years later, there are standards in place all over the world that serve to maintain compatible signals and assure the public that any television set they buy at Circuit City or Value City will be able to properly display their favorite programming. If you prepare graphics that are intended for broadcast over airwaves or cable lines, these standards are actually required by law to be upheld. Most broadcasters have hardware in place to adjust illegal color levels in favor of their respective guidelines. Instead of leaving this adjustment up to the broadcaster and risking what the results might be, you can exercise the control you already have.

The fact is that you can easily create colors that will violate these specifications with Photoshop. The easiest way to do this is to create a solid background layer with a simple default white. While most modern televisions can display this color (as well as other "illegal" colors) when transmitted over the air, the extra signal can bleed over into the audio stream, resulting in an unholy buzz in the speaker as well as creating hypnotizing streaks of feedback on the screen. You may have seen and/or heard these at some point. If you have, you will no doubt remember just how obnoxious it was.

In Chapter 17, we will take you through the ins and outs of color correcting. Among other things, we'll be highlighting Levels, Curves, and Color Balance. For now, open **Chapter 2 >> Fig 2-28.psd**. Follow along with the following examples to see how to make some basic changes.

Content on DVD

With **Chapter 2 >> Fig 2-28.psd** open, activate **Image >> Adjustments >> Levels**. The image we're working with is already color-balanced and optimized for printing

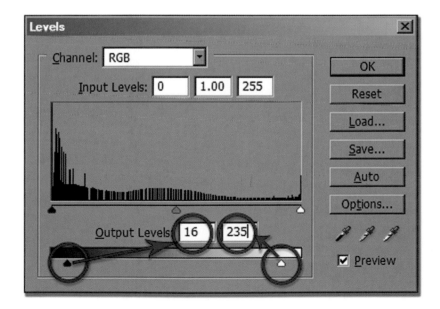

The highlights and shadows in this image are too intense for NTSC broadcasting specifications.

or display. However, the white levels extend all the way to 255, which is absolute white in an 8-bit RGB environment. The black level is set to 0. In the realm of NTSC video, absolute white should be 100 IRE and black is 7.5 IRE. For now, what's important for you to know (if you don't already understand video specs) is that 100 IRE equals 235 and black equals 16 on the 8-bit scale. Slide the right marker on the Output or manually type in 235 for the White Output, as shown in the figure below. Then slide the left marker to 16 and hit OK. This image is now broadcast legal.

You can bring an image within the NTSC color space by using levels.

Under the Filter menu, there is a video filter called Broadcast Safe. This filter not only affects the colors of an image in a horrifically unsightly manner, it will often leave many illegal colors unaffected. Open **Chapter 2** >> **Fig 2-30a** from the DVD. Apply the effect, **Filters** >> **Video** >> **Broadcast Safe**. You can easily tell on the computer monitor that what you end up with is a grotesque approximation of what you started with. If you go one step further and monitor this still through a Time Based Corrector (TBC), you will see that the brightness and saturation are both broadcast "unsafe."

Some of the colors are too bright and saturated for broadcasting in NTSC countries.

Simply applying the Broadcast Safe filter does not produce a desirable result.

Broadcast professionals are used to using hardware for checking their colors and luminance. Video editors will be familiar with vectorscopes and waveform monitors. However, the proliferation of affordable DV cameras and editing gear has led many intrepid souls to bypass any formal production training and to buy their own equipment to learn through trial and error (and, hopefully, our book). Whatever the case, it's beneficial to learn to use these tools properly, especially when your work is intended for broadcast or even VHS delivery.

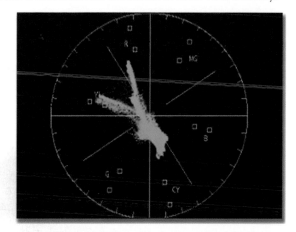

Vectorscopes measure chroma intensity.

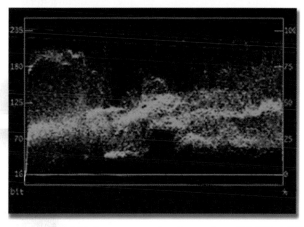

Waveform monitors measure luminance levels.

There is a paradigm shift in progress in the realm of $600–1600 category of video editing applications. Processors are getting faster, memory is getting cheaper, and disk capacity is growing. The current versions of all of the leading NLE packages are getting wise to include software versions of various signal monitors embedded within the programs.

For the fastest feedback possible on how your image will fare with broadcast standards, you have two options. One way is to install a plug-in such as Scopo Gigio. This is another version of a software vectorscope and waveform monitor that sits within Photoshop, giving you instant feedback as you work. The other way is to utilize a graphics card that can send out an appropriately sized image to a video monitor as you work. Some cards that are capable of this are the Matrox G550 video card and X.100 capture board. Once the signal is sent out to a video monitor, you still need to get a signal reading from a hardware vectorscope and waveform monitor.

Most current video editing applications come with extremely functional and accurate waveform monitors and vectorscopes.

TEXT COLOR

When it comes to dealing with type, the most crucial element concerning legibility is contrast and separation. A more concise description on this issue is covered in Chapter 10, but for starters, a good example of good contrast is black text on white paper or white text on a black screen. The more the text or the background is made darker or lighter and the difference in brightness is lessened, the more difficult it will become to read.

When the contrast between text and the background is low, steps need to be taken to separate them from each other. Chapter 6 will show you some great tools you can use to achieve as much separation as you need.

After you've selected the perfect font, you may have to get used to how colors will change somewhat when viewed on a video monitor or television set. The next section of this chapter will go into more detail, but the short of it is that colors tend to be a bit darker and richer on a computer monitor and a bit brighter and slightly washed out on a video monitor. When the concern is to get the text to a point where a viewer can read it from a video monitor, there are a few colors to favor and a few to avoid.

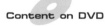

To give the best example we can, open **Chapter 2 >> Good Title Colors** and **Chapter 2 >> Bad Title Colors** from the DVD and view them on your computer monitor first. All of the colors should seem fine when over the appropriate background. Then bring both images into your video editing application and monitor the images on a standard definition video monitor. You'll notice that **Good Title Colors** is easily read and that **Bad Title Colors** shows some obnoxious twitter or interlacing artifacting on the edges.

Here are some tips for the best results:

1. Don't use text color that is opposite of the background – cyan text over a red background is a bad combination.

2. Use colors that are in the same wedge on the vectorscope, but keep one brighter and the other darker – bright yellow text over a dark red background should show up nicely.

3. When keying text over video that has too many bright and dark areas, use a contrasting drop shadow, outer glow or outline to keep it separated.

3
PIXELS

*P*ixels are the building blocks of video and Photoshop. Think of each pixel as a very small floor tile and Photoshop lays the tile down for you. Each tile can be one of 16.7 million solid colors, in a 24-bit image. These tiles are all the same size and rectangular, and you can see this with a magnifying glass. If the tiles are small enough, then your eyes will see an image.

RESOLUTION

The batman logo looks great on the right side, but the left side displays the chunky look of stair steps. You see stair-stepping most in the angular and circular lines, but not in straight lines as pixels are rectangular. Imagine this same logo created with bathroom tiles. If the tiles were 12 inches square, then the logo would look very blocky. Imagine the tiles being 1 mm squares

LO RES   VIDEO RES

laid over the same wall, then the image would have much more detail. If your tile image was of 12-inch wide lines, then there would be no problem using the big tiles, but the job would be impossible if it was a 12-inch circle that you wanted.

Most still images used in video come from digital cameras, scanning or exporting a frame from video. The amount of pixels you need for video depends if you are working in DV, Pal NTSC or another broadcast format. Video formats use rectangular or non-square pixels. Photoshop CS now allows you to create images with pixels that are rectangular, not square as in the past. DV NTSC video uses 720×480 rectangular pixels. How much resolution do you need for Photoshop images used for video? A basic rule is to prepare your Image in Photoshop at double the resolution of your final output. The reasons for this include the following.

Scaling and Panning

Suppose you have an image of the United States and want a video to zoom in on a state. You will need an image larger than 720×480 to do this. Depending on how far you zoom is how many more pixels you will need. If you zoom 200%, than you need 200% of $720 \times 480 = 1440 \times 960$). You may also want to pan around an image of a wedding couple, and having double your final video resolution is ideal for this.

Retouching and Color Balance

When retouching images for video usage, begin with an image double the resolution you need. When done with retouching, save your image down to the final resolution needed for video. Using the rubber stamp on a 720×480 will produce a poor result. The image will have soft areas where the clone tool was used with a soft brush. When you have so few pixels, there is not much detail and thin lines or edges can be difficult to clone stamp. It is actually harder and more time-consuming to get good results with video resolution images, and you will most likely finish retouching a 1440×960 image more quickly. You may also want to color correct an image, and the extra data helps you get a better color correction bringing out the detail. When your source image comes from a video grab, then unfortunately it is difficult to do major retouching.

Digital Cameras

You might also desire to shoot an image at exactly 720×480 if possible, so that there is no need to scale the image. Digital cameras have noise – especially in the blue channel that covers up detail. Shooting an image at double the resolution and then scaling down by 50% will give you a better image than originally shooting at the lower resolution, because the noise will be smaller and Photoshop can interpolate a better image.

You might also find that you want to crop the image after shooting, so if you were to shoot at exactly 720×480, then cropping the image would give you an image that is below resolution.

Scanning

Suppose you are scanning images for a simple slideshow in DV NTSC. Your video editing application will process images quicker, not having to scale pixels. Therefore, many video editors scan at a resolution close to 720 × 480. Never scan at 720 × 480, as you will regret having to rescan all your images. Removing dust and scratches will require using the retouching tools, which can soften the detail. You might also find that you need to crop in closer on the image later, and do not have enough pixels to do this. With more pixels, you can bring out the edges and shadows needed and then bring your resolution down to video.

Repurposing

The same images you use in video, you likely will desire to use for your printed DVD covers. Plan ahead and keep copies of your images at higher resolutions. You might save the day for that new business pitch, and your images will look better. In summary, you have to weigh the factors and estimate how much resolution you will need. In video, you can get away with an occasional bad image, because it is moving or flashed on screen. However, print is less forgiving because people can look at the image for as long as they want!

Guess what – you have just finished scanning 25 full body shots of executives, and now they've changed their mind and just want head shots. Next, you get a call from the print department, and they want your images to be printed in the company annual report. If you kept a copy of the original scans at a higher resolution than needed for video, you will be a savior. Working in video we are lucky because images we get from print are more than enough pixels – so why not return the favor and plan ahead? Drive space is less expensive nowadays, and you can always archive your data to a DVD.

Export from Video

When exporting from video you are limited to the resolution of the source footage. When exporting a still from video into Photoshop; remember to deinterlace. You can do it in your video editing application. Adobe Premiere Pro no longer has a stop motion command for capturing still frames. This is actually good, as making a still frame from a movie is better, the deinterlace has the neighboring frames to make a better still frame. If your video editing application does not have deinterlace, you can do it in Photoshop using **Filter** >> **Video** >> **Deinterlace**.

Once in Photoshop, double the resolution using Image Size before retouching. When done retouching, return your image back to video resolution. Image size helps thin angular lines which might need to be extended. This is actually good, as you get a better still frame by capturing a movie, so it gets the other half of the interlaced field to use for creating a still. Working in HDTV is great, because you get those extra pixels where they are most needed.

SAFE MARGINS

Every television set crops off the outer edge of your digital video file. Put a 1-pixel orange line around your digital video file, and play that back on your television. You will see that line is gone in most cases, and every television set crops off a different amount. In video you do not want critical information such as type too close to the edge. Your video editing application should have guides to show you the action and title safe zone. Premiere and After Effects are 10% for action safe and 20% for title safe. So imagine a frame on all four sides cutting off 5% for action safe, and another of 10% on all four sides for title safe.

Titles do not move, so you do not want to crop off any part of your title or "12 foot-deep pool" might say something embarrasing. A moving object is more forgiving because, if the title was moving you would occasionally catch the entire sentence. The action is similar to filming dancing couples at a wedding; with action it is OK if you occasionally cut off the top of the hair, but not if you are taking video of the couples standing still.

The defaults of 10% for each are very good. Create new files for video in Photoshop CS using the video preset sizes, so Action and Safe guides will be automatically drawn for you. If you are going to play the video back on the computer, you do not need to worry about using safe margins, for video which plays back only on computers.

IMAGE SIZE AND CANVAS SIZE

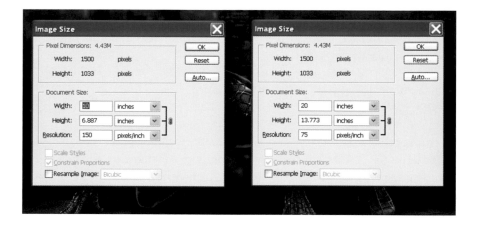

Both of these Photoshop commands deal with the quantity of pixels in your documents. Knowing how both of these work is essential to using Photoshop for web, print or video. The best way to explain it is to open the image **Chapter 03/Spiderman.psd.** Choose **Image >> Image Size** and you will see this image is 1500 pixels wide by 1033 pixels high.

Content on DVD

Image Size

Remove the checkmark from resample image, and the ability to change the amount of pixels goes away. Double the width to 20, and you will see that the height automatically doubles. The height automatically follows, because constrain proportions has a check, the check is grayed out, but it is there. Notice that the amount of pixels is still the same, this is because resample image was not checked. Change the resolution to 300 pixels per inch, and notice the amount of pixels is still 1500 wide, but the width is 5 inches. You could print this image 5 inches wide in a book like this, which has a line screen of 150 per inch (LPI). LPI is a printing term that is different than pixels or dots per inch (DPI). The standard rule for lithography printing is you need double the amount of digital pixels for every line of printed halftone dots (LPI × 2 = DPI needed for lithography). Click **OK**, and your file will process very quickly. This is because the quantity of pixels did not change, just the line of code that Photoshop uses for the density of pixels. The pixels have not been stretched or squashed, so you did not resample or do anything that would change the quality of the pixels.

In video or web, what matters is the amount of pixels you have. The physical dimensions of your image is meaningless. Forget about inches or centimeters – we are only interested in pixels, and in DV NTSC we are looking to get a final file of 720 × 480 pixels. Choose **Image >> Image size** and now **enable the Resample Image checkbox**. Notice with resample enabled, you can now change the amount of pixels in your document. Change the **width to 720** and do not be concerned about resolution, **your height should change to 496 if you had constrain proportions enabled**.

Canvas Size

This document does not scale proportionately to 720 × 480, so we will use canvas size to crop off a few pixels. With canvas size you do not change the density or resolution of the pixels; you either crop images entering smaller sizes or add background canvas color with larger sizes.

Choose **Image >> Canvas Size** and change the height to 480. On the nine squares, select the center one, so an even amount will be clipped off the top and bottom. You will get a warning that pixels on the image will be clipped, **click Proceed**. The final step before saving your image is to choose **Image >> Pixel Aspect Ratio >> D1/DV NTSC (0.9)**. You can now save this image and bring it into your video program at the same pixel settings.

One more very important addition to Photoshop CS is the new image size ability to scale styles. Open **Chapter 03/pizza.tif** and choose **Image >> Image Size**. You will want the scale styles box to be checked to scale all your layer effects. Change the height to 480, and if you had scale style checked than the drop shadow will scale OK; otherwise, your drop shadow will shift position and size as below.

Content on DVD

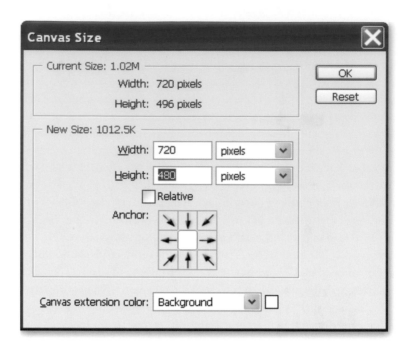

Urban Myths about Resolution

What can you do for an image without enough resolution for video? The best thing to do is to ask for a better image or accept the reality that there is no way to get a high quality image for a low res image. Using **filter >> median**, can help reduce raster, but that will soften an image. There are programs you can purchase which claim to improve image quality, but for video resolution there is no notice-able difference between them and the built-in Photoshop interpolation. Here are some comparisons of a 150 pixel wide image.

CROPPING

Photoshop has more than an ordinary crop tool, there are some often overlooked features. To crop an image, choose (**c**) to change to the crop tool, draw a cropping frame, and hit **Enter** [**Return**] to crop your image.

Squaring Off Perspective

Content on DVD

Open **Chapter 03/Julita Burgess.jpg** and you will see an oil painting shot with a digital camera. You will see by the guides that the image is not perfectly square. Choose **View >> Clear Guides** to delete the guides. With the cropping tool active, draw a cropping frame roughly around the gold frame of the painting. After you have drawn the frame, the options bar now has a perspective attribute.

Extensis Pxl Smartscale

900 pixel wide hi resolution image

Before Crop.

After Crop with perspective.

In the toolbar options, **check the box for Perspective**. With Perspective checked, you can **drag each of the four corner points of the cropping frame individually**. When the cropping frame closely matches the picture frame, hit **Enter [Return]** to crop your image.

Cropping to a Fixed Size

Open **Chapter 03/Rhino&Baby.png**, and you will see a portrait image of some rhinoceroses. Choose the Crop Tool and go up to the options bar and enter **720 for the width and 576 for the height**. You will notice that now the crop tool is always the same proportion, and it changes size at a 45 degree angle. Make sure

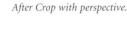

Content on DVD

Portrait image.

Cropped to PAL size.

you have Perspective turned off. Draw yourself a cropping frame about the size you need. You can reposition the frame by positioning your mouse inside the cropping frame and dragging. Hit **Enter** [**Return**] to finalize the crop on your image.

Additional tricks the Crop Tool can do are **Alt** [**Option**] dragging a cropping frame from the center. Dragging a cropping frame with shift will constrain it to a square. Move your cursor just outside the corner of a cropping frame, and it will change to a rotate tool. To enter the values of an existing image into the width and height click on the front image button, you can then go to another image and crop it to the same dimensions.

You can save presets for the Crop Tool, by clicking on the options bar flyout menu next to the Crop Tool icon. To get the presets for video you can **Alt** [**Option**] click on all the existing presets to delete them. The little page with a bent corner icon is handy for adding a preset of the existing size you have in the options bar.

Crop Menu Command

Another way to crop, is by using the Crop command. Open the original **Chapter 03/ pizza.psd**. **Ctrl** [**Command**], and click on the layer named "pizza". The marching ants will surround the pizza, but not the drop shadow. Choose **Image** >> **Crop** and the image will crop around the pizza but chop off the drop shadow. Drag the circle f icon for the drop shadow layer to the trash can in the layers palette to delete the drop shadow. This exercise demonstrates that the crop command works on the bounding box of a selection. It is usually better to create your drop shadow in your video editing application, because you can animate the drop shadow in programs like After Effects and have glass edge shadows and projection distance.

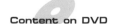
Content on DVD

SQUARE VERSUS NON-SQUARE PIXELS

Working with square and non-square pixels is such a minor aspect to editing, yet it still creates a real headache for many professionals. Without going into an engineering essay, this section will serve as a primer for understanding the difference between these pixels and when you should be aware of it.

The most common digital video formats in the realm of NTSC video are DV - 720 × 480, and D1 - 720 × 486. In PAL countries, DV and D1 are 720 × 576. They also come in widescreen formats, but these are rare by comparison. The important point to remember is that the pixels which make up these signals are rectangular. Video pixels are expressed as having a 0.9 aspect ratio. Computer graphics, and also Photoshop, are displayed with square pixels, and are expressed as having a 1.0 aspect ratio.

You don't always have to concern yourself with going between the two different shapes. The times when you do so are when you want and/or need the shapes created in one application to be identically displayed in the other. In the most basic of terms, if you create a perfect circle in Photoshop, you want a perfect circle to be displayed by anyone's TV set in their living room. Whenever you are creating graphics with an intended layout that you give any effort to, you will want it to look as close as possible to what you saw in Photoshop. There will be enough

A perfect circle created in NTSC video will look too wide in Photoshop.

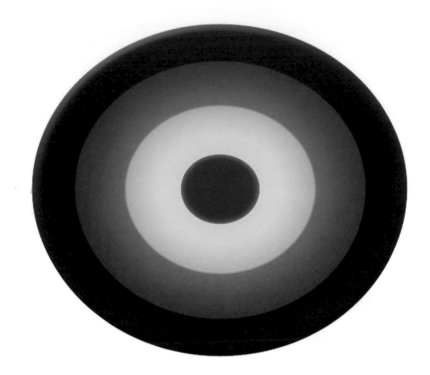

A perfect circle created in PAL video will look too tall in Photoshop.

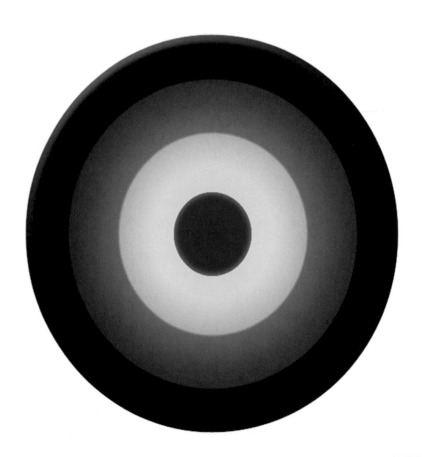

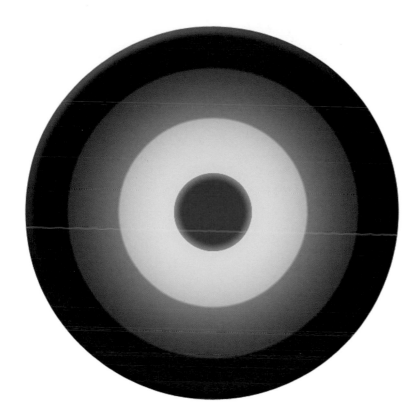

When proper conversions are used, a circle will look consistent in video editing applications and Photoshop alike.

variance in the brightness and color when bringing graphics into your editing application. You don't want the shapes to suffer changes as well.

BUILDING FOR DV, DVD, D1, AND HDTV

The conversions you need to write down or remember are commonly found as presets in various programs. Avid and Final Cut Pro have presets to export video frames as square pixel equivalents, and Photoshop has presets for those same equivalents when creating a new document.

Whenever you export a still frame from video, change the dimensions accordingly. Work with and save the image in Photoshop at the square pixel dimension. Import the finished image into your video editing application with the original non-square dimensions. When creating new artwork in Photoshop for use in video, open a new project with the corresponding square pixel aspect ratio, and import it into your video application with the non-square aspect ratio.

If you bring square pixel art into After Effects, create the composition at the dimensions and aspect ratio of your final video format. Apply the "stretch to fit" command, **Ctrl Alt F [Command Option F]**. If you are working on a large project with dozens upon dozens of images, you can highlight all of them in the timeline as you apply the scale layer to fit command, and they will all snap into place at once.

Format	Aspect Ratio	Non-Square Dimensions (Native Video)	Square Pixel Equivalent
DV (NTSC)	0.9	720 × 480	720 × 534
D1 (NTSC)	0.9	720 × 486	720 × 540
DV Widescreen (NTSC)	1.2	720 × 480	864 × 534
DV / D1 (PAL)	1.067	720 × 576	768 × 576
D1 Widescreen (PAL)	1.4222	720 × 576	1024 × 576
HDTV 720	1.0	1280 × 720	1280 × 720
HDTV 1080	1.0	1920 × 1080	1920 × 1080

4
WORKING WITH FILES

FILE FORMATS

Knowing file formats is very important, as each one has different features. We will first explain the features, and you can then use the chart to see which file format has the features you need. For video, we recommend using Photoshop's own PSD format. This has compression, no loss in quality or transparency, and supports layers, or merged layers. For a long time, Premiere and After Effects, had both fully supported blending modes and layer styles. You may hear incorrectly as some people became confused because blending modes did not rebuild correctly when importing as a comp in After Effects or sequence in Premiere, but it did if a single layer or merged layers were imported.

Lossy Compression

Compression is great because it makes smaller files, saving hard drive and server space. Do not use lossy compression on Photoshop images that will be used for video. Lossy compression means that you lose quality the more you compress. JPEG is a perfect example, as the file sizes are small from compression. Video editors will want to use JPEG for their web pages to get small files that download quickly over the internet. Many people do not realize, though, that each time you save a jpeg file it progressively gets worse. The quality slider ranges from 0 to 100, and each time you save it compresses and throughout data. So – keep an image for retouching and a separate jpeg, which is what you upload to your website. Open, save and close an image twenty times as JPEG quality 30, and you will see a blocky soft image come up on screen. Doing multiple saves on an open JPEG file, will only do one round of lossy compression, as it uses the data on screen – which is not the same as the compressed data in the file. If the file is open, it keeps using the original data and not recompressing those pixels each time, not from the saved pixels.

Non-Lossy Compression

The word "non" usually generates negative thoughts, but in this case it is a good thing. Non-lossy means there is no loss in quality when compressing. RLE stands for run length encoding. Imagine a data file of *AAAAAAAAABCCCCCC*, with RLE the file is written as A9B1C6. High-resolution files benefit greatly from RLE compression. Make a new document and fill it with a solid color and save it in PSD format, and you will see a very small file size.

Channels

Channels are usually 8-bit, and they define areas that are solid versus the transparent areas. Photoshop sees white as solid, and black as transparent. There is a range of 256 colors from black to white, with neutral gray being 50% transparent. Most file formats support channels, but TARGA is one that prefers channels to define transparency. Channels were the first way to define masks in Photoshop, but the feature of layer masks is so powerful that many people do not use channels anymore.

Transparency

Adobe took the concept of channels a step further than Barneyscan XP, and made actual layers each supporting transparency. This is what made Photoshop so successful when it first came out.

Layers

Photoshop PSD is a layered format, and since version 6 you have the layered option for TIFF. After Effects and Premiere Pro both allow you to import a layered PSD file and have the option of either importing merged layers, or selecting an individual layer, or putting all the layers together in a comp. Most video editing applications will place a PSD file and recognize the transparency, but not all can import a single PSD file and build a layered comp for you.

Print applications such as Quark will not let you place a PSD file, but Quark will let you place a layered TIFF file. Layered TIFFs are a very popular solution for Quark users. Adobe InDesign is the most advanced programs for handling file formats and it allows you to place PSD files and paste PDF editable vector paths.

Security

Do you want to send a proof to someone and make sure that they can only open it with a password? Open **Chapter 04/File Formats/white House.pdf** and you will be asked for a password. The password is mike. This way you do not have to worry if an email or disk is intercepted. It is usually more convenient to use your winzip or stuffit for adding security as it does it for multiple files in an archive. With PDF though, you can add security with Photoshop.

Content on DVD

Animation

Gif is the only animated image format in Photoshop, and you can only do that from Imageready. After Effects can render an animated gif from your existing video projects, but Imageready will give you smaller files. Gif is limited to 256 colors, so it is not good for video, just simple animations. Most people have Quicktime and Windows media players installed nowadays, so you can save a Sorenson 3 mov, avi or mpg for posting your videos to the web.

PSD has the smallest files size for a file format that accepts layers and is not lossy. These files and available for you to test-drive in your video editing application.

	Layers	Compression (Lossy)	Compression (Holds Quality)	Channels	Transparency	Notes
psd	YES	YES	YES	YES	YES	Excellent all around format for everything
targa	NO	Optional RLE	YES	YES	NO	Great format for TARGA only.
eps	NO	(Optional) JPEG	NO	NO	Hard Edged Path Only	Used in print, Holds clipping paths in Quark and older applications.
tiff	YES	(Optional) LZW	NO		YES	Improved since Photoshop 6.
gif	NO	YES (256 color limit)	NO	YES		Animated capability for web.
jpg	NO	YES	NO	NO	NO	
pict	NO	YES	YES	YES	NO	Similar to Targa, only has 16 or 32 bits per pixel.
pdf	YES	Optional Various	NO	YES	YES	Only format with security
png	NO	(Optional)	YES	NO	YES	Web format never took off, but interesting.

Content on DVD

They are located at **Chapter 04\File Formats**. While TIFF and PDF support layers, only PSD allows you to automatically rebuild the layers into comps in your video editing application.

Name	Size ▲
White House.jpg	51 KB
White House(Compressed).eps	113 KB
White House.gif	184 KB
White House(16bit).pct	442 KB
White House.png	546 KB
White House(Compressed).tga	753 KB
White House(Flattened).psd	777 KB
White House(32bit).pct	786 KB
White House.pcx	787 KB
White House.tga	1,013 KB
White House.eps	1,401 KB
White House.pdf	1,496 KB
White House(no compress).pdf	1,651 KB
White House.psd	2,118 KB
White House.tif	2,661 KB

LAYER COMPS AND SAVE TRICKS

Layer Comps

Photoshop layers are like the ingredients used to make a hamburger. Layer comps allow you to produce different versions of the completed hamburger, based on the information about the layer the comp saved. Open **Chapter 04\Big Mac(LayerCompsDone).psd** and choose **Window >> Layer Comps** if you need to make the window active. **Clicking on the little newspaper icon** to the left of the layer comp name Big Mac x2 changes:

Content on DVD

* ❖ Layer visibility

* ❖ Layer position

* ❖ Effects visibility

Notice the Bun Top layer moved upwards, another layer became visible, and the drop shadow is gone. Close this file and open **Chapter 04\BigMac.psd**, and we will do an exercise together that will help you understand the layer comp making process. The secret to using layer comps is to click the update palette icon often and at the proper moment.

Content on DVD

Step 1: Create and Name your Layer Comps

The first thing you want to do is **click** to the right of update palette icon which is the **new layer comp button**. Name the layer comp Big Mac and turn on all of the

three options. Do the same to make three more layer comps called Big Mac x2, Big Mac x3, and Big Mac x4. You will in most occasions want all three options on, except for when you want to change the position for all comps, with one mouse movement.

Step 2: Make Changes

Duplicate the Burger layer by **dragging the layer icon on the create a new layer button** to the left of the layer palette trash can icon. Change to the move tool, and **enable the option for auto select layer in the option tool bar at the top**. You can now just click on the pixels of a layer to select it, but remember to disable this option later as it can drive you mad when you forget it is on. **Click on the Top Bun and begin to move it upwards**, add the shift key to constrain to a straight upwards movement. Be careful about adding the shift key too early or you will link two layers prior to movement; if this happens, **shift click** on the layer again to unlink it. Next, **click on the Burger copy layer and move it upwards** until it is in perfect position. You will **probably have to adjust the Top Bun again** to get it perfect, and can use the cursor up or down keys to nudge in perfect position.

Step 3: Update Layer Comp States

Click on the name of the layer comp Big Mac x2 to select it. **Click on the update layer comp button** and the newspaper icon will move to Big Mac x2, confirming that is the state of that layer comp. Do the exercise for the next two layer comps, and you should be a layer comp expert now.

Step 4: Viewing Layer Comps

This part is easy, but it will explain the usage of the arrows to the left of the update layer comp button. Click on the previous selected layer comp button, which appears like a play backwards button. The layer comp state just changed to the previous one. You could do this by clicking the space where the newspaper icon goes, but during the review process this can be nice to utilize the arrow buttons.

The flyout menu for the layer comp window is useless and slow. You can simulate every one of the flyout menu options using the icons at the bottom, double-clicking, or dragging a layer comp to the palette icons. Layer comps and the interface are great, unfortunately layer comps are not recognized by video editing applications. There are two solutions, and read on below to learn them both.

Save Tricks

To save a Photoshop document with the Big Mac file open, click on the layer comp newspaper icon for Big Mac x4. **Choose File >> Save As >> psd**, and give the file a new name of **Big Mac(LayerComp)x4.psd**. Go into a video effects application like After Effects and import this. You get the tall x 4 Big Mac. Import the Big Mac(LayerComp)Done.psd file as a comp. All the layers will be there, but the visibility eyeballs will be turned off just as they were in Photoshop. You will also notice that the top bun is positioned incorrectly, as it is in the position for a single Big Mac. We had you do things the longer way, so you can appreciate the next tip.

Open **Big Mac(LayerCompDone).psd** and choose **Files >> Scripts >> Layer Comps** to files. For file name prefix, we recommend choosing a single character like a dash, or delete the name entirely. This is a great function, but when you run it your file names get very long. It will use the name of your layer comp and put a serial number in, so you are safe from having two files with the same name. Save the files to your desktop, review them and delete them.

Content on DVD

Export Layers to Files, and Naming Files

My rule was to never name files with anything but alphanumerics because Mac OS X and Windows do not like \/:*?>< % and those bullet points (whoever started that caused a mess for today's network managers – oops it might have been me back in 1985!). Before Photoshop CS there was no problem with naming your layers with special characters, because the problem comes from the OS not liking files named that way. This is because the new Mac OS is built on UNIX, and commands like "/rm" would reformat a drive. Stay away from those characters they are evil. Safe and useful characters to use for naming are dashes, parentheses, and brackets.

Open **Chapter 04/Fishing.psd** and choose **Files >> Scripts >> Export Layers to Files**. Create a **new folder on your drive called "Fishing Pics"**. Delete the file name prefix and run the script. You will get an error because I named one of the catfish 27 with an inch mark delete the inch mark in the layer name, and your script will work. Change the layer name and run the script again. The script is a little slow and is doing some extra work it does not need to, but hopefully Adobe will fix this in an update.

Content on DVD

FILE BROWSER

Wow – Photoshop CS made the file browser even better! Choose **Window >> File Browser** and then move the Photoshop window over so you can see the desktop of your operating system to the left. Find the folder for Fishing Pics you created, and drag and drop that in the Preview palette tab of the file browser. Yes, this works on both PC & Mac.

The file browser also has menu commands, and the default is a large thumbnail view. Choose **View >> Details**, and you will see a different view and that the script we ran saved the EXIF data which can be input and accessed by **Alt Ctrl I [Option Command I]**. This will tell you information about where the image came from, but if you left copyright notice blank, then nobody will see that in the file browser. In this view you will have interesting detail such as your color mode and pixels. So, if you are trying to find which files are CMYK and change them to RGB for video, this is where to go.

In the file browser filemenu you can:

❖ Create a new folder

❖ Purge cache (if you are having problems)

❖ Export cache (if you put files on a CD/DVD and wish others to have a fast thumbnail generation)

❖ Search (by filename, keywords and many other options)

Under Edit, you have preferences which we covered in Chapter 1. You have rotation and flagging, but that is better done by the icons above your thumbnails.

Now the automate menu is useful as you can run all the same automation, but you have the option of running them on file browser-selected files. You also have an additional feature we love to use called Batch Rename. Yes, you can select files in a folder and rename them all with a similar interface to the save for web feature. Neither the PC nor Mac have this feature built into the OS, and Adobe has it in a Photo editing program. Chapter 9 will cover automation.

The sort menu options work best if you are in view by detail. Under View, you can turn on the view for unreadable files, to see files which are not pictures. With this you can rename your movie files. The last interesting command in the view file browser is **View >> Reveal Location in Explorer (reveal location in finder)**.

If you have a library of images that you use as stock footage in your video projects, then you should look over the keywords options. You can make new keyword sets, and assign keywords to multiple images. To assign a keyword to an image, you only need to check the box in front of a keyword such as birthday. If this library is used by only one machine, then this option is great, as you have a file cataloger inside Photoshop. The biggest drawback is a person on the network will not see the keywords as the information resides on your machine. You could export your cache, but it will be a hassle to load the exported cache on each machine each time the keywords are updated.

EXPORTING

There are many scenarios that require an editor to derive a still image from video footage. Sometimes, a few hundred images may be needed to serve the interests of publicity, web content, DVD menu elements, collages, packaging, and a host of others. Unfortunately, the larger and more complex projects don't seem to come with forgiving deadlines, and a fluid work flow is needed to bring a project in on time. Chapter 3 provided a more comprehensive look at how to properly export images between Photoshop and a video editing application. This section talks about the strategy when dealing with large workloads.

FILE MANAGEMENT

The most important step is to plan ahead. You'll want to create separate folders for original images exported from the video application and for finished images waiting to be imported back into the video application. Both folders should be filed within a general "graphics" folder, within a master project folder.

Once all of the images are exported into their own folder, open a new document at the appropriate size. Save the new document as "MASTER" in a new folder within the same folder as the original images. You will do all of the work on each image within the MASTER file. The reason for this hierarchal structure will come to the forefront when you generate the new images to import into the video application.

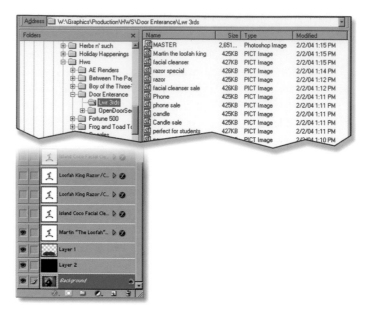

Maintaining symmetry between your layers and project folders will aid in keeping you organized with large projects.

Content on DVD

Open the file **Chapter 4 >> Homework Show** from the DVD. Notice how the layers and layer sets are organized. The Homework Show is a community service program produced by Jan Shimek III to fill an FCC requirement that all broadcasting stations must satisfy. The show is not intended to take in a profit, just to establish a relationship with Chicago Public Schools and create a little bit of positive PR. A week's worth of segments are expected from a single 8-hour session, and that includes the graphic elements. Organization is the only way this is even possible.

The first element created in this example was the background. Then, a custom banner was designed. The last elements needed were the various texts to go over the banners to create each lower third. Some time and care were spent on the first text layer to find the right blend of font, size, kerning, drop shadow, bevel, and gradient overlay. Once the right look is decided on, it becomes a template for all the other text layers.

With the first text layer selected, hit **Ctrl J [Command J]** as many times as there are layers needed. You can click and drag over the eye icons of all the layers you just created until you are left with only one layer visible. Double-click that layer and the text will be highlight in the window, ready for you to enter the new line of text for the next lower third. Repeat this process until all of your lower thirds are finished. Save the MASTER file.

Now is when you need to create the separate files for the different lower thirds. Some of the newer and more powerful editing applications on the market are boasting four, five, or more layers of realtime editing. Even if rendering is not an issue, working with 30 self-contained files is easier than dealing with 60 instances on the timeline. Also, some video applications allow for importing of Photoshop files as compositions with separated layers. This is a wonderful timesaver. However, unless your Photoshop composition contains no layer styles or adjustment layers or clipping groups, what you build in Photoshop will not be represented properly in your video editing application.

ALPHA CHANNELS

From the MASTER file, create a new bottom layer as straight black. Do this by clicking the new layer icon at the bottom of the layer palette, then use the Bucket tool, G, with the foreground set to black. Click anywhere on the blank layer and the Bucket tool will fill it with black. Now **Ctrl [Command] Click** the banner layer in the layer palette to create a selection. In the Channels palette, click on the mask icon on the bottom to create an alpha channel. Photoshop will automatically name it Alpha 1. You can see in the Channels palette that the selection you just made is now represented by white space and the area outside the selection is now black. When you bring an image with an alpha channel into a video editing application, the program will see the white area as visible and the black area as transparent. Creating the project with a black background will keep the "halo" phenomenon from becoming a problem when soft edges are used or when fading in and out in your video editing application.

Once the alpha channel is set, you're ready to create the separate lower thirds. Make the top text layer the only text visible with the banner visible beneath. Save **Ctrl Shift S [Command Shift S]** as a keyword in the text or as a sequential file. By default, Photoshop will assume you want to save it in the same root folder as the MASTER file. That is why we created its own folder. This way, we just go straight down the layer palette, saving as needed.

When in the Save As dialog box, be sure to uncheck the Layers box if you are saving as a flattened Photoshop file. If you don't uncheck it, a duplicate file is created with all the layers intact. This might be useful for other purposes, but for dealing with a large number of images, it's best to keep the clutter to a minimum. Also, you might want to consider saving as a .pict or .tga file. They can hold an alpha channel, and their compression is not too damaging for video purposes. The nice benefit to using a .pct or .tga file is that they can reduce the file size by 40% or more and are supported by most video editing applications.

IMPORTING

You have over 50 images that you made in Photoshop. You've got less than 2 hours before your project hits the air. You need to bring these files in properly and without delay. When bringing stills into Premiere, it works with the original files. The fastest way to bring in multiple images is to **Import >> Folder** into the project bin.

When working with Avid, create a new bin for the finished graphics and choose **File >> Import**. Click the Options tab. Make sure that the settings for **601 non-square pixels, 235 color levels, non-interlaced**, and **invert alpha** are all selected. Hit **OK**. When in the window for the folder containing the images, you

When you open an entire folder within Premiere, the folder stays separate and organized within the project.

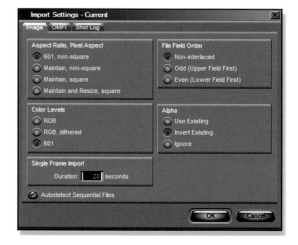

Avid gives you many ways to interpret footage and graphics.

can select them all by clicking and dragging over them, shift clicking the first and last files, or by hitting **Ctrl A [Command A]** and hitting Import. Once they are in the Avid bin, you are working with newly created OMFI files. Once you delete the media from inside Avid, the originals are still in their folders. You are able to delete or archive them for later use.

If changes have to be made to your lower thirds, such as spelling corrections, make the changes to the MASTER Photoshop file. **Save As** to the new file, replacing the incorrect lower third. Photoshop will double check that you want to do this, but we certainly don't want to work with bad content. After the changes have been made, reopen your Premiere project and they will automatically be replaced. If you are working with Avid, highlight the file in the bin and go to **Bin >> Batch Import** and hit **ALL**. Avid will open a dialog box with the original window where the first image was imported from and will automatically highlight the file with the same name. Hit **OK** and it is updated in the timeline. When importing and re-importing images with applications that do not convert them to a proprietary format like Avid does, such as Premiere, Final Cut Pro, Edition, and Vegas, you can reopen your project after changes have been made.

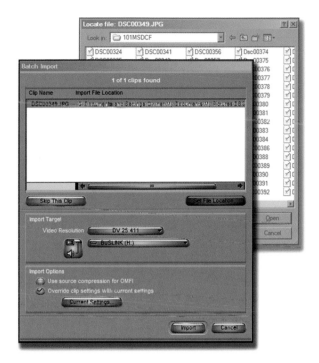

Getting used to Avid's conventions of re-importing corrected images is worth the trouble.

5
LAYERS

USING LAYERS

This chapter slowly introduces skills used by experienced Photoshop professionals, and builds your basic layer skills to include working with multiple layers at a faster pace. Open **Chapter 05/Manhattan.psd**, a file with only a background layer. An image can only have one background layer, and is always on the bottom in italics. Background layers are rarely used and more of a nuisance as most everyone has to convert them to a floating layer. Double-click on the italic background layer and rename it to the default layer 0. Now you can move the layer, and have transparency if you use the eraser. After converting thousands of background layers to non italics you will agree with me that background layers can be simulated by locking a layer, and are not needed in Photoshop.

Content on DVD

Making a Path Selection and Floating It

Click the Paths tab to view your paths palette and **Ctrl [Command] click on the name for path 1** making it the active selection. Marching ants will represent the boundaries of your selection. Hit **Ctrl J [Command J]**, and you will notice the marching ants are gone – this lets you know that you floated a layer. The menu command for floating a selection is Layer >> New >> Layer via Copy. In previous Photoshop versions the command was called "Float Layer", and some people remember J for jump. Click the Layers tab and you see a Layer 1, that is of the martini glass without the background. Floating a layer is one of the most essential tricks that a professional often uses.

Selecting Channels and Constricting Selections

Click on the Channels tab, and you will see we created a channel called Drink. **Ctrl [Command] the Drink Channel** to make that an active marching ants selection. Try changing the drink to a green apple flavor using **Image >> Adjust >> Hue Saturation**, dragging the hue until your drink is green. Once the hue palette is visible, you can hit **Ctrl H [Command H]** to temporarily hide the marching ants, but the drink is still selected – don't panic! We slid hue over to 60, and saturation to 10.

Renaming, Deleting, Creating and Moving Layers

Switch to the Layers palette and **double-click on "Layer 1"**; you will be able to change the name of the layer to "Apple". **Drag "Layer 0" to the layer palette trashcan** to delete it. To the left of the trashcan is a page icon you can click to create a new layer. Hit **(d)** to reset your default foreground and background colors. Hit **(x)** to switch your foreground and background colors. Now hit **Alt Delete [option Delete]** to fill the layer with a color. OOPS! – we still had the channel selection before and did not fill the entire layer. Hit **Ctrl A [Command A]** to Select All and you will confirm this by seeing marching ants along your entire document. Now again hit **Alt Delete [option Delete]** to fill the entire layer with white. Now **drag "Layer 1" below the "Apple" layer** in the Layers palette.

Manhattan made into an Appletini.

Visibility and Soloing Layers

Nacho & BBQ layers are linked.

Open **Chapter 05/FritosFloorstand(1).psd,** and inspect the layers. Notice the three layers at the top which do not have an eyeball to the left of the layer name "Nacho". Click in the space to turn on the eyeball and you will make it visible showing a blue Nacho Fritos bag. Click on the space again to turn the layer visibility off. Now click hold and drag downwards over the three empty spaces to turn on more than one layer with one mouse movement and let go of the mouse button.

Content on DVD

Hold down **Alt [Option]** and click on the "Nacho" eyeball to turn off all the layers in a document except "Nacho" – this is called solo. **Alt [Option]** click on "Nacho" again, and you will turn on all the layers – in other words unsolo the "Nacho" layer.

Linking and Targeting Image Adjustments

Now you will notice "Nacho" has a paintbrush and "BBQ" has a chain link. This brush means "Nacho" is the targeted layer for any painting, deleting or modification you would do. The chain on the "BBQ" layer means it is linked to "Nacho". Linked layers will be moved or transformed together, but effects only happen on the one layer with the paintbrush. You can never have more than one layer with a paintbrush.

These bags look strange as blue, and we will fix that. With the "Nacho "layer targeted, hit **Ctrl I [Command[I]** to invert the pixels into beautiful red Fritos bags. **Click on the BBQ layer to select it** and **invert the pixels, then do the same for the Original layer.** Now with the move tool selected **click and drag the Original bag**

Three flavors in position.

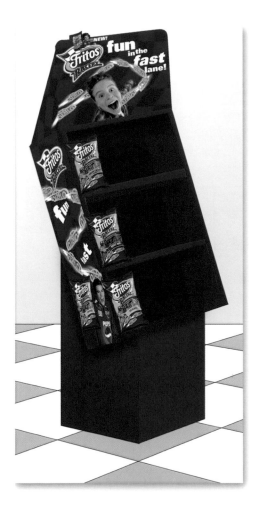

to the bottom shelf, left side, inside the floorstand. Now **select the "BBQ" layer and move that to the middle shelf**, and notice the Nacho layer also move. This is because those layers are linked. **Select the "Nacho" layer and notice** the link is still there, **click on the BBQ Link to remove the link** option. Now you can move the "Nacho" layer in place. You have to zoom in close to see that each of the three bags are different flavors indeed. **Ctrl + [Command +]** to 200% you should be able to read the flavor. Your image should now look like the one on page 70:

LAYER SETS AND LINKING LAYERS

Continue with the same file or open **Chapter 05/FritosFloorstand(2).psd**. Inspect the layers, and you will see folders such as "Midsection" which are called layer sets. **Click on the arrow to the left of the layer name "Midsection"** and you will expand the set showing five layers along with a nested layer set called "Rim". **Expand "Rim"** and you will find Layer nesting is a new option for Photoshop CS, and you can open CS files in previous versions, but the layers will not be nested. **Ctrl 0 [Command 0]** to fit the image on your screen and collapse the layer set midsection.

With "Nacho" as the active layer, **click on the BBQ link and drag over "Original"** so that the three flavor bags are linked. From the layers flyout menu **choose "New Set From Linked"** and name this layer set "Bags". The three layers will move into the layer set bags. **Open the "Bags" set and unlink the three layers**.

Move & Duplicate & Link Layers

With the Move tool selected, **enable Auto Select Layer** in the options bar at the top of the screen. **Alt [Option] drag a "Nacho" bag** to the right so a copy slightly overlaps the first bag. **Drag 2 more copies until you have four bags** across the front of the top shelf. Let's link the four Nacho bag layers together, and put them into a layer set. In the Layers palette, **drag across the empty row of boxes to link the four Nacho bags**. One of the bags will have a paintbrush, and three will have a link. The paintbrush symbolizes the active layer, and the three bags are linked to the active layer. If you **Choose "New Set From Linked" from the flyout menu. Double-click on "Set 1" and Rename it to "Nacho"**. From the **flyout menu choose Duplicate Set** and name that "Nacho 2". (Do not drag the layer set onto the icon for new layer set, as it will not duplicate the layer set in Photoshop CS, just create a new blank one. This used to work in previous versions of Photoshop.) **Turn off Auto Select Layer**, or else you will regret that you did not. Now **select the "Nacho 1" layer set and drag it up and to the right**. We dragged the Nacho 1 layer, because we want the row of bags in back to be the second row, so that the row in front is the top layer set. For practice, do the same to the BBQ and Original shelf until you have a total of 24 bags. You may have a little trouble on the bottom "Original" row as there is a guide and the snapping could make the image snap to the guide. You can delete that guide or turn off snapping in the view menu.

Masking a Layer Set

Continue with the same file or open **Chapter 05/FritosFloorstand(3).psd**. The bags are slightly hanging out of the shelves. To make it look more real, we will put a holdback mask onto the layer set called "Bags". We already have the shapes we need, and just need to make a selection from the transparency of the layer in the set called "rim". **Flip open the layer set arrow for the "Midsection" and the "Rim" layer sets. Ctrl [Command] click on the layer "Outer Rim"**, the marching ants will appear around the selection of outer rim. Continue holding **Ctrl [Command] add Shift and click on "Inner Rims" and "Left"** to add them to your selection. Now – do not do the foolish thing using the delete key on each layer. There is a non-destructive way called layer mask which you will want to use, and yes – they even work on layer sets. **Choose the layer set called "Bags" and choose Layer >> Add Layer Mask >> Hide Selection.**

The bags need a little separation between them, and shadows would help. We will do that very soon in Chapter 6 when we cover layer styles. We will next create a reflection of the floorstand on the dull tile floor; this will make the floor look shiny – as though it has just been waxed. Then, we will show you how to merge selected layers together.

MERGING SELECTED LAYERS

We will flip a copy of the floorstand layers and take the opacity down so that it looks like a reflection on the floor. First, we must merge the floorstand layers together into a new layer. We only want one layer for the reflection, so we can manipulate it as a whole. Turn off the visibility for the bottom layer set called "background". Create a new layer above the Nacho layer set, by **clicking on the new layer icon to the left of the trash can on the Layers palette.** Now **hold down Alt [Option] and choose from the Layer palette flyout menu >> Merge Visible. Rename the "Layer 1" to "Reflection".**

Choose **Edit >> Transform >> Flip Vertical.** Then **drag this layer below the layer set called "Base".** In the Layers palette, **change the opacity of this layer to 20%.** We need to move the image down, but there is not enough canvas. Choose **Image >> Canvas Size >> 3439 Height >> middle top square anchor.** Zoom out and see the entire canvas by hitting **Ctrl - [Command -] twice.** Now **drag the "Reflection" layer downwards holding shift** until the two bottom-most points of both floorstands touch.

Fixing the Skew

Hit **[m]** to switch to the rectangular marquee tool. **Drag a marquee frame around the left half of the reflection** as shown. Hit **Ctrl T [Command T]** to transform this selection. Begin to **drag the transform handle** indicated by the red circle 1, **in the middle of dragging add Ctrl [Command], and you will be able to freely skew**

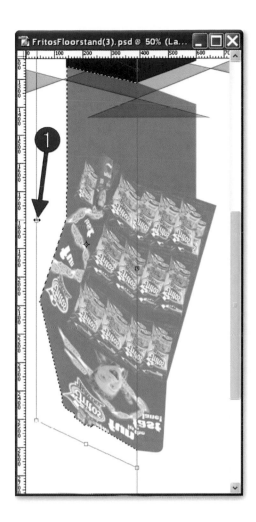

the left side as in the image above. You must hold down the **Ctrl[Command]** key for this to work, and you can even add the keys later but you need to drag while holding down those modifier keys. **Hit Return** to accept the transformation, and then with the **marquee tool do the same to the right half**. Now, we will just want to distort the entire reflection in another direction, so hit **Ctrl A [Command A]** to select all. **Hit Ctrl T and do a similar skew from the bottom middle handle** and try to get the final image above. We will get into layer masks in Chapter 15 to show you how to fade the reflection with a gradient.

MOVING LAYERS INTO DOCUMENTS

Moving Layer Sets between Documents

Continue with the same file or open **Chapter 05/FritosFloorstand(4).psd & FritosFloorstand(5).psd**. Version 5 does not have any bags, so you need to stock it, and everything has the same position as version 4. First, **highlight the layer set**

Content on DVD

Bags in version 5 to make it the active target. **Click the window for version 4** to bring that window to the front, **shift drag the bags layer set over to version 5.** A copy should come over, and it should be positioned perfectly inside the floorstand. This works if both images are the same size in pixels, or else it drops the layers in the center of the new document.

Copying Linked Layers between Documents

Often, you create alternate versions of something and want to borrow things from one document to another. There is one additional big secret here, and that is how to copy linked layers. The secret is to drag the image and not the layer name, and even the most advanced users don't believe this move is possible.

With **version 5 in front, hit F12 to revert** to the original version without any bags. On **version 4, flip open the bags layer set and link two bags together.** Then **shift click on the window for version 4,** and **drag the image – not the layer name – for bags, and release the mouse into version 5.** Many things can foul up this difficult move: such as

❖ if you have Auto Select Layer enabled in the options bar at the top

❖ if you do not have the move tool selected

To do this properly, you really do not have to click on a certain pixel in version 4, but anywhere inside the window and it is better to add shift afterwards and drag to version 5.

6

LAYER STYLES AND PATTERNS

STYLE AND ADJUSTMENT LAYERS

Targeting a Layer

As promised in Chapter 5, we will continue and add soft drop shadows to each bag in the floorstand. That is a lot of bags, but we will show you a shortcut, so open **Chapter 05/FritosFloorstand(4).psd**. Double-click the magnifying glass to get a 100% view. Hold the spacebar down, to temporarily get the hand tool. Use the

Content on DVD

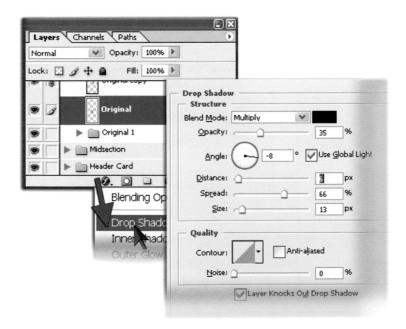

Add Layer Style Palette button.

hand to center on the bags. **Hit (v)** for the move tool and **choose Auto Select Layer in the options bar** at the top. We want to start by adding a drop shadow on a bag in the bottom row. **Click on the bottom left Original flavor bag** and your layer sets should flip open to highlight and **select the layer called "Original".**

Creating and Modifying a Drop Shadow

Click on the circle f icon at the bottom of the layers palette and choose the Drop Shadow Layer style. A huge layer style window will open and a checkmark will be in front of Drop Shadow. Keep the layer style window open, and **drag upwards inside the image to move the drop shadow.** By dragging in the image window you adjust the angle and distance values in the Layer Style palette. We prefer to structure my drop shadows beginning with the spread, so that is why the chart is in that order. Experiment with the settings or input the values supplied in the image.

Spread   Outwards expansion distance in pixels

Size   Hardness along the spread

Distance   Offset distance along angle in pixels

Drag Copying a Single Layer Style

Click on the arrow to the left of the circle f on the original layer to expand the layer styles assigned to that layer. You will see the word Effects and then the words Drop Shadow. You can drag the words Effects to copy all the layer styles from one

Drag Copy effects between layers.

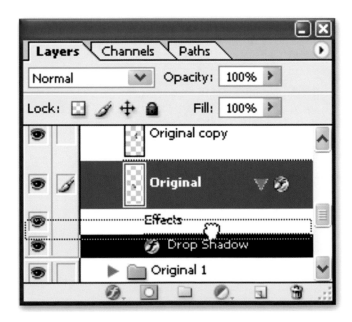

layer to another. Since there is only one layer effect, it does not make a difference, and we just drag copy the drop shadow. **Drag the words Drop Shadow upward until you see a black line just below the "Original Copy" layer above and drop it**. This will drag and drop a copy of the Drop Shadow layer style onto the other layer. With so many bags to add drop shadows to, there must be an easier way. YES – there IS a way to apply a layer effect to multiple layers.

Copy and Paste Layer Effects

Select a layer that has the drop shadow and choose **Layer >> Layer Style >> Copy Layer Style**. Next, resize your Layers palette as large as it will fit on your screen. **Flip open the arrow for all the bags layers sets** so you can see the name of each layer that is a bag of chips. **Select the bottom most bag layer to target it, then click and hold in the empty space above the paintbrush and drag upwards**

Final File with drop shadows between each bag.

until you link all the layers. Here comes the grand finale – choose **Layer >> Layer Style >> Paste Layer Style to Linked**, and you have a drop shadow on all your bags.

We prefer to assign drop shadows in my animation program because we can animate them, but in this case you do not need to animate them so it is easier using Photoshop to add all these little drop shadows for depth.

Stacking Layer Effects

Content on DVD

You can enable 12 layer styles, plus blending options for every layer. Open up **Chapter 06/Layer Styles.psd** and you will see a layer with seven layer styles configured, but the visibility is off. **Turn on the visibility for each layer style** and watch the type come alive. Though the visibility is off, the settings are remembered, which is a great feature if you are going through an approval process. If you want to get back the big Layer Style palette, just **double-click on the word Effects or on any of the Layer Styles.** In the styles screenshot, you can see the word Drop Shadow is highlighted in blue, which tells you that the settings to the right will be for Drop Shadow. You can choose any of the other 11, and even the blending mode at the top.

Blue highlight shows that Drop Shadow is active for editing.

Stroke Layer Style

There is a new style button that you can pick, and if you like this set of layer effects, it will add this to your styles palette. Click cancel or OK to get out of the Layers palette. We can delete all the layer effects by dragging the word Effects to the trash, which leaves us with black type on a black background. Add a layer effect of stroke, and say OK to the default of three red pixels. To get multiple strokes, duplicate the layer, and change the stroke width of the bottom layer to let's say a 6-point white stroke to see an outer stroke of 3 points on the type. With Photoshop, you do not have a choice for the endcap shape of strokes, so they always look rounded as they get heavier, and there are no dashed lines. You will want to use Adobe Illustrator for more options to create a custom strokes. Once you start stacking multiple strokes in Photoshop you begin to get a 1960s style look, as in Layers **Chapter 06/Styles(Strokes).psd**.

Content on DVD

Satin and Adjustment Layer Styles

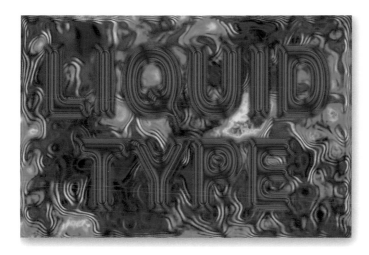

Open **Chapter 06/Liquid Type.psd**, and you will see some of the tricks to making Satin work for you. **Turn on the visibility for the "freaky color" layer** and watch what power an adjustment layer can have. Don't be afraid to use the Satin layer style. It is useful for getting liquid effects, and it works with the transparency of a layer. It produces these waves of chrome on the edge of transparency so similar to painting with liquid mercury. To control the complexity of the amount of waves, **double-click on the Satin Layer Effect and change the contour of the Satin layer** effect. The contour is the graph icon you get in the Layer Styles palette. To get the edges of the type to fade into the background, a new layer was created called "Expansion". The "Liquid Type" layer was Ctrl[Command] clicked on and then the command select >> modify >> expand, was used to get a fatter selection. This was filled with blue and then a Gaussian blur faded the edges. You can delete the "Expansion" layer and try to create your own.

Content on DVD

Pass Through versus Normal Layer Set

The default Photoshop layer set blending mode is Pass through. Layer effects will pass through the Layer Set, affecting everything else underneath. The way to

Change a layers set from pass through to normal to contain adjustment layer.

Content on DVD

constrain layer effects to a layer set, is to set the mode to normal. The word "normal" does not sound exciting, but this is something really important that every Photoshop user should be familiar with. Open **Chapter 06/Satins Fire.psd** to see a Layer Set called type. **Turn the visibility on for the Fiery Gradient adjustment layer.** The type will turn into colorful fire, but we destroyed the nice effect of the smeared crossed x gradient background. The problem is that the gradient adjustment layer is not only affecting our type layer in the set, but also the layers outside of the Layer Set. Luckily, we can keep the gradient effect within the type Layer Set, by changing the blending mode. Change the **Type Layer Set Blending Mode from Pass Through to Normal,** to get the final result.

TILED PATTERNS

Healing the Seams

Content on DVD

Let's start out by making two different types of tiling patterns, and then we will show you the advantage to applying them as layer effects, rather than fills. Open **Chapter 06/Grass.psd**.

Offset the image so the edges meet in the middle showing where they would overlap. Choose **Filter >> Other >> Offset, and input the values 650 and 550** as in the screenshot.

You will see a seam down the middle which would look worse, if you were to repeat the tiles next to each other. Change to your Healing brush (**j**) and hit your right bracket (**]**) **key shortcut to increase your brush size to 100 pixels.** Hold down **Alt [Option]** and **click on the red circle 1 to define the source point and release** the mouse button. Then **click and hold the mouse button on the red circle 2 and drag to the right, when you get to the right edge release** the mouse button. The amazing Healing brush will do a great job and fix the seam. There also is a vertical seam, and you will want to repeat the same procedure. The vertical seam is not that evident because the color and tone of the grass are the same along the

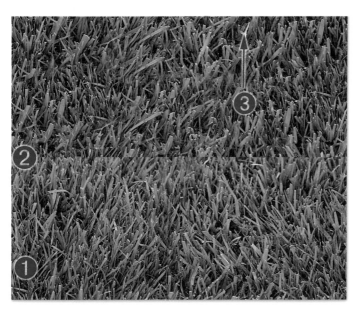

horizontal axis. You do want to show more grass blade tips and just randomize the seam area for a good tiling pattern.

Remove Eye-Catching Objects

The red circle 3 is pointing to a larger yellow blade of dead grass. It is very hard to see, but you should hit **Ctrl** + [**Command** +], to zoom in on your window until it says Grass.psd@200%. **Use the Healing brush to remove any elements that would show a repeating pattern.** This image is already very clean, but had there been a rock in the grass, you would see that rock every 1330 × 1100 pixels, and your pattern would not look realistic. The original image had smaller blades of grass towards the top, because they were farther away from the camera lens. The square we chose towards the bottom had similar size blades of grass, and gave us enough area so that the pattern would look real.

Defining and Applying Patterns

Choose **Edit >> Define Pattern**, and you will get this dialog box of which you can name the pattern grass. Now make a new document using one of the video presets, and go to your Layers palette. **Click on the Layer palette icon for Create New Adjustment Layer >> Pattern.** For scale change this to any number you like, we chose 25%. Smaller than 100% is good, but you have to worry about pixelization larger than 100%. Patterns do not care what dpi your file is, so if you create a 720 × 480 pixel document, it will look the same in 300 dpi as it would in a 72 dpi document. While in this dialog box, use the Move tool on the image to adjust the position of the pattern, as if you had the Hand tool.

Offsetting Logos for Wallpaper

In this next example, you will practice what we learned and use maths to create a tile pattern similar to gift wrap. **Open KahluaTile.psd** and choose **Image >> Image Size.** You will see that this document is 1000 × 1000 pixels, and has a logo in the top left. We will make three more copies for a gift wrap or wallpaper-style repeating pattern. Duplicate the "Kahlua.ai" layer once, then choose **Filter >>**

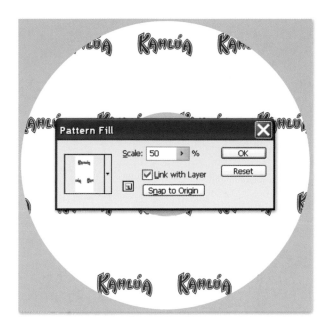

Other >> Offset 500 to the right. You now have two Kahlua logos horizontal to each other, and to make things easier we will merge the two layers. **Ctrl E [Command E]** to merge the layer down, then duplicate the "kahlua.ai" layer which should have two logos in it, for a total of four logos in the document. Choose **Filter >> Other >> Offset 250 to the right and 500 down, with Wrap Around enabled**.

Define a pattern as you did before and name it. Instead of throwing out your Kahlua wallpaper file, save it. The reason for this is that patterns do not recognize transparency. If later you desire to put the logo on a background of Kahlua brown, you will regret not having saved a worker file. You could try using the Blending option of a layer to get rid of white, but the aliasing will leave a halo of white. Open **DVD Kahlua.psd** and **double-click on the "pattern Fill 1" layer**. You can resize and shift position as the pattern has been applied as an adjustment layer and not as a fill.

Content on DVD

7

VECTOR SHAPES

*S*ave yourself production time, and build video files to be repurposed for print by understanding the vector capabilities in Photoshop. You can create or import a vector logo in Photoshop. This will be covered in the final bonus chapter—Illustrator for Video. The exercises in this chapter are designed to help you combine shapes in Photoshop. Those who know how to use the pen tool from Illustrator already have much useful experience for working with shapes in Photoshop.

BITMAPPED OR VECTOR?

Computer images are made with vector and bitmapped data. Bitmapped objects are simply made up of many colored rectangles called pixels. Vector objects use mathematical equations to describe their shapes. Curves and corners are defined by handles that extrude from points. Vector files are usually smaller in file

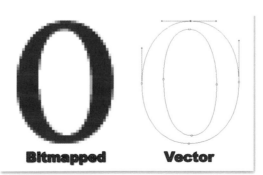

Bitmapped and Vector.

size, and therefore faster to work with. Vector files are also resolution-independent, so you can scale and transform them without any loss of quality. Type and shape layers are actually vector objects, until you use a command such as rasterize. You can always transform a vector object to a bitmapped object, so build your objects as vector rather than bitmapped, when you have that option.

Often, your only option is to build your graphics as bitmapped. Photographs can only be accurately represented by pixels, and not by mathematical shapes. Bitmapped graphics are better when you need soft edges and more colors, but vector is better for flat tints, or something that needs a crisp hard edge. Ultimately, everything you make gets bitmapped before it goes to tape; all vector graphics turn into bitmap when you render your movie file from your video editing program. Without vector graphics we would have to scan all our type, and we could not make changes without retouching the type as pixels, rather than as a vector object. The mistake that many people make is not to use the vector capabilities of Photoshop enough, and to build better vector layers we need to use shapes.

SHAPES

Making Shapes

We often forget that shapes in Photoshop go well beyond just drawing squares and circles. You can also paste clipboard data from a vector-dominant program such as Adobe Illustrator. The toolbar at the top has very useful options and custom shapes. There are three ways in which shapes tool draws shapes:

Shapes   Draws a solid adjustment layer, and uses your shape as a vector mask

Paths   Draws a work path in the paths palette that you will add to, until the name of the path is deselected in the paths palette.

Fill Pixels   Draws bitmapped pixels into the current selected bitmapped layer. Will not work if current selected layer is a type, or adjustment layer without a layer mask.

The rectangle, rounded rectangle and ellipse tools all have similar options, and each can be very useful when needed. Suppose you want to draw shapes of all the

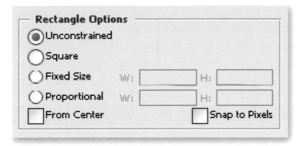

same sizes, then you can set a fixed size. The circled numbers which we use occasionally in the book were set so the size matched on all of them.

The polygon tool has different options, and you can draw a triangle if you set the sides to three. The Smooth Corner option is not that useful except for three-sided

figures and stars. There is no radius for a smooth corner, so everything quickly becomes a circle once you use more than four sides. Drawing stars is easy when you check the option, and you can make them pointy by increasing the inset percentage.

The line tool gives you the options of arrowheads at the beginning and end. The width and length are confusing, but the default is 500%, or five times the weight

of the line. Using numbers below 200% for width or height will not make a good arrowhead, since you would barely see it. A negative concavity makes an arrowhead look like a spear, and a positive number makes a pointy arrow. At the default concavity of 0%, the arrowheads come off at 90 degrees from the line. Arrows are very useful in video, and are great for focusing attention.

Width	Length	Concavity
10% to 1000%	10% to 5000%	−50% to 50%
of weight of line	of weight of line	

Custom Shapes

You can create your own useful sets of shapes containing: logos, dingbats, icons, or whatever common object you need. Open the file **Chapter 07/Custom Shapes.psd**, and you will see two shape layers for the Dolby and DVD logos. Adding commonly used items to our preset shapes would be a great time saver. Here is how to do it:

Content on DVD

    Select the Dolby shape layer, and then go to the Paths palette. You will see a path called Dolby vector mask. From your Photoshop menu choose **Edit >> Define Custom Shape**. Once you have named the shape and it has been added to your current shapes, from the option bar at the top **click on the shape picker and select the Dolby logo**. Photoshop does not automatically switch to your newly defined shape, so you have to do it. **Make a new document and then hold down Shift and drag to draw a Dolby logo** using your existing foreground color. Now you can quit and reboot Photoshop. The custom shapes you have just created will be there, and by quitting you saved the shapes to your Photoshop preference file. If your computer crashes, you could lose shapes if you do not save them. A very smart thing to do is use the **Custom Shapes flyout menu >> Save Shapes**. Many people do not do this, only to find that they lose their shapes in future procedures. Load a library of shapes using the **Custom Shapes flyout menu >> Load >> Chapter 07/Number Circle Shapes.csh**.

PATHFINDER

There is no pathfinder in Photoshop, as in Illustrator, but you do have the ability to add, subtract, intersect, and exclude shapes in Photoshop. Making compound paths in Photoshop is a little tricky, but can save your day if you follow along and learn these techniques. Open **Chapter 07/Adidas.psd** and you will see a shape layer for the Adidas logo, but the middles of the letters are not cut out.

Content on DVD

Make Compound Paths

Hit **Shift [A]** until you switch to the solid path selection tool. **Click on the middle of the letter a, to select the middle of the circle** you need to knock out. Go to the options bar above and **click the fourth icon in the group called Exclude**, and you will have fixed the first letter. **Click on the next circle to knock out, which is the middle of the d. Hold down Shift to select the remaining two letters**, and then **click the Exclude** button in the options bar.

Now the hard part – change to the zoom tool and zoom in on the register r symbol (®). **Click on the inner circle and fix this as you just did using Exclude.** Now what do you do? If you try to change either the outer or inner shape of the r, you get the wrong result. What you need to do is change the layering order of the paths for the r against the circle. **Shift select both the inner and outer shape for the r,** then hit **Ctrl x [Command x]** to cut them to the clipboard. Hit **Ctrl v [Command v]** to paste them back in place. Notice that two important things happen: first, the paths paste back in the same position, and second, because of the layering, they are now on top of other paths stacking order. The center of the r needs fixing, but you can do that using the Exclude trick.

Combining Paths

Open up **Chapter 07/combine.psd** file and you will see a gray snowman. With the solid path selection tool you can select individual paths and move them around. You can hit **Ctrl T [Command T]** to transform the paths you have selected to rotate scale or skew. Now suppose you want to merge the three body sections of the gray snowman into one path, here is what you do. **Shift select the three body parts of the snowman,** then **click the Combine button** in the top options bar. The Combine button only appears when you have one of the two path selection tools selected. You will not have the Combine option with the move tool or the shape tools.

Content on DVD

Vector Masks

Open up **Chapter 07/Bellagio.psd** and you will see an image with two layers and one path. Now for the advanced people, you won't believe this until you see it! The gradient at the bottom is actually created by the stroke effect being graduated by the layer mask applied. For this project we will take the path call "Bellagio" and use it to apply a vector hard mask to the "Blue" layer, which already has a soft, bitmapped mask.

The top layer "Blue" may already be selected, as that is how the file was saved. Go to the **Paths palette and select the "Bellagio" path.** To add a hard mask to the blue layer choose **Layer > Add Vector Path >> Current Path.** Wow!! The layer effects of the drop shadow and blue stroke have taken effect, and you have an image which will make a lovely postcard style intro to a video.

Content on DVD

8
BRUSHES

*W*hen a painter creates a painting, they have to choose a canvas, which can be anything from paper, a car hood, or a brick wall. Respectively, they can use a number of tools to express their message from a paintbrush, an airbrush, or a spray can. As authors and readers of this book, we've already chosen video as our ultimate

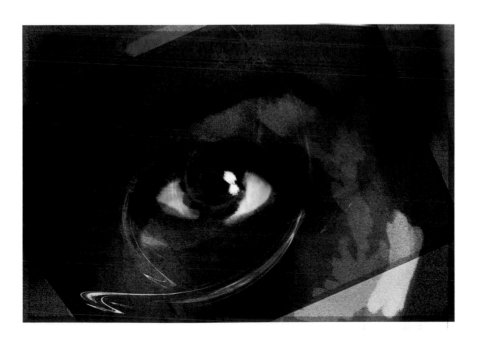

canvas, but the tools we can use to paint with inside Photoshop are quite extensive and flexible. Even if you are not a gifted drawer/painter, becoming intimate with the various brushes and their control settings will empower you nearly every time you open an image inside Photoshop.

THEY'RE NOT JUST FOR PAINTING ANYMORE

Your first thought might be that the brushes in Photoshop are just for drawing things. While you certainly can draw with the brush tool, the controls and characteristics of all the brushes apply to over a dozen separate tools in the program including (but not limited to) the Healing Brush, Clone Stamp, Eraser, History Brush, Blur Tool, Dodge Tool, Burn Tool, and Sponge Tool. The adjustable brush parameters are exactly the same for dialing in the characteristics you want when you will be using any of these various tools utilizing a brush metaphor. Memorizing the shortcuts listed in this chapter and Chapter 1 will help you to hone your skills and increase your speed when performing tasks such as painting, erasing, smudging, sharpening, blurring, masking, cloning, dodging, burning, healing, and using the History Brush. These tools become even more powerful and intuitive when used in conjunction with a pen mouse for advantages such as controlling opacity, flow, size, and color by the pressure of the stroke, which we'll get into later in the chapter.

BRUSH PALETTE

Open a new document, **Ctrl N [Command N]** in Photoshop with one of the video presets, using RGB color, white background, and 16-bit color. If you don't have Photoshop CS, or your computer is on the slower side, stay in 8-bit mode. Click on the brush tool or type **B**. Type **D** to make the default foreground black and background white active. Click and drag anywhere in the document and Photoshop paints in the black for you. Not very impressive at this point, but it's where we begin. To have a serious selection of strokes, we need to get deeper into the options bar and brush palette.

The Brush Tool options bar.

In the top left of the options bar shown in the figure above, is the brush icon located in the Tool Preset Picker. When you click on it, you will see three presets (unless you or someone else has modified them). Clicking on any of these presets will instantly change the brush settings to the preset parameters. When you spend

10 or 15 minutes tweaking the perfect brush for a critical project that you will have to duplicate a week later, you can save yourself another round of adjusting the brush by saving the brush settings in the preset window. To save your brush, click the tiny New Preset icon in the lower right corner of the preset window. You can **Right Click [Command Click]** the on preset to delete or rename it.

The Tool Preset Picker menu allows you to load some fantastic brush presets that come with Photoshop.

Just to the right of Tool Preset Picker is the Brush Preset Picker. If you click on the Brush Preset Picker you will have a window that you can resize as large as you like. The two adjustment sliders from the top control the diameter or size of the brush and the hardness or feathering of the edge. In the upper right corner of the window, click the arrow to bring down the drop menu, as illustrated in the figure above. You will see a smattering of different styles of brushes to load listed at the bottom. After clicking on a brush style you are given the option of adding them to the existing list of available brushes or to replace them so you can save window space. Replacing the existing brushes will not delete them permanently. There are hundreds of brushes to choose from, each with their own strengths. Give yourself some time to explore them and discover what effect they have when applied.

In the middle of the Options Bar are the settings for Opacity, Flow, and Airbrush. Opacity works the same as if you were to change the opacity of a layer by making it more or less transparent. Flow controls the blending of the stroke to allow each brush shape to be visible along a stroke which you can scrub the values by placing the cursor over the words "Flow" or "Opacity", and then clicking and dragging. Clicking on the Airbrush button will allow the brush to paint continually while holding down the mouse button in place. Just like a real airbrush, the Photoshop brush will continue to add color and intensity in one spot while you hold down the mouse button.

On the right side of the options bar is the brushes palette icon. When you open this palette you are given a very comprehensive set of parameters. Understanding

The Brush palette is where the
Brush Tool gets its real
strength.

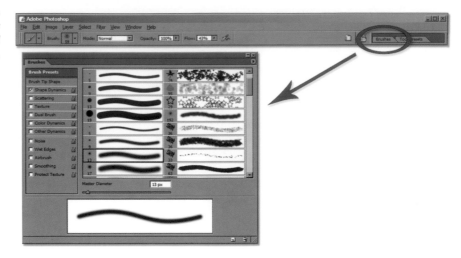

this interface and the different settings will allow you to become much more
expressive and far more expedient when creating certain imagery. The figure
above shows the Brush Palette with the preset tab open. On the bottom of the
window, you can use the slider to adjust the roundness or diameter of the brush.
If you slide the controller back and forth, you will get an instant preview in the
bottom box of the palette. It will only show you an accurate preview in size up to
48 pixels in diameter. Beyond 48 pixels the preview will remain the same size,
but will be larger when used in the document.

Brush Tip Shape.

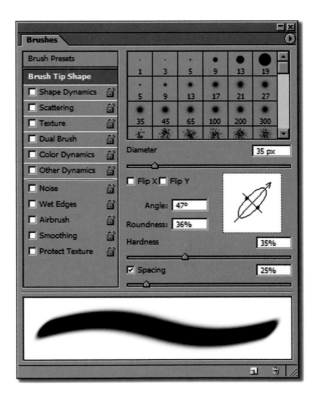

In the Brush Tip Shape interface, you can select a completely different brush shape from this window as well as the diameter, angle, roundness, hardness, and spacing. Unlike versions 6 and 7 of Photoshop, un-checking the Spacing gave you a solid draw. With version 8/CS, you need to check Spacing and bring the percentage down to 1%. When making adjustments to the angle or roundness, use the Compass tool to the right and drag by the arrow or black dots to get an instant preview of your input. You can also scrub the Angle and Roundness values. This is especially useful when working with patterned shapes.

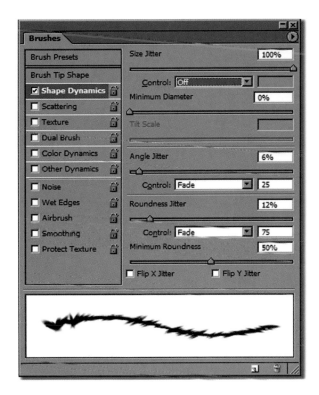

Shape Dynamics.

Continuing straight down the palette menu is the Shape Dynamics settings. From here, you can determine how much random variation you want your brush to exhibit. As with the previous settings, you still get an instant preview at the bottom. The settings for Size Jitter, Angle Jitter, and Roundness Jitter offer further control where the use of a pen mouse, stylus wheel or fade is optional. Taking advantage of these controls may require additional hardware, but give you increased articulation and control. For brush strokes that are less mechanical-looking, dialing up the jitter settings for size angle and roundness will help give you an organic-looking result.

Scattering lets you determine how far and how many shapes are to be displaced along your stroke path. It's good to go back to the Brush Tip Shape window and use the Spacing slider along with the Scattering controls to achieve your desired effect. Checking the Both Axes will scatter the shapes left and right, as well as up and down. The Count slider creates a similar effect to the Spacing slider, but while

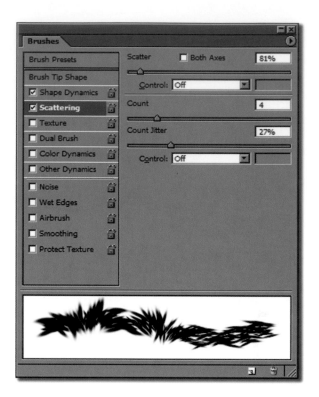

it adds more shapes to the stroke, they are more random in their placement, as opposed to a uniform alignment. The Count Jitter will vary the number of random shapes by your desired amount. A pen mouse can control both the Scatter and Count Jitter.

Chapter 6 goes over Layer Styles. A similar feature between the Layer Styles and Brushes Palette is Pattern and Texture. The same textures are available for both. Instead of applying a pattern over an entire layer, a brush can paint a texture exactly where and how you want it. By keeping the Texture Each Tip unchecked, the brush will act as though painting onto a textured surface or canvas. Different Modes will change how the foreground color will behave when painted. For a detailed description on different blending modes, see Chapter 16. The Depth slider will control how much color will cover the texture of the canvas. Wherever you can see any shade of gray in the preview window is where the color will not penetrate the canvas. The black areas are where the color of the brush will be applied.

If you enable Texture Each Tip, each brush tip will be rendered separately and you are also given a few extra controls. Minimum Depth will restrict how deep the Depth Jitter will penetrate the canvas. A pen mouse can also control depth Jitter.

The Dual Brush offers some familiar parameters to work with. They have the same effect that the same parameters in other menus have. The difference is that this second brush is what you see within an area defined by the other brush settings. You can start by defining a 50-pixel wide, hard-edged brush with

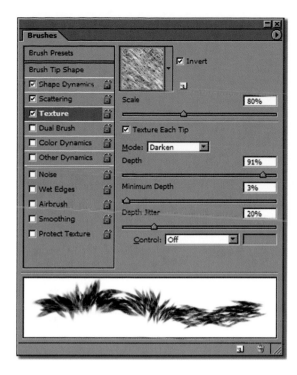

Texture.

1% spacing, no shape dynamics and no texture. So far, this will give you a normal solid stroke. However, when you select Dual Brush, the tip you select in this window will be what you paint with. Any diameter, spacing, scattering, or count that causes it to randomize outside of the defined area of the primary brush will

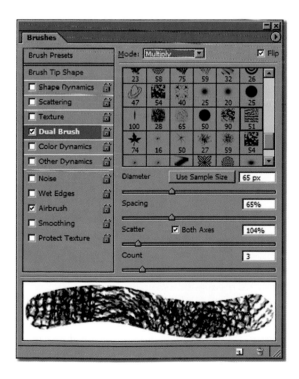

The Dual Brush selected is confined within the parameters of the original brush tip.

Color Dynamics will not give you a colored preview. You will have to stroke the canvas to see the effect.

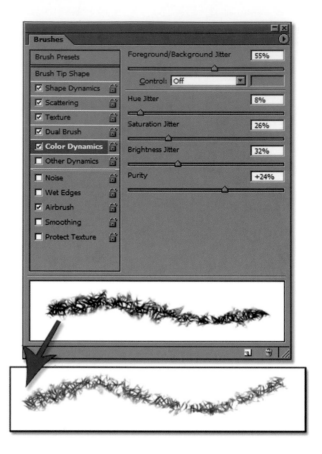

be clipped. Keeping an eye on the preview window is critical. If you want to use a special brush tip like the one in the figure above, you have to be sure that the dual brush tip does not overextend the primary brush, unless you desire this effect.

There are five parameters you can alter in the Color Dynamics menu. These controls will help alter the color over the duration of the brush stroke. For controlled randomness you can set the foreground and background colors to meet your needs and then enter an amount for them to jitter between. This is the only parameter in this menu that can allocate the use of a pen mouse. For an added boost of chaos, experiment between the Hue Jitter, Saturation Jitter, and Brightness Jitter settings. The last slider in this menu is Purity. Purity will increase or decrease the saturation of the colors used, but will not vary the amount. To see the effects of Color Dynamics, you have to use the brush on your document. The preview window is only in grayscale.

There are only two parameters in this menu. Opacity Jitter and Flow Jitter will vary their perspective characteristics over a stroke by the entered percentages. A pen mouse can control them both. While the Opacity Jitter will vary the transparency of the stroke along the path, the Flow Jitter will vary the opacity of each brush tip, giving a more organic behavior and look to the end result.

Below the menus are five additional options to choose between Noise, Wet Edges, Airbrush, Smoothing, and Protect Texture. Noise will add a random

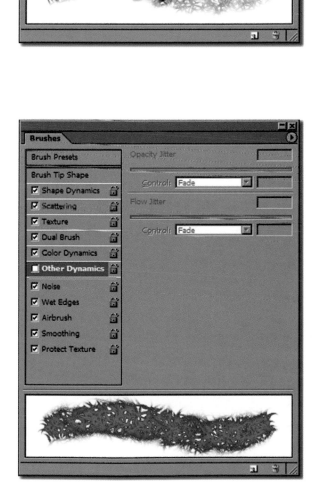

Other Dynamics.

Noise and other check marks.

grungy edge to the brush shape. Wet Edges creates a watercolor effect by concentrating the color on the edge of the brush shape. Airbrush simply turns on or off the airbrush feature at the top of the Options Bar. The Smoothing feature helps to take out the shakiness of your own hand as you draw the brush stroke. The final option in the Brushes Palette is Protect Texture. Select Protect Texture when you will be working with multiple brushes that you want to use for the same texture settings. The end result will appear that all brushes have painted onto the same canvas.

INSTANT AUTUMN

Open a new document with the video preset of your choice. Hit **B** or click the brush tool icon. In the Brushes Preset picker, click the arrow in the upper right and select **Load Brushes**. Navigate to the DVD and load the **Chapter 8 >> Instant Autumn** brush. This may or may not be of some use to you, but after you load it into your preset window, select it and begin to draw inside of the document. You will find that you've quickly drawn a few hundred leaves with varying colors, sizes, and angles. It should look something like the figure below. While you have this preset chosen, take a quick tour of the Brushes Palette and see what settings have been customized to achieve this effect. If you like this custom brush, feel free to use it anytime. You are encouraged to modify the settings as you like. If you prefer the original preset, you only need to click on it in the Preset window in the Options Bar.

Content on DVD

The leaves were created with about 6 seconds' worth of strokes using the Instant Autumn brush preset included on the DVD.

TABLETS

The brush settings mentioned in this chapter that take advantage of a pen mouse are not fully realized until you have the opportunity to use one. Instead of using a bulky chunk of plastic, (your mouse), a pen allows you to take advantage of the most dexterously developed expression you have – your writing hand. Wacom tablets offer the most precise control over a computer's cursor that you are ever likely to find. Not only do they offer precise placement of the cursor or brush, but the pressure you apply to the pen and the tilt of the pen can control attributes

Wacom is one company that makes tablets that use an optical pen mouse and can express pressure as a value such as opacity or jitter.

such as opacity, size, jitter, or any one of the other settings mentioned in this chapter. Tablets come in sizes from 4 × 5 inches up to 12 × 18 inches. As helpful as they are with painting, their true power lies in masking, cloning, healing, dodging, burning, and working with the pen tool.

INDEPENDENT PRACTICE

One of the best ways to acquaint yourself with the inner workings of the Photoshop brushes is to open an image and trace or paint over it. The first figure in this chapter began as a simple photograph that was scanned into Photoshop and painted over using various brushes, colors, and blending modes. Start out with something simple like a person's face. Scan in your own picture, video frame, or open **Chapter 8** >> **Face** from the DVD. Don't try and recreate photorealism – you're working with brushes. Be as abstract as you like, and experiment. You'll learn more about these tools if you give yourself a chance to safely make mistakes and try wild attempts at craziness.

Content on DVD

CUSTOM BRUSHES

Custom Brush Tips

Do you need a brush that paints with texture? If so, make a custom brush. You can use this for retouching to add a more random rough look. We used this on an image of a white wooden fence to weather some blue type with wood texture for

a Red Lobster® promotion. You can also make brush tips that simulate chalkboard writing, and we will do this together in this next example.

Open **Chapter 08/Chalkboard.jpg**, and bring the Path palette to front. **Ctrl [Command] click on the path palette name for the "Scribble" path to make it an active selection. Choose Image >> Crop** to crop the image to that size. You will have an image of bluish-white chalk against a black background. We need an image with a white background and black chalk to define as a brush preset, so invert the colors using **Ctrl I [Command I]**. To round off the edges, the eraser tool and the background color set to white. Hit (**e**) then (**d**) which will switch to the eraser, and set the colors to default of foreground black and background white. Use the **eraser tool to round off the edges to get a brush, which looks like the brush in the red frame above.** You can do a color correction to get rid of the light blue tint, by choosing levels, and pulling the triangle on the right towards the center until the gray turns to white. When done rounding off the edges, choose **Edit >> Define Brush Preset** and name the brush chalkboard scribble. **Make a new document about 720 × 480 pixels**, and switch to your paintbrush tool using (**b**). Pull down your Brushes palette, and make sure that you **have your new brush selected and begin to paint**. The brush name will appear if you let the mouse hover over the brush palette swatch. If you did a good job cleaning off the corners, your brush will work well. There was a thin line of pixels around the edge, which was left intentionally in the file. If you did not delete the pixels on the edge, your brush would look square rather than round. If you had trouble with creating these brushes, you can load then into your Brushes palette using the supplied file. You can right click [**Control Click**] **and choose Load Brush Chapter 08/brushes.abr from the fly-out menu.** Photoshop has two palettes for brushes: one is the brush palette, and this one is for managing your brush presets. The new brush at 300 pixels is large enough for print graphics, but make it smaller for usage on your video resolution file.

Content on DVD

Content on DVD

IMAGE HOSE

Corel Painter has a very interesting brush called Image Hose that paints full color images from your brush. You can set the Image Hose to spatter the images randomly, controlling the amount of scale, rotation, and distance from the brush stroke. You can do this in Photoshop also, but are limited to 8-bit gray and not 24-bit color. You can set the brush to print with random luminosity and tints, making the brush have color. Painter additionally can also put a drop shadow with transparency between each image that comes out of the hose, and choose from more than one image stored in your brush. Though the current version of Photoshop is not as advanced, you can create some amazing artwork, and it is a great way to learn more of the control in the Brush palette.

Open **Chapter 08/Fiji Warmask.jpg**, which is a digital camera image, and **Ctrl [Command] click** on the path. Choose **Edit >> Define Brush Preset, and name your brush**. Your new brush should be 401 pixels in diameter. Having a larger brush size than you ultimately need is good, as you can always make the brush smaller, but not larger. Photoshop allows you to make a brush larger, but then you are up-sampling the pixels, and your artwork will eventually look rastered and soft.

Bring your Brushes palette to the front. The default location is in the well (if your display has more than 800 × 600 pixels), and you can leave it in there or

Content on DVD

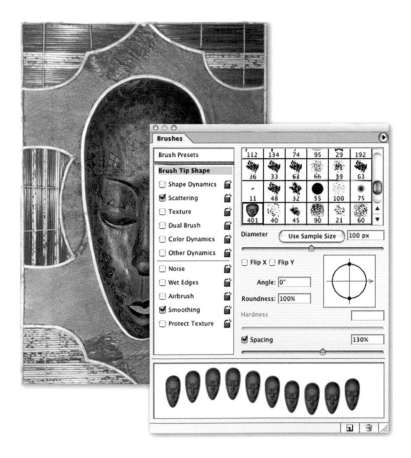

drag it out if you prefer. It is such a large palette that Photoshop leaves it in the well so that it will not clutter up your work area. **Click on Brush Tip Shape and set the Spacing to 130%.** This puts space between each image so that we can see each mask we draw with our new brush. **Make a new document of 720 × 480 pixels,** and using the left bracket keyboard command **change your brush to 100 pixels** and begin to paint.

STROKE PATH

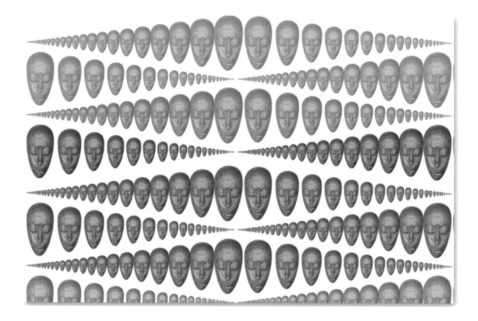

This final image was created by drawing a straight path with the pen tool, naming the path, and then applying the Stroke Path command from the paths palette flyout menu. Enabling Simulate Pressure from the Stroke Path command causes the brush to scale at an even rate, creating the bow-tie effect. The Brush Preset of Shape Dynamic was set to 70% to vary the size. The layer was duplicated, and some layering work was done to flip the bow-tie sizing effect. So you could draw a spiral in Illustrator, bring that path into Photoshop, and apply the Stroke Path with a brush set to an image for a spiral of images effect. Hopefully, the next version of Photoshop will allow full color images for brushes, as this could make brushes even more useful.

9

SPEED UP PHOTOSHOP

$\mathcal{E}$*ach section of this chapter goes through features and techniques that will save*

you steps, clicks, guesses – and sometimes even hours of work. If you want to take

the necessary steps toward becoming a bona fide Photoshop professional, this chapter

will help you to finish a project on time and to handle a seemingly impossible

workload.

KEYBOARD SHORTCUTS

Moving Around an Image

If you have ever had a client sit in during a video edit session or a photo-enhancement session, you may have felt impatience coming from them at one time or another. If you are performing tasks with someone's eyes peering over your shoulder, you can start to feel intimidated if you are not in control of your application. A professional at the helm of an application like Photoshop is something akin to a magician because they can usually perform tasks and corrections faster than someone can describe it. It's very reassuring to a client when an editor or graphic artist has confidence and speed.

The first way to gain speed and confidence is to learn your shortcuts. Chapter 1 offers some invaluable shortcuts once you've selected a particular tool. However, you can select any tool itself from the keyboard as well. Chapter 1 also gives an easy reference to the shortcuts associated with each tool. Remember that you can cycle through stacked tools by holding down **Shift** as you hit the appropriate key. However, I find it easier to set the tools to cycle through without the Shift key. If you'd like the tools to cycle without using the Shift key, go to **Edit** >> **Preferences** >> **General** [**Photoshop** >> **Preferences** >> **General**], or type **Ctrl K** [**Command K**] and uncheck **Use Shift key for tool shift**.

In addition to the Screen Navigation shortcuts listed in Chapter 1, there are some shortcuts I use on a daily basis. When working with images that have dimensions larger than the computer workspace, you may often want to see the entire image for purposes of composition analysis. However, when making alterations to a large image such as applying filters, you always want to view and preview your image at 100%. Open **Chapter 9** >> **Snare** from the DVD. By default, Photoshop opens the image at an appropriate size so you can view the entire image within your workspace. In the bar at the top of the window, it will read Snare@(whatever)%. Unless you have an abnormally huge monitor, with extremely high resolutions, the percentage will most likely be less than 100%. To look at the image at 100%, you could use View >> Actual Pixels, or you could use **Ctrl Alt 0** [**Command Option 0**] – using the zero on the number pad at the right of the keyboard, not at the top. To see areas of the image that are beyond the window borders, you can use the Hand tool, (**H**), and drag the image around for viewing. If you are using another tool such as the Lasso tool, (**L**), or the Pen tool, (**P**), you can just hold down the space bar, which will give you a temporary Hand tool. Another often overlooked feature is the Navigator Palette.

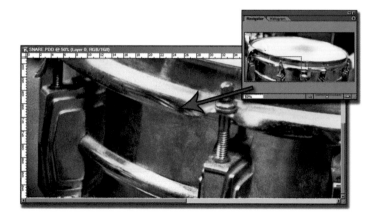

A quick quide for the tool shortcuts. Most tools have a corresponding letter, such as M = Marquee Tool and L – Lasso Tool

The Navigator is a very intuitive way of resizing and getting around your image. When you want to shrink your image to fit entirely in your viewable workspace, use View >> Fit on screen, or **Ctrl 0** [**Command 0**] (zero on the number pad).

Perhaps the most obvious way to resize your image is to use the Zoom Tool, (**Z**). Another handy trick when viewing a large image is to double-click the Zoom tool, bringing it to 100% view.

In the Zoom Options Bar, you can set it to zoom in or out. The cursor will identify which direction the tool will zoom by adding a + or − inside the magnifying glass. Holding down **Alt [Opt]** will reverse the direction. Chapter 1 gave you the shortcut of Ctrl +, [Command +] and Ctrl -, [Command -] but if you include Alt, [Opt] you will resize the window along with your image – which is extremely helpful when working with multiple open files.

The Status Bar not only allows you to enter the viewable scale but will also give you hints at other shortcuts for an active tool.

Make sure the Status Bar is visible, **Window >> Status Bar**. The Status Bar will be located on the bottom of the screen. On the left side, the viewing percent is given. You'll notice that it is exactly the same size as the top of the file window. The difference with the Status Bar is that you can highlight the number with your cursor and enter in the exact value you want to view your image. For quality purposes, you should evaluate your image at 100%, 50%, 25%, 12.5%, or 6.25%. When viewed at any other value, Photoshop will not redraw the preview with even proportions and will likely give you inaccurate feedback, such as aliased or jagged diagonal lines. Keeping those recommended viewing percentages in mind, there is one last shortcut that Windows users can take advantage of. If you are using a scroll-wheel mouse, the scroll-wheel can resize your image too. Scrolling toward you zooms in, and scrolling away zooms out. When you use the scroll-wheel, the viewing values usually won't fall on the preferred percentages that we would like. If you hold down **Shift**, the zooming will snap to 100%, 66.67%, 50%, 33%, 25%, 16.67%, 12.5%, 8.33%, and 6.25%. If you are already zoomed in past 100%, the scroll-wheel may behave as it would in a web browser, by scrolling down the image. You can engage the zooming behavior by holding down **Alt [Opt]**.

Layer and Selection Helpers

Open **Chapter 9 >> Selections**. This is a multilayered image with different layers of text and a logo. It's very common to create a lower third banner for use in video. When moving separate layers around to compose a final image, it's often beneficial to move multiple images together instead of one at a time. Select the Move tool, (**T**), and check the Auto Select Layer box in the Options Bar. Click on any object and take note that the layer will be highlighted in the Layer palette. If you want to move any combination of the layers in the document together, you can click between the Layer snapshot and the eyeball, and you will see a chain link.

Content on DVD

You can select many layers together by clicking on one link and dragging the mouse straight down the Layer palette. This shortcut also works with the eyeball, allowing you to switch multiple layers on or off. If you want to view one layer and turn off every other layer, **Alt Click [Option Click]** the eyeball of the layer. Repeating this step will bring back the layers that were previously turned off. A more intuitive way of selecting multiple layers in a composition is to hold down the **Shift** key while clicking on the layers you want. Don't forget to make sure Auto Select Layer is turned on. You can also deselect a linked layer by **Shift Clicking** it again. When the Move tool is selected, you can also move a selected layer using the arrow keys. They will move the layer by one pixel at a time unless you hold down the **Shift** key, moving them 10 pixels. It's also nice that Photoshop will view all of the nudging around as only one history state. So after you enter two moves and 50 keystrokes to nudge a single layer, you can undo it all at once by entering **Ctrl Z [Command Z]**.

You can select different layers and even rearrange their order from the keyboard. The table below gives you the Layer palette shortcuts.

ACTION	PC	MAC
Select the next layer up	**Alt]**	**Option]**
Select the next layer down	**Alt [**	**Option [**
Select the top layer	**Alt Shift]**	**Option Shift]**
Select the bottom layer	**Alt Shift [**	**Option Shift [**
Move the selected layer up one space	**Ctrl]**	**Command]**
Move the selected layer down one space	**Ctrl [**	**Command [**
Move the selected layer to the top	**Ctrl Shift]**	**Command Shift]**
Move the selected layer to the bottom	**Ctrl Shift [**	**Command Shift [**

Windows users can Alt Tab between open applications.

Bonus

If you work on a PC and you tend to have multiple programs open, you can jump to a different open application by **Shift Tabbing!**

Customizing Keyboard Shortcuts

Users of Avid, Maya, 3D Studio Max, and a host of other top-level applications have enjoyed the ability to thoroughly customize their keyboard for many years. Thankfully, one of the most overdue and greatly anticipated enhancements given to Photoshop CS (and Premiere Pro or Windows) is the addition of a customizable keyboard. This book is written to conform to the standard preset shortcuts included with Photoshop, but not all of the existing shortcuts work for everyone. Photoshop CS is the 8th version of the quintessential image editing application employed throughout the globe. It's used by professionals in pre press, desktop publishing, magazine editorial, wedding photography, real estate and, of course, videography and broadcasting. With so many different demands on one application, there are more features built into Photoshop than any single profession can use. Photoshop is a highly refined instrument, to say the least. So if a videographer gets into Photoshop just to create slates, open pages, lower third banners, and credits, they will never see a use for the Slice tool, (**K**). It might make more sense for them to assign **K** to the Paint Bucket tool.

Go to Edit >> Keyboard Shortcuts, **Ctrl Alt Shift K [Command Option Shift K]**. This will open the dialog box for creating your own customizations.

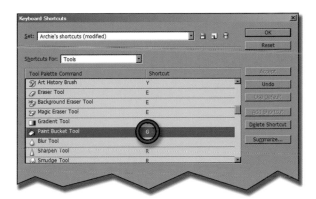

The long overdue customizable keyboard has been added to Photoshop.

From the top, you can create and save different sets of custom settings – which is ideal for a workstation used by more than one person with different tastes. Just below that, you can select the category of shortcut for Application Menus, Palette Menus, or Tools. Click on the **New Set** icon at the top between the Save and Trash icons. Photoshop will prompt you to save it in the presets under Keyboard Shortcuts. Name this set **Temp**. Select Tools in the Shortcuts For bar. Scroll down to the Paint Bucket tool. Notice how the shortcut (**G**) is listed to the right along with the Gradient tool. Click anywhere on the Paint Bucket too line and enter (**K**). You will now be given a notice that says "The Shortcut K is already in use and will be removed from Slice Tool and Slice Select Tool if accepted". You can select

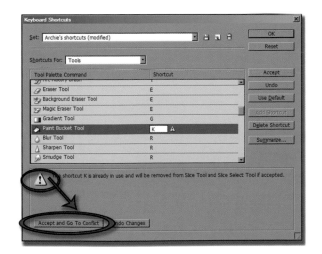

Photoshop warns you when you choose a shortcut that was previously used by another tool or command and lets you jump right to the conflict to enter a new shortcut that suits your needs.

Accept or **Accept and Go To Conflict** if you want to assign a new shortcut to the Slice tool.

Go ahead and accept it. Now you can either save the set or delete it using the icons at the top of the window. Avid still wares the crown for having the most intuitive and fluid interface for customizing your keyboard, but Photoshop is very powerful in its own right. Once you start working on any large quantity of tasks, the heavily repeated steps will reveal themselves to you. If there is no shortcut for it, go ahead and make your own!

PALETTES AND WORKSPACES

This section not only helps to speed up your work inside of Photoshop, but it is also essential if you are not fortunate enough to have a large monitor or dual monitors.

The default layout of Photoshop may or may not work for you. However, you are not confined to one layout or workspace.

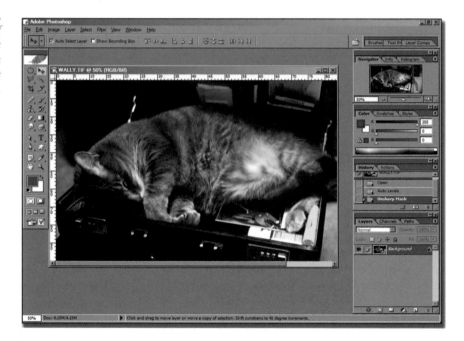

The figure above shows the default layout of palettes when you open Photoshop. This default workspace will not meet your needs if you work with any number of layers with large icons and layer styles. Not to mention if you like the Text Character and the Styles palettes to be open, your screen real estate will quickly vanish, leaving no room left to view an image.

The next figure shows my typical workspace. I'm lucky enough to be able to work on a dual monitor system, so I can fit most every palette I need on my second monitor. However, if my main workstation is preoccupied with transcoding a 2-hour file for DVD authoring, I need to use my old computer to print up labels while the new one is busy. A 14-inch monitor with 800 × 600 pixel resolution is all I have to work with.

If you have the screen space at your disposal, use it.

IA screen with 800 × 600 pixels can get cluttered up rather quickly.

The figure above shows the workspace on the 14-inch monitor. As you can see, it's far too cluttered with all of my palettes open. Hitting the **TAB** key will make every palette, tools, and options bar disappear.

Hitting **TAB** again brings them back. A similar shortcut is **Shift TAB**, which will just take the palettes away and leave the tools and options bar.

Open **Chapter 9 >> Arizona**. Hit **F** and see how it affects the view. It should look like the bottom figure on the next page. This shortcut is the same as selecting the Full Screen with Menu Bar button on the tools palette.

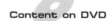

Content on DVD

While this view does conserve screen space by taking away the windows of the operating system, the task bar will still be present, covering the task bar. If you hit **F** again, you will be in the Full Screen mode. The task bar will be hidden and the status bar is visible. What's nice about this view is that the background is black and if you use the TAB trick and resize shortcuts illustrated in this chapter, you can give your image the most objective evaluation with less graphical noise on screen

Hitting Tab on the keyboard hides every palette and the options bar to give you added room to work.

The Full Screen Mode with Menu Bar helps to unclutter your workspace.

to distract you. Hit F one last time and you are back to the standard view. One final benefit to PC users when in the Full Screen view is that, although the menus are gone from the top, the small black arrow on the top right of the tools palette will access all of the menus.

This section would not be complete if we didn't mention the ability to save different workspaces. It's a common technique in video editing to jump between different workspaces that complement different tasks such as audio sweetening

The Full Screen Mode even hides the operating system's task bar, giving you maximum real estate on your monitor.

or effects work, and it's no less helpful to do the same in Photoshop. If you have a small monitor, you can further customize your workspace to include only what you need to perform a certain task. Examples might be to create a workspace with only the Layers and Characters palettes open when you create different Text layers and different workspace with only the History and Navigator palettes open when you plan to use the Rubber Stamp, Healing Brush, and History Brush.

Switch between the three different views from the Tool palette or cycle through them with the F key.

Select **Windows** >> **History** and **Windows** >> **Navigator**. Close all other palettes on the screen by clicking the X in the upper right corner. Move and resize the open palettes any way you like, giving yourself ample room to work with your image. Remember you can always hide them by hitting **TAB**. Save this workspace by going to **Windows** >> **Workspace** >> **Save Workspace** and enter **History & Navigator**. Now close both palettes and open **Windows** >> **Layers** and **Windows** >> **Layer Comps**. Again, mold the palettes to fit your tastes. Save this workspace by going to **Windows** >> **Workspace** >> **Save Workspace** and enter **Layer Comps**. Unfortunately, Photoshop CS does not allow you to enter a shortcut for different workspaces, but it is still a valuable feature to take advantage of.

CROP AND STRAIGHTEN

If you've ever been commissioned to create a photo montage using over 100 pictures, you've been praying for this feature. Adobe has heard the prayers, and crying, of

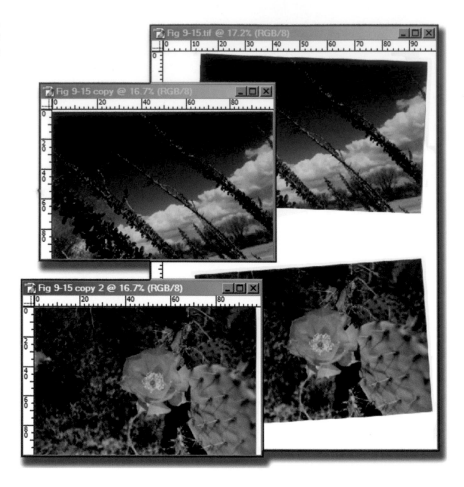

Photoshop can help automate the process of creating multiple files from a batch scan.

us who need to scan multiple images on a flatbed scanner and create separate files for each one. Open **Chapter 9 >> Flatbed Scan**. You can see that there are three different pictures that we put on the scanner. Before Photoshop CS, we would have had to draw new selections, create a new file, drag the selection to the new file, rotate, and finally crop before we could get to the real work on it. Go to File >> Automate >> Crop and Straighten Photos, and you should get three new files from each of the pictures. For best results, try and lay out your pictures as straight as possible and leave a little bit of space between them. Photoshop needs to see blank space to tell them apart, and the final straightening it does is a bit crude, as you will want to do some minor cropping to clean up the edges sometimes.

HISTORY BRUSH AND HISTORY PALETTE

History Palette

If you are worried about the limitation of only one level of undo, worry no more. The History Palette is there to put you at ease. Open **Chapter 9 >> Pretty Face** on the DVD. Open the palette by entering **Window** >> **History**. Go to Filters >> Blur >> Average. This filter will average the colors to a gray, completely erasing the original image. Select the Brush tool, (**B**), and draw a few strokes. Now go to **Filters** >> **Blur** >> **Gaussian Blur** and bring the slider to about 10 pixels and hit OK. What we now have is a completely unusable image, but that's fine because we have the History Palette to help us.

If you look at your History Palette, it should look something like the figure to the right. From the top it shows the Pretty Face image snapshot with a History Brush icon to the left of it. Below that are all the steps you just performed in the order they were executed. If you click on the different history states or steps, you will see the document revert to that state in time and the steps that followed will be slightly faded to indicate where in your history you are. Clicking the snapshot at the top history state, will revert the document to its original state. Once you apply another change to the document the faded history states will disappear and free

The History palette allows you to experiment with an image without worrying about whether or not you can undo multiple steps.

up more memory for Photoshop. The default limit of history states is 20. You can change this number to go as high as you like in the preferences, but you need to keep in mind the limitations of RAM you have on your system in relation to the size of the image you want to work on. Photoshop will technically allow you to enter 100 history states, but if you're going to work on a document that is 80 MB, even a computer with 1 GB of RAM won't manage more than a dozen history states.

As you perform steps to an image and the History Palette builds a list of those history states, the standard undo shortcut, **Ctrl Z [Command Z]**, will toggle between the current and previous history states, unlike Premiere or After Effects where it will continually take you back through your previous steps. This is nice if you like to evaluate "before and after" previews, but if you want to quickly step back through the history states, hit **Ctrl Alt Z [Command Option Z]** to go back and **Ctrl Shift Z [Command Shift Z]** to go forward.

History Brush

The History Palette becomes even more relevant when we start to use the History Brush. Keeping the Pretty Face open from the previous section, click on the snapshot at the top of the History Palette to revert it back to its original state. Reapply the Gaussian Blur filter by hitting **Ctrl F [Command F]**, which applies the last filter you used with the same settings. You should still be able to make out the general placements of the eyes, nose, mouth, and so on. Select the History Brush, or hit **Y**. Make sure the snapshot in the History Palette still has the History Brush icon activated. If not, click in the box to the left of the snapshot. Once the icon is there, paint over the eyes of the blurred face and you will see the original image begin to reappear beneath your strokes. When multiple history states are in the palette, any one of them can have the history brush icon activated, making that particular state the source the History Brush will paint from.

As you work on your own projects and images, you may run into a situation where you apply a change to an image or layer, but only a small part is undesirable. The techniques described above are extremely helpful to achieve your desired result.

ACTIONS

Actions work the same way as Macros work on Microsoft Word, or Scripting on 3D Studio Max. Each action is a list of steps bundled together that you can have Photoshop perform with a single click. What's more, you can edit the individual steps inside of these actions and even create your own actions from scratch to help with your most commonly used tasks – saving you many clicks and a lot of time.

Working with Actions

Content on DVD

The Actions palette can reduce many steps to a single click.

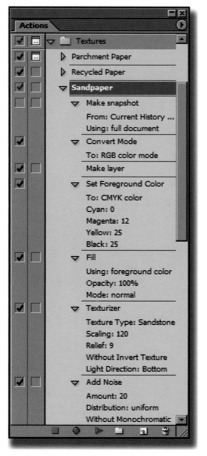

Open **Chapter 9 >> Actions** on the DVD. This is just a 720 × 540 image to keep memory usage down while we work with some of the actions. Open the Actions palette, **Window >> Actions**. If this is the first time the Actions palette has been activated, it should only have the Presets set open. These include a sampling of the other sets contained in Photoshop. All together, Photoshop ships with about 100 actions. Some are helpful, some are useful, and some are just not worth mentioning to 99% of us. But they are all there for you to use as you see fit. Click on the menu arrow in the top right corner of the Actions palette and select Textures at the bottom. The Textures set is now added to the Actions palette. Twirl it open and click on Sandpaper. Twirl Sandpaper open as well to see all the different steps that make up the action. Each step can twirl open too and give specific information about its characteristics.

With Sandpaper selected, simply click the play icon on the bottom of the palette. What you are left with is an image that looks like sheet of sandpaper. Take a look at the History Palette now. From the top to bottom there should be the opening history state snapshot, Snapshot 1, and four steps below. Drag the Snapshot 1 to the trash can at the bottom of the palette to delete it then click on the opening snapshot at the top. The image reverts to its opening state and the other steps are faded to indicate that you have gone back in history.

In the Actions palette, below the Sandpaper action, uncheck the Make snapshot step on the left. This will omit this step the next time you play the action. Notice how this will cause the checkmarks next to Sandpaper and Textures to turn red. The red checkmarks are telling you that one or more actions have been altered. There's also another column worth noticing in the palette between the checks and the actions. Clicking in this box toggles the dialog box on and off. If you turn it on, each step will wait for you to confirm the settings before moving on to the next step. If you are familiar with a given action and are confident in the end result, you can keep it off. However, some actions may be best suited to have the dialog box turned on to allow more precise customization on the fly for a particular image. Turn it on for the Sandpaper action and hit Play. The action will play until the Texturizer filter step is reached. Go ahead and bring the scale slider to 200% and hit OK. The action will continue to the final step.

You can solo steps and dialog boxes within an action the same way you solo a layer by Alt Clicking [Option Clicking]. Only the steps or dialog boxes within that particular action are switched off. Repeating the process will turn every step or dialog box in the action back on, so if your Make Snapshot step was turned off before you soloed another step, it will be turned back on after you unsolo another step, so be aware. If you click on any step within an action, hitting play will begin the action at the selected step, bypassing all preceding steps.

Making Your Own Actions

Open a new document, **Ctrl N [Command N]** with 720 × 540 square pixels and a black background. Don't use any of the presets in Photoshop CS. If you have a version of Photoshop earlier than version 8/CS, this section will show you how to build your own guidelines for action safe and title safe regions.

Type **Ctrl R [Command R]** to bring the rulers into view on the top and left of the new image. **Right Click [Command Click]** on the rulers and select **Percent**. Now click and drag from the top and place the guideline at 90% on the left ruler. Drag another line from the top to 10%. Drag two more lines from the left ruler at 10% and 90% as well. You now have set title safe guides that will help you when you create text that you want to ensure are viewable on a monitor. These guides will also allow layers (and text) to snap to them when moved around.

As helpful as title safe guides are, if you are going to be working with titles on many of your projects, you'd be foolish not to create an action to do it for you. So click on the opening snapshot at the top of the History Palette to revert your document back to its opening state, taking away the guides you just made. We're now going to make the same guides, but this time, we will start by clicking the New Action button at the bottom of the Actions palette.

You will be prompted to name the action, to put it in any of the open action sets, or to assign a function key shortcut. Name it Title Safe Guides and give it a

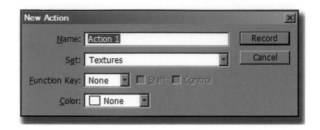

shortcut of F11 and hit the Record button at the bottom of the Actions palette. The Record button on the Actions palette turns red to indicate that your steps are being recorded. Make the four guidelines just as you did earlier, then hit the Stop button on the Actions palette. You've just created your first custom action. You can click the New Set button on the Actions palette and give it any name you like. You can even move actions between different sets. If you want to move a copy of an action, **Alt Drag** [**Option Drag**] it to another set or within the same set and "copy" will be amended to the action's name.

Editing Actions

Upon thinking about it, you might want to add action safe guidelines to your action. You don't have to start from scratch. Select the Title Safe action you just created in the Actions palette and twirl it open. Click the Play button on the bottom of the palette. It's not important what order the lines are created in, but in another action the order of steps may be crucial. You can click on any step within an action to insert a new step or series of steps after it when you hit the Record button on the bottom of the palette. With that in mind, select the last step in the action and click the Record button. Now drag four new guides at 5% and 95% from the top and left rulers. Hit the Stop button on the Actions palette. You've now just edited your first action.

   Working with actions can be extremely simple, as this section demonstrates. Staying organized and conducting your experimenting before you begin recording your steps will help you to build a nice healthy collection of custom actions. Happy programming.

Bonus Action

In the Workspaces section of this chapter, we mentioned that Photoshop does not allow you to program a keyboard shortcut to activate a given workspace. You can get around this limitation by creating a new action that records you simply opening **Window** >> **"whichever" Workspace**. You'll be limited to some combination of function key and maybe **Ctrl Shift** [**Command Shift**], but it's worth it and it's very easy.

BATCH AUTOMATION

With all of the keyboard shortcuts, history states, workspaces, and actions that we have at our disposal, there still may be a faster way to do certain tasks. It's common for me to receive a dozen images for a single project from the graphics department at the television station where we work. Sometimes the personnel in graphics are so inundated with work that they forget to correct the colors for broadcast-safe specifications. We could correct them in Avid, but that would include me stacking a color effect on each image or turning down the luminance and saturation of the master output. Neither option is favorable.

We could open each image in Photoshop and simply apply my custom 601 Curves action to it and save it before importing into Avid. However, one project we had to turn around very quickly included well over 50 images, and just about every one had uncorrected colors for broadcasting. Instead of crying to the already overtaxed graphic artists, we used Photoshop to do it all for me.

When you have an action that you want to apply to multiple files, such as in the case we just described, go to **File** >> **Automate** >> **Batch**.

From the Batch dialog box, you can select the action you want to play and what you want to apply it to. In my scenario, we clicked on Choose... to select the entire folder that held all of the images, checked Include All Subfolders because they were organized by subject, checked Suppress Color Profile Warnings, and set the destination to Save and Close. After clicking OK, all 50 images were ready for us to work with about a minute later, thanks to the Batch function.

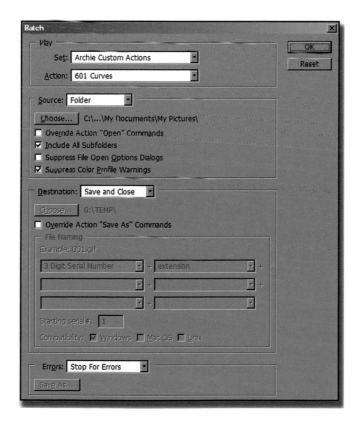

The Batch command lets you apply any action to an entire folder of images in one step.

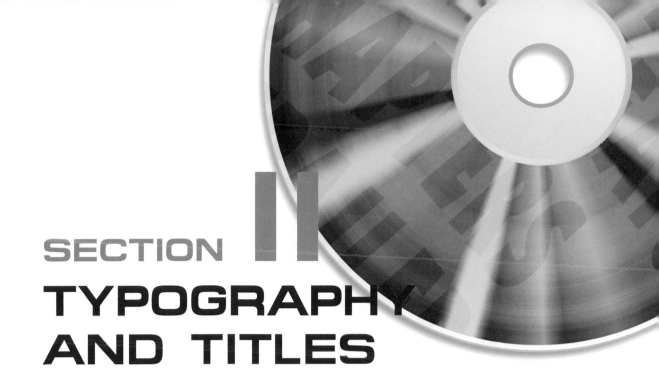

SECTION II

TYPOGRAPHY AND TITLES

10
TYPOGRAPHY

MANAGING FONTS

Font Management Utilities

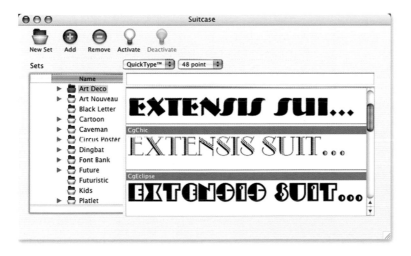

The best way to open and close fonts is with a utility such as Suitcase or Font Reserve by Extensis, which is available on both PC and Mac platforms. The time and aggravation you save are worth purchasing a font management utility. If you need to load different type on your projects, then this investment is one you will not regret.

A font utility also gives you the ability to preview fonts without loading them. Not having to load the font allows your machine to quickly provide a preview. Suitcase for example gives you a Quicktype option where you choose which letters you want to preview, and chooses a set of fonts to preview the letters of your choice. This is extremely useful when you are designing, and trying to find a typeface that fits your project. Once you find fonts you like to use, you only need to activate them, and not copy the file to your operating system. This helps you to have a font library separate from you operating system and to not need multiple copies of fonts on your hard drive.

Loading Fonts with Photoshop

You can load fonts into your operating system, by copying them physically to your **windows [system]** folder. Additionally, Photoshop uses font files from these folders:

❖ Windows: Program Files/Common Files/Adobe/Fonts

❖ Mac OS X: Library/Application Support/Adobe/Fonts

We intentionally started this chapter with font utilities, because it is the best way to go. Even though you have a font utility, it is important to know how to load or disable fonts from your system. Fonts occasionally conflict with each other because they have the same FOND ID number. A FOND is like a social security number for a font, and if two of them have the same FOND number you will find that only one of the two fonts will work, or possibly neither. You also have many fonts installed on your system that you will probably never use. Mac OS 10 comes with many extra international and miscellaneous fonts that make your operating system take longer to boot, and your font menus really long. Fortunately you can disable them on the Mac using the next font application we will discuss called Fontbook. On the PC, you can use ATM or remove them manually. Most fonts from your system are not good for video, and your creative will look better and more original using the purchased or some of the downloadable free fonts on the net.

Fontbook [Mac OS]

When Mac OS 10 first came out, you had to manually go into your system and remove fonts to get rid of all those extra ones you will not use. Since Mac OS 10.3 Fontbook is in your applications folder, and you can disable the fonts by using a button. There are some fonts you will not want to disable in Mac OS 10 because of these reasons: Lucida Grande and Geneva: cannot be disabled because it is used by the operating system

❖ Times & Times New Roman: Serif font used in many office documents and web pages

❖ Arial & Helvetica: Sans Serif font used in many office documents and web pages

❖ Verdana: Sans Serif font used in many web pages

Fontbook is actually very good, and try it first if on a tight budget, or have a very large studio with many machines. Features like hitting the first few letters of the name of a font will not automatically scroll to that font, but you have a search, which works just as good. The worst thing about Fontbook is you must copy your fonts to your system, and they cannot reside separately or on a shared server. Double-clicking on a font will bring up Fontbook, and there is an option to copy the single font to your users library for you. You also cannot preview multiple fonts.

Summary

It is difficult to say what Extensis will do in the future, now owning both Suitcase and Font Reserve. Mac users will probably see Fontbook get even better in future versions. PC users do not have a font management utility built into the OS. Many people on the PC still use the old Adobe Type Manager, which you can get by with. Adobe Type Manager only works on the Mac in the old OS 9. Though ATM can load Opentype fonts, you will get crashes as a result. The auto loading of fonts can also cause crashes with certain newer applications.

The PC has a utility for accessing special characters in **Program files >> Accessories >> Character Map**. The Mac has an even better utility which can be accessed from Mac OS 10 Edit >> Special Characters. Overall, the Mac is a little better with handling type, and the Extensis PC version of Suitcase has not been updated from version 9 for quite some time.

TYPESETTING

Photoshop has a Type palette which you can access by choosing **Window >> Character**. All your typesetting controls are found in either the Character or Paragraph palette. You should try not to use the Character palette, but use the following keyboard commands instead. Once you begin to use them, it will be much easier to design type.

SPACE 1967.®

SPACE 1967.®

Kerning Tighten by 20/1000 ems	Alt Left Arrow [Option Left Arrow]
Leading Decrease 2 pts	Alt Down Arrow [Option Down Arrow]
Baseline Shift Down 2 pts	Shift Alt Down Arrow [Shift Option Down Arrow]
Type Size Decrease 2 pts	Shift Ctrl < [Shift Command <]
Make Superscript	Shift Ctrl + [Shift Command +]
Align Left Center Right	Shift Ctrl L, C or R [Shift Command L, C or R]
Select All characters in layer	Double-click any type layer

Content on DVD

Open **Chapter 09 >> Kerning.psd**, and you will see a layer set called "kern me". **Using the keyboard commands above, make the layer inside kern me look like the image above.** Kerning is the spacing between individual letters, and tracking is for a range of letters. The type is set in the font New Baskerville, which has pretty good kerning, but the letters PAC have too much space on both sides of the A.

Other areas needing to tighten up kerning are between 19 and between 7 and the period. These are common issues to look for. Once you have finished kerning the type, you will agree that it is much easier using the keyboard commands. When you select letters, an underline appears under the type to let you know that it has been selected. You can get rid of that underlining by removing the check in front of **View >> Extras**. Adobe may fix this in a future release, but in most cases you are able to use the keyboard command of **Ctrl H [Command H]** to toggle your visual aids, which might be distracting. When you are done, turn your visual aids back on.

Now **double-click on the 1967®** line to select it, and use the keyboard command of **Alt Up Arrow [Option Up Arrow]** to reduce the leading. Leading is the space between lines and named that because typesetters would use thin lines of lead to increase that space. Using keyboard commands is the only way to go, and the character palette is more useful to confirm you numbers.

Select the ® by dragging the cursor bar over that letter. **Use the keyboard command from the previous chart to make it superscript**. Most other Adobe type programs allow you to change the amount Adobe uses creating a superscript character. **Use the keyboard command to make the type smaller and then baseline shift** to get it up higher so the tops of all letters are even. You can also change the typeface of ® by using the tool bar above. Keep your type selected and hit **Ctrl H [Command H]**.

OPENTYPE

What is Opentype?

Multiple master fonts, a technology previous to Opentype, allows you to take MM fonts and create your own custom versions controlling boldness, track, and slant. MM fonts are barely used by anyone, but can be very useful when you need a bolder version of a font.

Opentype is the latest Adobe type technology, and has a good chance of staying around. Opentype is 100% cross platform, and the same font file can be loaded on Mac or PC. Your documents do not reflow with Opentype because the same file is used on both platforms. The main feature of Opentype is you have access to over 65,000 characters in each font. The extra characters are called glyphs in most Adobe applications. The glyphs you get with Opentype are swash characters, ligatures, symbols, old style, ornaments, and even fractions. Photoshop will recognize Opentype characters, but is not as sophisticated as Illustrator or InDesign.

Let's explore and open **Chapter 09 >> Opentype.psd**. You will see letters in red that are special characters, not available in a standard true type or type 1 font. Each line of type has one of the checkmarks enabled from the flyout menu of the Character palette. You could enable them all, but it is best to just select the letters you like to be fractions, and enable the fractions checkmark for those letters.

Content on DVD

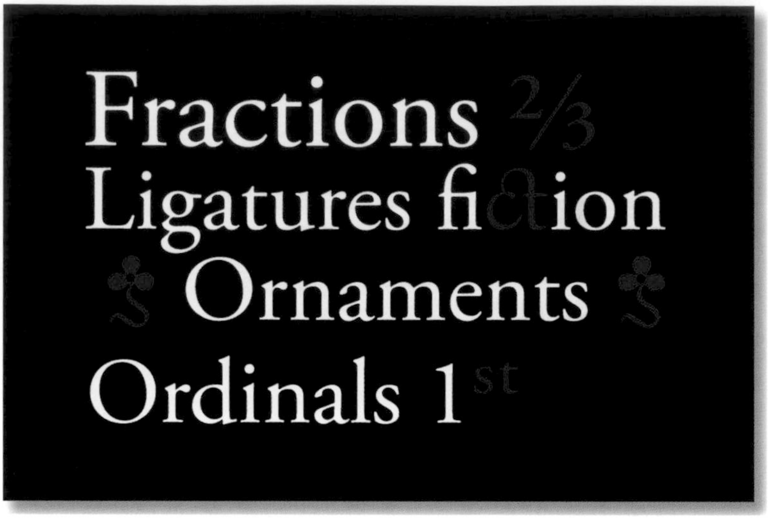

Fractions ⅔
Ligatures fiction
Ornaments
Ordinals 1ˢᵗ

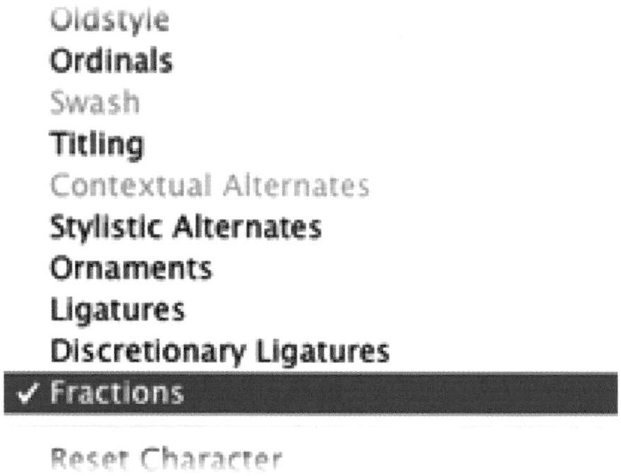

Oldstyle
Ordinals
Swash
Titling
Contextual Alternates
Stylistic Alternates
Ornaments
Ligatures
Discretionary Ligatures
✓ **Fractions**

Reset Character

TYPOGRAPHY FOR VIDEO

What does a professional designer consider when setting type for video? It is much more than what font or color they like. The professional designer considers technical, readability, usability, and emotion. All of these are affected by all attributes you apply to type, and the copy you have. Video is different than web, and even more different than print.

Make it easier for your audience to read and comprehend your type by giving it contrast. If you are doing a credits roll, you will want the characters' names to have contrasted separation from the actors' names. This will help your viewer so that they can quickly find information, such as who played a certain role. This allows the user to quickly scan and read only what is needed. If you were to try being really creative, and set all your type in different fonts, your credit roll would be hard to follow.

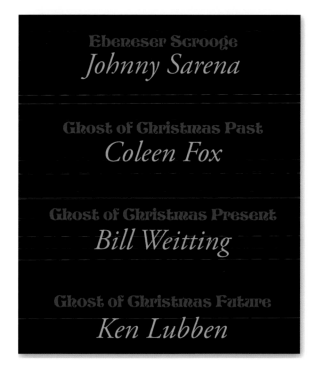

Compare the two credit rolls in the two figures above, and you will see there is enough contrast to separate the second example, even though both are a shade of green. The type size is smaller on the dark green character names, but since it is a thick gutsy type it is still readable. The light green actor names are in italic and share the same font, which unites them, but separates them from the character names in the thick sans font. The lower-case and customized leading helps the readability and separation of the credits roll. Lower-case letters have descenders in letter like **jyg**, and ascenders in letters like **ltkhd**. Letters without ascenders or descenders only have an x-height such as **xacoeurs**. You can set alternating lines in all caps, but it is usually difficult to read if you have all the type on your page in capitals. The difference in the height of the letters ascenders and descenders, gives the brain a visual resting place. Be creative though in using anything to provide contrast in your type (text warps, blurs, lines, rounded boxes, tracking, animated tracking, animated color, glows). Don't limit your creativity – think out of the box, as the possibilities are endless.

Type Size

In print, the standard page size is 8.5 × 11 inches. At 300 dpi that gives you 2550 × 3300 pixels. The average print canvas has more pixels than video, so you can go with smaller type and it is still readable. In web, you only have a few more pixels, but the viewer is sitting closer to the screen, and it is a progressive scan. In print, a typical copyright line of type is set at 6 points, but try 6-point type in video and it will be unreadable. For video you use larger type, and there is no rule for minimum size as every typeface has a different level of readability. You may have chapter names of a DVD set in 18-point type. You are asked to change the typeface, to a font with a smaller x height (the height of lower-case letters that do not have ascenders or descenders, such as x). It may now be difficult to read the type at 18 point, so you may have to make the chapter names larger.

Less is More

You have received the copy for your DVD from the copywriter. Each chapter name has a description, and you are to set 10 chapters per screen. If the copy is too long, then the viewer will lose interest and have a hard time finding the chapter they are looking for. Reduce the amount of copy so there is less to read. It is easier to find a needle within a few straws of hay, than in a big haystack. There might be extra features on the DVD such as the biography of the main characters, but readers will lose interest if they have to choose "next page" too many times. A printed brochure that comes with the DVD would be able to have longer descriptions than on the DVD.

Boldness

Beefier, gutsier, bolder type usually does better in video. You might have an extra-light font that looks good on the computer screen, but if you preview your DVD on a television, the thin horizontal lines might appear to flicker because of the interlacing. For the same reason, you do not want to use 1-pixel lines. If you have a font to make bolder, you can apply the stroke layer style. You do not want to apply more than 1 point of stroke for a DVD menu, as the stroke will begin to round off your letter. When adding a stroke to type, it is a good idea to increase the tracking so the space between the letters does not get too tight. The viewer needs to be able to scan DVD menus quickly, and they will appreciate if you give them less to read. Did you ever watch a movie, and want to read the credits to find who the soundtrack is by? Would it not be aggravating if the credits role lasted for 15 minutes?

Tracking

In video, you might use more drop shadows, strokes, and glows around your type, but the space between the letters can get tight with these added effects. Even without any layer effects, use more tracking in video – especially on smaller type. Video has less resolution, so the type is not as crisp as in print. The extra tracking can help the readability of the type, especially on monitors. There also might be glare or a reflection off the television, which makes it harder to separate the letters.

Text Color

You will notice that white is used more in video than in print. Paper is not as white as a video screen, so white type on a black background has more visibility. Colorful text against a colorful background does not always work too well in video, as there might not be enough contrast between the type and background. For example, red type over a purple background is not very readable. You can put a white stroke around the text to help separate it from the background. If the type was yellow it would help, as yellow is a bright color that would contrast better with the purple background. Color can imply emotion, and a wedding video might use flowery and pastel colors, while a travel channel jungle safari might use more earthen colors. Company colors are important, and Kodak would prefer to see Gold in their corporate meeting than a color such as green, which is used by Fuji film.

11
CREATIVE TYPOGRAPHY

*V*ideo editing applications come with a variety of titlers. Premiere Pro (for Windows) ships with the best titling tool ever to be included with the program. Final Cut Pro (for the Mac) boasts a full-featured Live Type tool that includes some very nice presets. Boris, Pinnacle, and a handful of other companies develop third-party plug-ins that greatly improve the more bland variety of titlers, such as Avid's limited text tool which is included in many versions of their application. While all of the various developers of video titlers have their own strengths, the vast majority of the titling you're likely to create will be better served by Photoshop than any other application. This chapter will illustrate just how fast and powerful Photoshop's Text Tool is, and how to get the most out of it.

THE TEXT TOOL

Ever since version 6.0, Photoshop has had the best solution for working with text this side of Illustrator. The past two versions have only improved upon the new tool design. Open a new document with the D1 Square Pixel preset using a black background. This preset will give you the extremely important title safe guides automatically. I prefer to compose all of my titles with a square pixel aspect ratio because the non-square settings in Photoshop are for previews only, and can knock down the quality. It's important to view your text at full quality and full resolution to make good decisions when choosing fonts and composing the final image.

The Text Tool options bar.

Select the Title Tool, **T**. The cursor will turn into a book, indicating the Title Tool. The options bar will look something like the figure above. Just like the brushes, the Text Tool has presets you can select, load, and save. In my opinion, none of the Text presets is worth loading because they all have the quality setting too low. However, it makes all the sense in the world to save text presets for specific attributes when you know you will be revisiting a project or client. Just to the right of the presets is the orientation indicator. This button will toggle the direction of the text between horizontal and vertical. As long as a text layer is selected, you can toggle this button and see the layer update immediately.

Next is the font family selector. If you want to cycle through various fonts and see what they look like, make sure the text layer is selected in the Layer palette, then click the font name in the options bar. Now you can use the up and down arrow keys, home, end, and even a scroll wheel. You can cycle through all four windows in the options bar for the Text Tool. One important thing to remember is that every time you change a font, a new history state is created. If you have lots of fonts you want to preview, it's very easy to preview a few dozen fonts within a minute and that will eat up your History palette very quickly. Next to the font family selector is the font style selector. If the font you have selected has a bold, italic, or other setting built into it, you can make a selection here.

Moving further down to the right of the options bar is the font size window. As a general rule, I try to stay away from font sizes smaller than 24 pixels. That includes bold fonts too. You have to remember what your final delivery medium will be. If it's NTSC VHS, you definitely want to be sure your font sizes are not too small. Even if 35 mm film is your target medium, you still want to think about font size because this summer's biggest blockbuster will soon be available on DVD and VHS. The final scrolling window in the options bar is the anti-aliasing selector. As a rule, I don't use anything but Smooth. Strong doesn't seem to change too much about the appearance, but as soon as you select Crisp, you can easily notice the quality of the font fading. The next three buttons are the text justification selectors. They will affect the text just like any word processor. One space over to the right is the color selector, which doesn't necessarily reflect the foreground color. The button with the T over a bowed line is the Text Warp editor. We'll go over that in more detail later in the chapter.

The final button on the options bar is the Character and Paragraph palette button. Whenever working with text, I like to have at least the Character palette viewable. It has most of the options already found in the options bar, but it includes some essential attributes like leading, tracking, kerning, baseline shift, horizontal or vertical scaling, and eight faux settings. Faux settings can be switched on or off at any time. They include bold, italic, all caps, all lower-case, superscript, subscript,

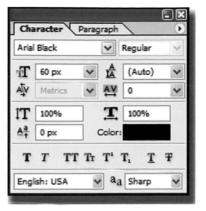

When you want to bring the quality of your text formatting to a higher standard, using the Character palette will give you a very high degree of control.

underline, and strikethrough. If a text has any faux attributes applied to it, the warping feature cannot be turned on, and vice versa.

Text Containers

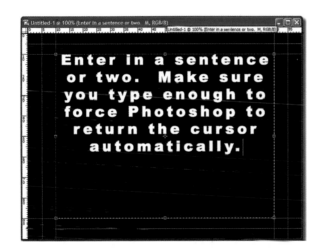

Drawing a container will prompt Photoshop to return the text to a new line automatically when typing or re-sizing the text.

With the Text Tool selected, click and drag from the top left of the document to the lower right within the title safe boundaries. The cursor will be flashing inside the container you just drew, waiting for you to start typing. Enter in a sentence or two. Make sure you type enough to force Photoshop to return the cursor automatically. If you cannot see any text but the cursor is moving, you may have to change the text color to something other than black. You can change the color by hitting the number pad enter, then clicking the color button on the options bar. If you hit Enter on the main area of the keyboard, you will

You can type on any kind of path – including shapes.

start a new paragraph. After you've made your change, bring the cursor back to the end of the text you've entered. When the cursor loses the bookends and is left with the middle, click and you will be editing the original line of text. When you're done typing, hit Enter on the number pad. If you just click the Title Tool in the document without drawing a container, you will have to decide when to start a new line by hitting Enter. This isn't so bad, but after you type your text and start altering the fonts, sizes, and other attributes, the text may become too large for the canvas and run off out of view. Having a container will keep the text inside. If it gets too big for the container, you can either resize the container by dragging the corners to fit the text, or adjust the font size, scale, spacing, or tracking.

Text Paths

Another fantastic feature that Photoshop has borrowed from Illustrator is the ability to type text on a path. Chapter 7 goes over paths and shapes in more detail, if you haven't read it yet. For now, we will keep this somewhat basic. Select the Circle Shape Tool, **U**. In the options bar, you can select the shape attribute. Both the shape and paths settings will create a path for us to type on. Turn off all layers except for the background. Hold down **Shift** and drag the cursor in the document to make a perfect circle. Hit **T** for the Text Tool and place the cursor at the top of the circle. Notice how the cursor will change shapes based on whether you are on the outside or inside of the shape. If you click when you are on the outside, you will be typing on the path of the circle. You can keep typing until you run out of space. This technique works with any path you can create.

To edit the starting and ending point for the text on the path, select the Path Selector Tool, or hit **A**. Make sure that you haven't selected the Direct Selection Tool and that the text layer is selected in the Layers palette. Bring the cursor to the first letter of the text. There will be a small "x" on the base of the path just before the

To move the starting point of the text, use the Direct Selection Tool to drag the "x" forwards or backwards to suit your taste.

letter. When the cursor changes to a Text Tool cursor with a black arrow, you can click and drag the x in either direction of the path, changing the starting point of the text. At some other point on the path, there will be a tiny "+" with a circle around it on the path. This mark indicates where the text will end. You can drag this around the path with the Path Selection Tool the same way as you did with the little "x".

If you switch to the Direct Selection Tool, **A**, you can alter the text's path just like any other path, and the text will update along with your changes. Select the text in the Layers palette and its path will be visible. Use the Direct Selection Tool to drag the corners around to suit your needs. You can even **Ctrl Alt Shift Click** [**Command Option Shift Click**] a corner to convert it back and forth from a straight corner or a rounded corner with handles. Once a text layer has a path associated with it, you can turn off or delete the shape layer you used to create it. The text layer saves the path as a part of itself.

After you've typed on the path, open the Path palette. You will see a new path named after the text layer. Go back to the Layers palette and click on the Shape 1 layer, then hit **T** for the Text Tool again. This time, click inside the circle. A container is already made for you to type inside of with a corresponding path in the Paths palette. The circle container will behave the same way as if you clicked and dragged your own container, but will keep the text within the circle's boundaries instead of the rectangle's. Using the Direct Selection Tool on the container's path will alter the layout of the text accordingly, updating as you edit.

WARPING TEXT

Another enhancement brought to Photoshop's text tool since version 6.0 is text warping. This feature is not as sophisticated as typing on a path, but nevertheless

has some usefulness. Hide or delete all layers except the background layer. Use the Text Tool to type "Warping Text" then hit enter on the number pad. Click on the Create Warp Text button on the options bar. If you have any faux settings on the text, you will be prompted to cancel the Warp Text or to automatically turn off the faux settings and proceed to the Warp Text.

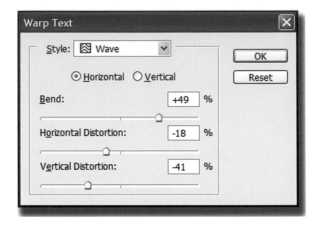

These are the settings used for the previous figure.

The Warp Text window has a style selector, two buttons and three sliders. The default setting for every style is horizontal, 50% bend, and no horizontal or vertical distortion. Keep Horizontal checked, unless you are working with vertical text – then select Vertical. The Bend slider will give you the most variation based on the style selected. The Horizontal Distortion and Vertical Distortion will give the appearance of perspective and distance.

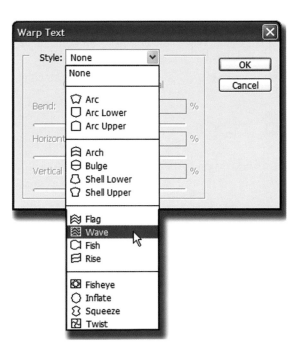

The Warp Text dialog box gives you 15 different styles to choose from.

If you open the style selector you will see the 15 different warp styles, separated into four categories based on their characteristics. Every style has an appropriate icon to the left that gives a very succinct illustration of what you can expect if you apply a given style. Some styles are more useful than others, but you shouldn't be afraid to experiment with any of the settings because you can come back and change them at any point in time. As long as you have the room on your monitor, you can watch your text update as you make changes in the Warp Text window. Just hit **OK** when you're done. If you want to go back later and make changes, just make sure the text layer is selected in the Layers palette, hit **T**, and click the **Create Warp Text** icon on the options bar.

SHORTCUTS FOR TEXT

Moving the Cursor and Selecting Text

Open **Chapter 11** >> **Paragraph** on the DVD. The text takes up most of the title safe area. Hit **T** for the Text Tool and click anywhere on the text. Photoshop allows you to use the same shortcuts that most word processors use – so if you don't already know them, you can use them on your word processor too.

Content on DVD

Using the arrow keys to move the cursor in any direction is fairly basic, but if you hold down the **Ctrl [Command]** key, you will jump to the beginning of the next or previous word. Hold it down with the up or down arrow keys and you will go to the beginning of the previous or next paragraph. If you hold down the **Shift** key while using the arrow keys, you will create a selection of the text you pass over in whatever direction. If you hit **Shift Up** or **Shift Down**, you can select an entire line of text, starting or ending at the cursor. **Ctrl Shift Left** or **Right** [**Command Shift Left or Right**], will select one word at a time in either direction and **Ctrl Shift Up** or **Down** [**Command Shift Up or Down**], will select one paragraph at a time. To select all the text at once, you can either hit **Ctrl A** [**Command A**] when the cursor is in the text or double click the T icon in the Layers palette – it won't even matter if the Text Tool is selected.

EDITING TEXT

If you have to create a number of lower third banners for the names of 20 different people to be seen on screen, start with only one name. Spend your time getting the font, size, color, style, banner, and composition exactly how you want it. Then you will make however many duplicates you need of the text layer by hitting

When creating lower third banners, Photoshop gives you more creative power and flexibility than any video editing application.

Ctrl J [Command J], replacing the names and titles. This workflow will ensure consistency because each copy of the text layer will contain the same formatting and style effects.

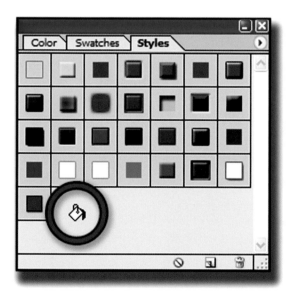
Open **Chapter 11 >> Lower 3rd** on the DVD. This is just a generic lower 3rd. If Jane Doe is the host, we will most likely need a guest. Click the T icon on the Layers palette. Hit **Ctrl J [Command J]** to duplicate the text layer, and turn off the original. The copied layer retains all of the attributes of the original, including the layer style. Hit **T** for the Text Tool and click into the text. Move the cursor around and watch the options bar change settings as you move to name, title, and description. Highlight the only the name Jane Doe and enter "Joe Somebody". Then highlight the title and description and enter "President - Tasty Food Restaurants". Before you hit the number pad **Enter**, move the cursor back to the name and leave it between the "J" and the "o". For getting the truly best typesetting, manually adjust your kerning, or space between letters, by using **Alt Left** or **Right [Option Left or Right]**. Some fonts will not give a favorable space between letters by default. It may be technically legible, but not on target for purposes of an esthetically pleasing title.

Text Styles

While you have Chapter 11 >> Lower third open, make sure one of the text layers is selected in the Layers palette. Open the Styles palette, Window Styles. Place the cursor over an empty area of the palette and it changes to a Bucket icon.

When you have made a style that you want to save for repeated use, select the layer associated with the style and click on a blank space in the Styles palette.

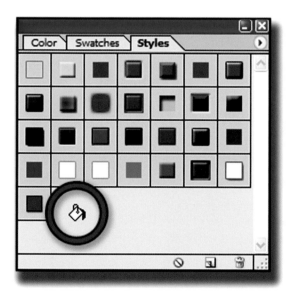

Click inside the palette and a New Style window opens. A preview box for the style is on the left, you are given the choice of including the layer effects, the layer blending options, or both, and a name for the custom style is waiting to be entered. We would name this style "Text - What's On Now?" so we could identify it quickly in the Styles palette.

You can create and save your own styles.

12
DVD MENUS

*T*he subject of DVD authoring is the basis of entire books. This chapter will illus-

trate easy menu design tips that will give any DVD project more character, impact,

and distinction by using Photoshop. Digital Versatile Disc or DVD is the fastest-growing

format the planet has ever seen – including VHS and CD. It's no surprise when you *consider the quality of the video and audio it can hold. All videophile and audiophile interests aside, the real innovation of the DVD format lies within its interactive potential. If you have ever rented or bought a movie on DVD, you've seen the menu pages. Different titles or movies will have their own unique menu layout and interface design. A well-planned and executed menu layout will have a similar feel and tone of the content contained on the disc, (hopefully) wetting your appetite or raising your curiosity.*

DVD AUTHORING APPLICATIONS

DVD authoring is within the reach of most professionals and many enthusiasts. There are many options to choose from when considering a DVD authoring application. The price of entry ranges from $49 to over $2000 in the United States. It doesn't matter if you have formal training or if you are only a hobbyist, there is a solution that is right for your level of skill and budget. The following table is a mere sampling of the DVD authoring applications available for less than $1000.

COMPANY	TITLE	COMMENTS
Sonic	My DVD	Arguably the world's most popular consumer-level authoring application. Extremely easy to use. Basic menu design allows for still images to be used as a menu background.
Sonic	DVDit!	A deceptively powerful application. Very intuitive interface and preview function. Allows you to import a layered Photoshop file as a background and separate buttons.
Sonic	Reel DVD	Highly functional application. Unique storyboard interface design may or may not appeal to a given user. Allows you to import a layered Photoshop file as a background and separate buttons.
Ulead	DVD Workshop	Very good value with few limitations on authoring. New version supports more audio formats and allows you to import a layered Photoshop file as a background and separate buttons.
Pinnacle	Edition	First and foremost a video editing application, Edition is the first to offer complete DVD authoring within the program using the original DV files. Allows you to import a layered Photoshop file as a background and separate buttons.
Apple	iDVD	The easiest solution for the Mac. Offers innovative interface design and integration with iTunes and iPhoto.
Apple	DVD Studio Pro	Perhaps the most full-featured solution for under $2000. Originally developed by Spruce Technologies, Apple has since acquired the program and has given it a new facelift and changed some of the menu terminology to conform to Apple's way of communicating. Three different interfaces: Basic, Extended, and Advanced offer an environment and toolset to fit your level of expertise. Final Cut Pro users will feel very comfortable in a familiar environment. Allows you to import a layered Photoshop file as a background and separate buttons.

| Adobe | Encore | As to be expected, Encore offers the tightest integration with Photoshop, as will be explained later in this chapter. Extremely versatile and well equipped to author a truly high-end DVD experience. Puts a great deal of control in the author's hands. Not only allows layered Photoshop files to be imported as background and buttons, but also allows Photoshop to create specific highlights for button states. |

DESIGN TIPS

All of the DVD authoring applications previously mentioned in this chapter offer some level of menu design, including pre-made backgrounds, animations, buttons, and even music. All of the included materials with any of these programs are undeniably of professional quality. However, as beautiful as a stock footage waterfall background can be for a wedding video menu, it will never touch the impact of a photo showing the newlyweds locked in a kiss, a wide shot of the ceremony, or even the cake before it's been cut. If the menu background itself doesn't communicate anything about the content it navigates, it is nothing more than decoration.

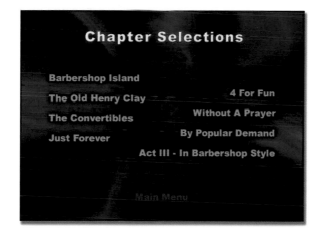

Some graphic backgrounds may look interesting, but do not communicate anything important to the content.

Layout

Chapter 3 goes over resolution and pixel aspect ratios in detail. When you work with a DVD authoring application that is Photoshop-aware, your best strategy is to create your artwork in a video preset that matches the DVD project. So in the United States, a DVD project would be 720 × 480 non-square pixels. The Photoshop equivalent to those dimensions is 720 × 534 square pixels. The authoring application will resize the image to fit the screen, and will look correct when viewed on a television monitor.

The basic principles of general design apply to DVD menu layout design. You want to be aware of action and title safe areas. Coordinate the eye of the viewer by leading them from left to right and top to bottom – unless you are authoring in a language that reads from right to left such as Hebrew, or up and down such as Chinese and Japanese. Stay away from placing your subject dead in the center as it will tend to anchor the viewer's eyes there. Maintain a healthy amount of "white" space to keep from over-cluttering the screen.

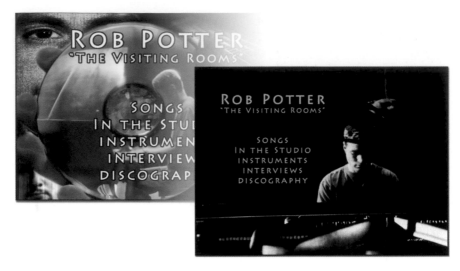

Even if you only create a single page menu for a DVD title, keeping the design uncluttered and streamlined makes for easier navigation, and communicates elegance.

The most effective way to begin a project is to storyboard or sketch it out on paper ahead of time, in the same way you would plan a complex production shoot or a complex web site layout. Start with your main menu at the top and branch it down to include all submenus. This approach gives you a visual queue to help you stay organized and can act as a checklist as you build your assets.

Spending 5 minutes mapping out a DVD's navigation scheme can save you 5 days of redoing your work.

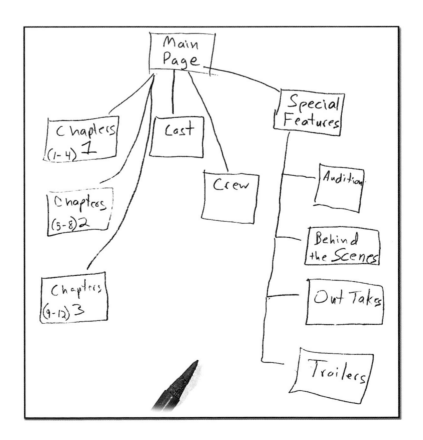

We would always suggest working with a DVD authoring application that supports layered Photoshop files. The different layers can import separately with the layer name attached to it. However, if you use any layer styles on any of your layers, they will not appear when imported into the DVD project. You will have to create a new layer, **Ctrl Shift N [Command Shift N]**, link it to the layer with the layer style applied, and merge the two together, **Ctrl E [Command E].**

Theme

The real fun in designing menu backgrounds comes from establishing an appropriate theme to complement the content contained on the DVD. Taking still frames from the video content is an easy way to get started. The figure above shows a simple

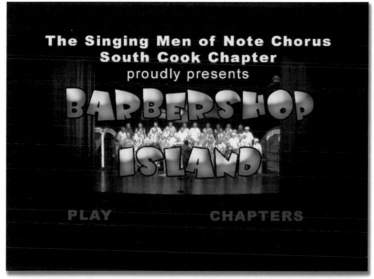

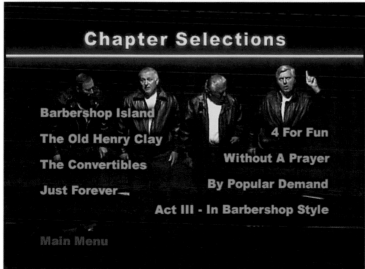

Personalizing menu pages may be less flashy than some stock backgrounds, but will produce a harder impact on the client and will complement the content on the DVD.

layout of a two-menu DVD that we authored for a client. The main menu was taken from the open shot of their performance and the chapters menu was taken from the group that included the performer who hired me – a little bit of PR goes a long way! Notice how the text doesn't violate the faces on screen for the chapters menu, and the font and treatment of the title reflects the jovial nature of a Gilligan's Island spoof. This attention to detail and inclusion of their style helped me to get a unanimous decision from the group to hire me again for their next annual show.

A very common function of most DVD authoring applications is the ability to drag the first frame of a chapter point from the timeline and make a thumbnail icon out of it. This feature can be extremely useful most of the time. Sometimes, however, the first frame of a chapter point might be a black screen, a wide shot, a frame with the subject blocked by something in the foreground, or a frame with too much motion blur. The more advanced programs, such as Adobe Encore, allow you to set the beginning of a chapter at one frame and the reference frame for that chapter as another.

For the most flexibility in setting a visual icon to identify a chapter, Photoshop is right for the task. If you want to use thumbnails that show elements from the content to clue a viewer in on what to expect, you might be better off exporting the frame of video to Photoshop where you can crop and resize the image to best meet your needs. If you're working with NTSC DV footage, a full frame scaled down to a thumbnail might be too difficult to recognize, but a 720×480 resolution might be plenty of leeway to allow you to grab just a portion and repurpose it as an icon.

A) In the context of a DVD menu, a full screen capture may be too small to make out any detail when scaled down as a menu button.
B) Cropping part of the image might be the best solution, as long as you select an area the same size or larger than the final button.

Keep in mind the principles of typography outlined in Chapters 2, 10, and 11. Don't use fonts that are too thin or too bright. Use complementary colors to separate them from the background, or use outlines and drop shadows. Finally, make sure it's large enough to read. Instead of overcrowding a menu page, split it up between two or more submenus.

PHOTOSHOP FOR ADOBE ENCORE

Adobe Encore is a DVD authoring application that currently exists only for the PC. Most of the DVD menu design is done in Photoshop, especially if you are using

Encore. Mac users can also prepare files for usage with Encore and save them as layered documents in Photoshop format. You need to know how to properly name your layers so Encore will give them special features. Open **Chapter 12 >> Hummer Menu.psd** and inspect the layers. When you want a video to play inside of a button, you must define the area you want the video to play in. This is the purpose of layers named "(%)", which is used to define the area for these animated thumbnail buttons.

Content on DVD

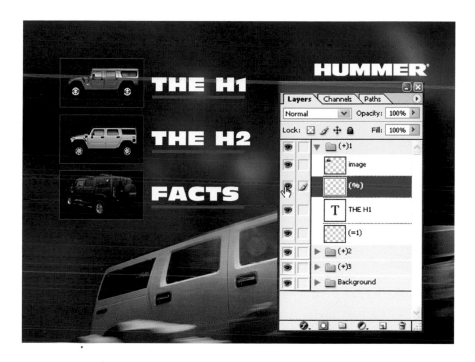

   Ctrl Alt [Option] click on the "(%)" **layer visibility eyeball** to solo the layer. This will hide all the layers except the one you **Alt [Option]** clicked on, so you can see it is just a white square. **Ctrl Alt [Option]** click on the "(=1)" **layer visibility eyeball** to solo the layer. This is a subpicture layer which will change colors when selected. The color will change to what Encore preferences are for color state #1. There are three color state settings you can configure. A subpicture is similar to a rollover in web design, as it has an activated and selected state. The following chart will help you understand how to name your layer sets and layers in Photoshop.

Layer Sets

(+)   The characters you put after the (+) will be the name for the button.
         Specifies this layer set is a button.

Layers

(%)   An area you fill that represents a placeholder for either a thumbnail or
         animated button, that you set a link to in Encore.

(=1)	The pixels in this area change to the color and opacity Encore has set in the
(=2)	highlight group. There are three possible color sets, and the state changes to
(=3)	selected or activated.
	It is important to use only a single color and to stay away from anti-aliasing.
	This is a limitation of DVD Technology, but not of Encore.

Layers named anything else will have no special function.

SECTION III
MASKING AND TRANSFORMATIONS

13 SELECTIONS

*M*asking is the single most important skill you can learn in Photoshop. Photoshop has many tools and commands for masking, and it is good to learn them all. Chapter 14 deals with layer masks, which is the best method to use, since it is non-destructive. Before you learn to work with layer masks, it is best you know the selection tools first. Various combinations of masking tools help you get a perfect layer mask. Once you have a good mask, you can float the part of the image to its own layer. This allows you to fix tonality, do selective sharpening, or apply effects to that part of the image. We assume you are familiar with the basic Photoshop commands of select all **Ctrl A [Command A]**. To deselect, there is actually a command, but many people find it quicker to just click and release or use the keyboard command of **Ctrl D [Command D]**.

ERASER

You rarely want to use the eraser on an image, as it is destructive. When applying the eraser to a background layer, the color of the image changes to the background color. Double-click your background color swatch, and set it to a green, and open the **Chapter 13/Eraser.tif file**. Run the eraser set to about 50 pixels over the background layer, and it will change to the background color of green. Undo this, and hit (**d**) on your keyboard to change to the default colors. Run the eraser over the background and it will now change to white, which is how we normally think of erasing a pencil mark on white paper. Turn on the visibility of the red layer, by **clicking on the eyeball in front of the layer named "Red Layer"**. We want to erase this red field and show the layer underneath. First you must target which layer you will erase by **clicking the name of the "Red Layer" to highlight that layer in the layers palette**. Hit (**e**) to switch to the eraser, and **begin to erase** – you will notice the Fiji bottle layer showing underneath the red. **Turn the visibility eyeball off for the background layer**, and you will see a checkerboard pattern. The checkerboard symbolizes transparency, and is actually transparent when you import the image into your video editing application. There is also a layer effect of bevel and emboss applied to the red layer, and it reacts with the transparency of the layer. If you used a hard brush, you will see a beveled edge where the opaque part of the image meets transparency. You can also **change the opacity of the eraser tool in the options bar at the top to 50%, now rub the eraser over the red.** You will see that the eraser can have an opacity setting, which erases at a reduced intensity. You can also have an eraser tool follow a path, as we did in the previous chapter on custom brushes.

MAGIC WAND

The magic wand is used for selecting pixels of similar colors, depending on the tolerance you assign in the options bar. The tolerance can be set from 0 to 255, which is the range of colors that will be selected, depending on where you click with the magic wand. Open **Chapter 13/Magic Wand.tif** and **set the tolerance of your magic wand to 0. Click anywhere on the grayscale gradient, and you will select only one rectangle. If you click below the grayscale gradient, you will select the bottom half of the page,** because the transparency is seen as a color.

Click on the top left square, hold down shift on your keyboard and click on the third square, and then the fifth. Holding down shift adds to your selection.

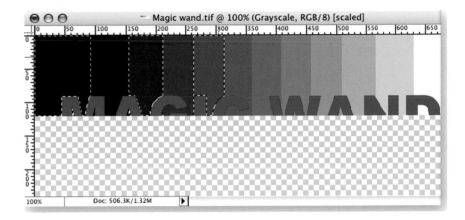

Hold down **Alt [Option] and click on a selected square to subtract from your selection area.** Now **change the tolerance to 44 and click on a square, and you should select about three squares.** Increasing the tolerance, increases the range of pixel colors that the magic wand will select. Now **click on the visibility icon for the blue layer** to show the layer with the blue gradient. You can now read the type MAGIC WAND, but how can you select it with one click. This is easy, but you must change two settings in the options bar at the top. **Remove the check for contiguous** so that it will select red pixels even though they are not neighboring (contiguous) pixels. You will also want to **check the box for use all layers,** because the type is in two different layers. Now **click with the magic wand tolerance set to 0 on a red pixel** and you will select the entire word magic wand. There are four icons to the left of the tolerance setting in the options bar, but they are rarely useful, as the keyboard command to add and subtract to your selection are quicker to use than depressing those buttons.

PEN TOOL

The Pen Tool is used to draw shapes of vector quality, which are stored in the paths palette. These shapes always have a reference in the paths palette and are also referred to as paths or bezier curves after their inventor. You can always **Ctrl [Command]** click on an item in the paths palette to change a path to a bitmapped selection. Open the file **Chapter 13/Pen Tool.tif** and we will change the sign that says "Le Car Rental". Hit (**p**) to switch to the pen tool and look at your toolbar options, you will see three icons (Shapes, Paths, Pixels) in a group which are very important. Choose the second icon, so that we will be drawing an unfilled path. Find the Le Car Rental street sign, **and click on the five corners of the red field and finally on the starting point** to close the path. **Double-click on the name work path in the paths palette and hit return.** This saves and names the

Content on DVD

path – the default name of path 1 is acceptable. You can have only one work path in a document. If you do not name your work path, you will very quickly lose that path when switching tools. If you select a path by highlighting it, then you will be adding to that path when using with the pen tool. **Ctrl [Command] click on the name of path 1 in the paths palette** to select it, then hit **Ctrl H [Command H]** to temporarily hide the marching ants of your selection. **Switch to the eyedropper tool and sample the red color on the left edge of the sign**, your foreground color should change to red. Next hold **Alt [Option] and click on the right edge of the sign** to sample a darker red color, which will fill your background swatch. Switch to your gradient tool by hitting (**g**) on your keyboard and you will see your options bar at the top switch to the options for the gradient tool. **Click in the middle of the gradient in the options bar** to bring up the Gradient Editor, and **choose the first swatch which is foreground to background color.** Many people have a hard time finding the gradient editor, as they expect there to be a gradient palette as in other applications. **Make a new layer**, and **drag across the sign to fill your new layer with a red to dark red gradient**. Make visible the layer set called "new sign" to show you the finished sign. The type was set in a straight line using the sampled color of bluish white from the previous sign. The type was then transformed to match the angle and skew to give the pictured result.

EXTRACT

This filter can quickly extract images if you are good with a mouse or digital tablet. The quality is not as good as layer masking covered in the next chapter. Open **Chapter 13/extract.tif** and choose **Filter >> Extract** to pull down the interface for extract. **Enable Smart highlighting** and **draw a green border around the edge of the bird**. Smart highlighting works well in most areas, only highlighting the black of the bird and not the background. If you make a mistake, use the eraser tool to erase parts of the green highlight if it went outside the bird.

Once you have finished highlighting the entire edge of the bird, **switch to the paint bucket tool, and click inside the bird** to fill it with blue. When your results look satisfactory, **click OK** to have it extract the image.

Extract is destructive and erased the background, and you will probably have a few areas where the edge does not look good. There is a workaround we want to share with you, in case you like using the extract filter. **Revert to the original image, duplicate the background layer, run the extract filter on the duplicate layer.** The top layer will be destroyed, but you have a back-up. What we like to do is use the result of the extract, and apply it as a layer mask to the original layer. **Ctrl [Command] click on the extracted duplicate layer,** this selects the transparency of that extracted layer. **Double-click the background layer,** and name it so you can add a layer mask. Once the background layer is not in italics, **choose Layer >> Add layer mask >> Reveal selection** to add a layer mask to the layer.

You can then paint on the layer mask in black to erase the background, or in white to bring back the raven image. Layer masks are non-destructive to your color data, and can be used together with the extract filter in this method to make it more useful.

COLOR RANGE

Content on DVD

This selection technique is extremely useful, and similar to the magic wand, but allows you to choose multiple colors and a tolerance range. Open **Chapter 13/Color Range.psd**. Notice the orange paint on the rope and other various parts of the white rim of the lifesaver. Choose **Select >> Color Range** and the default will show your image in color, and your preview in grayscale. You can change both by **clicking on the Image radio button, and changing selection preview to grayscale**. If you hold down **Ctrl** [**Command**] you will temporarily toggle the Selection/Image radio buttons. Color Range will select colors similar to the value you initially have in your foreground swatch. The colors that will be selected are in white, and the unselected colors will be in black.

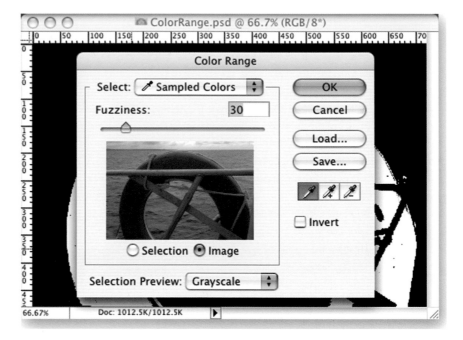

Slide your fuzziness to the right and you will be selecting more colors, and also notice more gray pixels. Gray symbolizes a partial selection with transparency. The closer to white the gray is, the stronger the selection; until it is white, which is full strength. **Click in your image or in the color range window** to sample a range of colors based on the fuzziness. Each time you click a range of similar colors are selected depending on which pixel you clicked. **Slide fuzziness down to about 30**. You could keep sliding fuzziness to the right and select more of the orange, but you will do better by adding a highlight, midtone and shadow of your orange lifesaver. **Hold down the Shift key** and notice that your eyedropper has added a plus. This means that you will be adding colors to your selection range, and the same fuzziness value will be applied to that range. Try to **select your darkest orange and lightest orange**, until you get a nice selection. You can also hold and drag the eyedropper over the lifesaver, but often you may inadvertently include a black smudge on the lifesaver, which has the same color as the shadows in the water. **Click OK when you are satisfied with your selection**, then do a **Ctrl H [Command H]**, to hide your selection edges.

Now choose **Ctrl U [Command U] and change the hue to 40** to get a yellow, or choose your own favorite lifesaver color. Colors closer to orange such as red are more forgiving, but the color range works so well on this type of image that you should not need to do any touchup. We will go over the color replacement tool in Chapter 17, and how to set your brush mode to color/hue, to help fix color leaks on an image. You can also in the color range filter hold down **Alt [Option]** to subtract a sampled color from a selection. The three eyedroppers are quite useless, as it is much more convenient to use the keyboard commands of Shift plus **Alt [Option]**. The Invert button is also quite useless, as you can always inverse your selection by choosing Select >> Inverse. There is also an alternate method to using the eyedropper. Change the sampled colors option to red in this case which is similar to orange, but there is no fuzziness so you will find it more accurate staying with the sampled colors option. For this image the red option worked well, but you can get better results with the eyedropper, and with the keyboard commands, it is very quick to use.

MAGIC LASSO

Open **Chapter 13/MagicLasso.psd**, and we will select the coconut on the beach. You can select the magic lasso by **hitting Shift L, until the lasso tool switches to a lasso with a magnet**. Position the bottom-most point of the magic lasso rope on the edge of the coconut and **click and release the mouse button once**. This sets the initial starting point, and you will drag, and additional points will be created by the magic lasso tool once the tool needs to create a point. If the magic lasso tool laid down a point in a bad position, stop drawing and hit **the Delete key to delete the last point created**. You can hit the Delete key to keep deleting single points, until you have deleted them all. Once you get to the bottom of the coconut where the shadow meets the ground, the tool will not work as well and you have to manually set a few points, to assist the tool.

Click and release the mouse button to set a point near the start of the shadow. The magic lasso really is a smart tool, but it appreciates help when it encounters an area where the edge is not defined. Now the lasso tool has been setting vector points and Bezier curves to define your selection; so this tool works well on hard-edged objects, such as product shots. You could use the pen tool instead, but the magic lasso is for faster selections, which do not need perfect quality. Video can be more forgiving than print, because it is difficult to notice imperfections in animated objects. When you are near to the end, you will want to close the path by **clicking over the starting point**, double-clicking or **hitting Enter [Return]**. This draws a line that follows the edge of the coconut, and is the preferred method in this case. If you need your final line to be straight, such as for a polygon shape, you can **Alt [Option] and double-click.** The **Alt [Option]** is useful for when you need to draw straight lines by clicking and releasing, or drawing freeform by click dragging. Now you can copy this to the clipboard and paste it into another document, which we will distort to match another image in Chapter 15 transformations.

QUICKMASK

The QuickMask was modeled after prepress houses usage of rubylith. They would put a ruby red vinyl over a sheet of mylar, and then tape this over film and cut a mask out of the rubylith. When you turn on the QuickMask mode, the word "QuickMask" appears up in the document title. When you paint with black, it now puts a red color over the area, symbolizing what will be deselected. We will now use QuickMask to extract a head from the background, of which you might want to replace it with a flat tint – as in a news broadcast graphics.

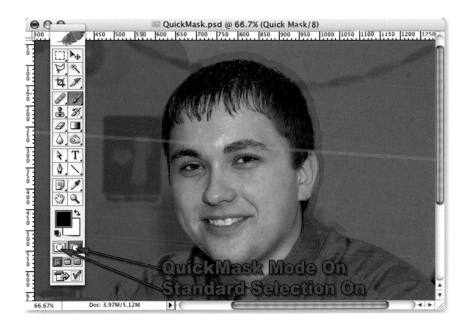

Open **Chapter 13/QuickMask.psd** and click in the toolbox to enter the QuickMask mode. You can enter and exit the QuickMask mode at anytime using the buttons below your Foreground and Background colors. **Double-click the magnifying glass** to change your view to 100%. Choose your paintbrush by **hitting (b), change the diameter to about 50 pixels, and paint the border on the area you want to delete.** If you make a mistake, you can hit the x keyboard command to switch colors, and erase the red. **Increase your brush size to about 100, and paint in the remaining background.** The bigger brush allows much quicker painting, and you can quickly increase your brush size each time using the right bracket keyboard shortcut. Painting in the background should be much easier. Now you can easily make that a selection by switching from QuickMask mode to standard mode. Don't worry, as you can keep going between the two modes without losing your selection, unless you deselect. There are not many hairs on this image so you can do a rough QuickMask, if you have a good mouse hand. QuickMask is not the best quality method, but it can be fast. QuickMask works well with cleaning up a color range selection, but does not work as well as the density masking achieved by using layer masks. This is described in the next chapter, and is one of the most useful skills you can master in Photoshop.

Content on DVD

14
LAYER MASKS

*T*he topics of QuickMask and Extract were covered only briefly in Chapter 13, because we want you to learn thoroughly the best method— layer masks. You still need to use the selection tools, so you can modify and create your layer masks. Once you have a selection of marching ants, all you need to do is choose a layer, and use the command Layer >> Add Layer Mask >> Reveal Selection. This creates a grayscale swatch to the right of the active layer when that command was invoked. Once you have a layer mask you can **Alt [Option]** click on the layer mask to see what it looks like. You can work directly on the mask using brushes to improve your mask. **Ctrl [Command]** click on a layer mask, and you select the white pixels of the layer mask. You could use a Select >> Modify >> Contract, then Select >> Inverse, and fill that with black to mask deeper into your image. Think of the layer mask as a transparent material over a spotlight. Paint on a mask with black to hide parts of the image, or white to show the image. Because you paint on a mask, the original image is left *untouched. Video and stage professionals can think of a mask as a gel mask for stage lighting.*

Every image is different, and so are the masking techniques you will use. If shooting with a digital camera, try and shoot your subject with a blue screen background. Green works better for DV, but any color is useful as long as it is different from the subject. These screens are called chroma keys, and the important part is to light the chroma key and subject properly to get a good range of color in your image.

HAIRY MONKEY

Results of a vector mask.

We will start with an easy layer mask to create, so you can learn this advanced technique. You will also find your existing stock images more useful, and want to use them more often. Open **Chapter 14/Hairy Monkey**, which is a stock image against a white background and a clipping path. Vector masks are hard-edged, and we need a soft density mask. A soft mask makes the edges of hairs semi-transparent, as they should be. Look at a hair under a microscope, and you will see that the edges are semi-transparent. The clipping path has so many points that it can slow down your computer. **Enable the visibility eye-con for the layer set called**

Content on DVD

"vector mask test" to see that the vector mask is unacceptable. Vector masks are great for shots with hard edges, such as product shots of a can of soda pop. With hair, vector masks take too long to draw with the pen tool, and you need them to blend softly with the background, and not be blurry. A layer mask has pixels which each have their own opacity strength; so you can actually have the hair combine better with any background you choose to use. We are going to rebuild this the proper way, so **drag the "Vector Mask Test" layer set to the Layers palette trash can.**

Select >>All and copy the monkey layer to the clipboard. The monkey is so dark and the background is white, that this is an easier layer mask to create. **Click on the Add layer mask icon in the layers palette. Alt [Option] click on the layer mask** to enter the mask and **paste your clipboard contents.** It is important that you **Alt [Option]** click prior to pasting, or else you will not paste into the layer mask, but create a new layer. You will see a grayscale version of the monkey in the layer mask. If you **click on the color layer swatch for the monkey** you will see that it looks like most of the monkey is transparent, which is the opposite of what we want. Have no fear, this is so easily corrected, but first **click on the layer mask.** Invert the pixels of the layer mask using **Ctrl I [Command I].** Now you should see some of the transparency squares showing through the middle of the monkey. **Alt [Option] click on the layer mask** and you will see light gray colors in the center of the mask. We could paint out, but it is a much easier and accurate to color correct out the light gray. First zoom in to about 100% view by **double-clicking the zoom tool.**

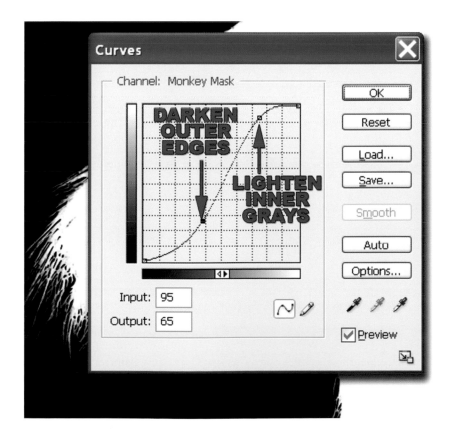

Mask "S" curve correction.

Choose **Image** >> **Adjust** >> **Curves and click to set two points as shown**. This is an S-shaped curve, which adds more contrast to the mask, but still holds some grays near the edges. You will want to **drag the right point upwards to get rid of the grays** in the center and watch the preview to know how far to go. Now remember the white halo we saw in the first monkey image – we can crop in on that using the **left curve point and dragging it downwards to darken the outer edges**. If you are having trouble with using curves, just click Load and load the "Monkey Mask Curves.acv" file (we will cover that better in Chapter 17). **Click on the "Monkey" layer swatch to see your results**. Not bad – but there is still a small halo of white on the hairs; that's because the monkey was probably shot on a white back ground. We could use the Select >> Modify >> Contract command to squeeze in a pixel, but the length of the hairs would be shortened. We are going to cheat this by using the Burn tool to darken the edges of the hairs. Hit **Shift O until you switch to the Burn tool** – it looks like a hand about to strike a match. Set the Burn toolbar options to a **65 diameter, 0 hardness brush, and range to midtones**. Now just **rub the Burn tool over the edges where you see a white halo** and it almost seems to act like an eraser. This part can be destructive if you go too far inwards, so stay outwards and drag in to avoid going too far. A Wacom pen also gives you nice pressure-sensitive results here. **Create a new adjustment layer of solid color of green** to test your results. Everything should be perfect around the edges, which is the most important part. The monkey's face and toes will have some unwanted transparency if you used my curve, but you can correct that using the paintbrush. **Alt [Option] click the layer mask** to see if you have any light grays in the face and toes. **Switch to the Dodge tool set to Highlights, and paint over the grays in the layer mask** to lighten them. Be careful not to use midtones, as you would probably lighten the edge of the mask where the dark grays are. Notice that the Dodge tool lightens the pixels you do not need, but does not erase the dark blacks because it is set to Highlights. **Switch to the paintbrush with a foreground**

Good masks are very useful.

color of white, and paint out any light gray pixels in the center. Test out your monkey, and your results should be good enough. The final results here had a slight Gaussian blur to the mask, and a slight curves correction in the midtones to pull the mask inwards. A slight blur to the edge of the art pixels was done by selecting inverse of the mask pixels and using expand of two pixels. Don't worry if you did not understand the last part – you are on your way to becoming a masking pro, and the next example is a more difficult image that builds upon the techniques you learned.

MARSHALL FIELDS CLOCK

To separate the clock from the rest of the image is a difficult task. This clock has colors that are also in the background, such as the black shadows. This advanced technique will build your skills in additional hand-cutting techniques to masks, using tricks to make the process easier. The creative possibilities are endless, and you could animate the background and transform into any of these variations.

Black and white.

Colored chalk.

Prep the Image

Open the file **Chapter14/Clock1.psd. Drag the background layer onto the page icon** at the bottom of the layers palette, to duplicate the layer.

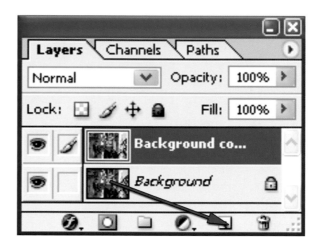

The background layer should also now be highlighted to let you know that is the active layer. We will color-correct the layer copy to over saturate the pixels and help the Color range command make a better selection. Hit **M** on your keyboard to switch tool to your rectangular Marquee tool. **Draw a marquee to include the clock,** but not the background. This will help the next color correction and the color range command to have less to process.

Hit **Ctrl U [Command U]** to bring up the Hue/Saturation palette. Change **Edit to Green,** to match the clock color. Notice the triangles around the green at the bottom right. You can fine-tune these in/out points if needed, but the default green is perfect for this lesson.

Increase saturation of the green clock to the point just before the background begins to change color. You are looking to separate the edges of the clock from the background. The edges are more important than the center which we

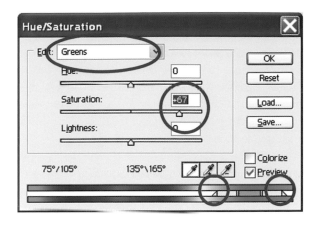

will paint in later, as with the monkey. Hit **I** to switch to the eyedropper and check that it is set **to 5 × 5 average in your Tool Options** taskbar at the top. Using the eyedropper, click on a color representing the clock green edge. This will sample a 5 × 5 pixel average color into your foreground color swatch.

Color Range Select

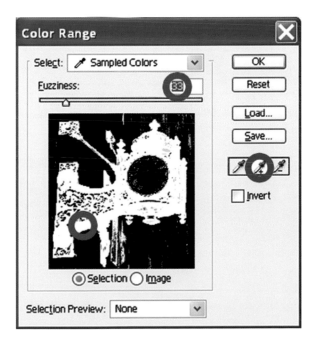

Choose **Select >> Color Range and change fuzziness to about 33**. It is good to have a lower value and to add more colors so that you define more precisely the range of colors you want this technique to use. You will notice that the foreground color was used, just as if you would have clicked with the first eyedropper in the

Color Range menu. Now **hold down Shift**, and you will do the same thing as if you switched to the second eyedropper with the plus in the Color Range selection filter. **Click to add about three additional colors** from the lightest to darkest colors of the clock. If you choose a bad one, immediately do a **Ctrl Z** to undo. When you have got the best selection, you can Click OK, and you will create a new selection and the marching ants will display the boundaries of the selection. With the ants still marching, click the background layer to make that the active layer, so we can apply the next step to the layer with the original color.

Before we can create a layer mask, we need to change the background to a layer. Double-click on the background and rename it to Clock. Choose **Layer >> Add Layer Mask >> Reveal Selection**, or just click on the add a layer mask icon on the bottom of the Layers palette. **Delete the background copy and create a new blue adjustment layer under your clock** layer, so you can test your mask. This blue layer also helps you find the problems areas so you can make a better mask.

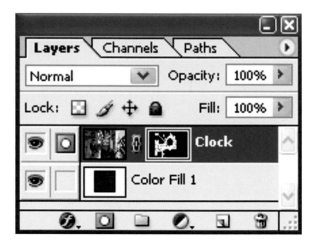

Layer Mask Cleanup

Content on DVD You can open **Chapter 14/Clock2.psd** and use that file, if you had difficulty getting to this point. **Click to the right of the color layer swatch to select the layer mask** and a very thin border appears around that swatch to notify you that the mask is the active layer. Notice that your foreground color switched to a grayscale color, which verifies that the layer mask is active and not the layer artwork. You will also see the word Mask in the title bar of your file name.

❖ Hit (D) on your keyboard to reset the foreground/background swatches to black and white.

❖ Hit (B) to switch to your brush tool.

❖ Hit (]) on your keyboard until you increase the brush to 300 pixels.

❖ Hit (**Shift**) a few times to ensure that your brush has a hard edge. This keyboard command increase hardness by 25% each time.

Since your foreground color is white, you will paint your mask white; therefore the mask will reveal your image. Change your brush size as needed, using the left and right bracket to decrease or increase your brush size. **Now paint on the clock face, to reveal pixels you want back.** You are actually painting on the mask, bringing back the image you need. Color as much as you can without going over the edge. Try to fix the other parts of the image using x to switch between black and white for your foreground color and changing your brush size. Alternate between **Alt [Option]** clicking on the mask swatch or the color layer swatch to see what needs to be cleaned. You can paint with either showing; just make sure that the layer mask is active by clicking on it prior to painting. Once you feel comfortable with these techniques, open the file **Chap12/Clock 3.psd** so we all have the same image.

Content on DVD

Median and Drawing Straight Lines

A very useful command to reduce rough edge is to smooth out the noise using a median command. **Alt [Command]** click the layer mask to reveal the grayscale mask, and zoom in on the bottom middle. Choose **Filter >> Noise >> Median >> 3**, and toggle the preview to see how it clumps together pixels and gets rid of garbage. Click on the color layer swatch and zoom in on the top left area where there are two red circles. **Click on the layer mask to make it active, and set your foreground color to white.** We will now show you how we cleaned up the mask by drawing a line between two points. **Change to a 20 pixels brush, and click circle 1 and release the mouse.** Next, **depress and hold down the Shift key and click on circle 2**, and you will have brushed a straight line between the two points. The green bar is about 20 pixels thick, that is why we set the brush to that value. You can now use this technique to clean up the square area at the top of the bar.

Drag the Clock Copy blue layer to the trash can, and you now have knocked out the background of a difficult image.

You now have separated the clock from the background using a non-destructive method of layer masks rather than using the eraser tool. Should you want to view the original image without the layer mask, you can disable it. **Right Click [Ctrl Click] on the "Clock" Layer Mask >> Disable Layer Mask**. There is also an Enable Layer Mask command in the same location, or you can **Alt [Option] click on the mask and then on the Layer Thumbnail.**

15
TRANSFORMATIONS

$\mathcal{E}$dit >> Transform *has the basic transforms of scale, rotate and reflect. Open*

Chapter 15/Transform1.psd *and you will see the coconut we extracted in the*

Content on DVD

magnetic lasso chapter (Chapter 13). The background has a pile of wooden logs shot very close with a lens set to give the image perspective. Mirror the coconut layer using **Edit >> Transform >> Flip Horizontal.** *The lighting on the coconut will better match the logs, but we have to distort the coconut to match the perspective of the logs. Choose* **Edit >> Transform >> Distort** *and pull the four corner handles to match the screen shot. To get the proper angle we can match the frame edges of the distort transform to the angle of the log edges. Hit* **Enter [Return] or double-click inside the transform frame,** *to apply the transform. On bitmapped images, you will want to try and apply only one transform when possible, as multiple transformations degrade the quality of the image. This coconut is quite big, so the degradation will not be noticeable, but if it was a logo with small type you would see the pixels breaking up if you did for example four transformations to get to that point. The degradation only happens when the transform is applied, so you can pull the handles as many times as you want.*

TRANSFORM TOOL

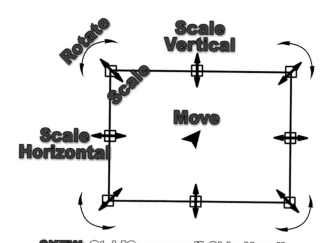

SKEW: Ctrl [Command] Side Handle
FREE DISTORT: Ctrl [Command] Corner Handle
PERSPECTIVE: Shift Ctrl Alt [Shift Cmd Option]
on any of the 8 handles

Hit **Ctrl T** [**Command T**] and you will again see a square with eight handles surrounding the pixels of your layer. You have four handles on corners, and another four in between – these are called side handles. If you are, on or near, one of the corner handles you will be scaling your object and could add Shift to scale the same amount in both directions. If you were to pull a side handle you would either scale vertically or horizontally only, adding Option in either case would scale from the center. You do have in the toolbar a Rubik's cube which allows you to select one of nine points to be the center of scale, and if you drag the center target you can make that the center of transformation. Now if you would like to rotate your object, just move your mouse outwards until your cursor icon changes to symbolize rotate. You can hold down Shift to rotate in 15° increments, or manually enter a value up in the tool bar. Should you wish to reposition the coconut, move your mouse inside the transform frame, until the cursor changes to an arrow and drag your item to a new position. What you see on the screen is a rough representation, until you hit **Enter** [**Return**] to finalize the transformation. You also should be in a 100% view (double-click on the magnifying glass) to judge pixel quality.

We will make our own drop shadow, and first create a new adjustment layer for the logs. With the **logs layer selected** >> **click Layers Palette** >> **Adjustment Layer** >> **Hue Saturation**. Set the adjustment layer **saturation to –25 and lightness to –50, and fill the layer mask with black**. Filling the layer mask with black, will temporarily remove the adjustment layer color correction, but we will add it back only in the areas we need. **Ctrl** [**Command**] **click the coconut layer** to get marching ants on the coconut. With the **adjustment layer selected, Ctrl T** [**Command T**] and transform your machine ants to **skew a shadow shape** coming from the bottom right of the coconut. Choose **Select** >> **Feather** >> **16 and fill your targeted layer mask with white**. For a darker shadow, double-click on the adjustment layer and reduce the lightness setting even more. This technique is better for creating drop shadows than the layer style. Not only does your shadow get perspective, but it also has realistic tones and desaturation as in real world shadows. A final optional touch you can do to the coconut layer to help it look realistic is to **Ctrl** [**Command Click**] **on the layer, Select** >> **Inverse, Select** >> **Modify** >> **Border** >> **3, Filter** >> **Blur** >> **Gaussian Blur** >> **2**, to soften the pixels on the edge of the coconut. You can also run the burn tool on the highlights of the coconut to adjust the lighting.

EFFECTS

Displace

Content on DVD

Displace

Horizontal Scale [10]

Vertical Scale [10]

Displacement Map:
- ○ Stretch To Fit
- ● Tile

Undefined Areas:
- ● Wrap Around
- ○ Repeat Edge Pixels

Open **Chapter 15/Displace.psd** and **leave the layer effect off and the layer mask off**. The layer mask is the black outlines of a puzzle shape. The black in the layer mask makes those areas transparent, which then allows the layer effect of bevel and emboss to round off the edges. There is one more thing to make this puzzle effect look more convincing; that is to displace the pixels on the edge of the puzzle pieces, to make it look like they are wrapping around the edge of the puzzle pieces. The displace filter uses a file you create for a displacement map, and save in the Photoshop file format. Pixels of 50% gray in the displacement map are neutral and will not displace the image. Pixels which are solid black displace the image the amount you specify in a negative diagonal direction. White pixels displace the image the amount you specify in a positive diagonal direction. You can use a color image, and it will base it on a darkness value of 0 to 255 for the shift, but grayscale are the easiest to control the shift.

With the coconuts layer selected choose F**ilter >> Distort >> Displace>> 10**. This filter prompts for a displacement map, choose **Chapter 15/puzzle.psd** and your image will look distorted. On the Mac you will have to flatten puzzle.psd, because the displace filter does recognize files with adjustment layers for displace maps. Notice the chain icon between the coconuts layer and layer mask is disabled. This was done intentionally so the displace filter does not displace the pixels in the mask. **Turn on the layer effect visibility eyeball**. Turn on the layer mask by **Right Clicking [Ctrl Clicking] on the mask and choosing**

Content on DVD

Enable Layer Mask. Your image looks very convincing. Look at how the image bends around the puzzle edges now.

Let's look at how the displacement map was created. It is optional whether you want to follow along as the file has already been created for you, called **Chapter 15/puzzle.psd.** **Alt [Option]** click on the layer mask to take a look at that and you will see black outlines of a puzzle shape. Select all the pixels and copy them to the clipboard, make a new document and paste in those 720 × 480 pixels. For a good map you will want to blur the pixels to get a gradation so that the displacement of pixels is smooth. We also applied a curve to darken the pixels above 50% to fatten the lines. Finally, make a new layer of 50% black and set that layer to blending mode of multiply; this neutralizes the images to 50% except for the gradating black lines of the puzzle edges which displace the image.

Content on DVD

Spherize

Open up **Chapter 15/Spherize&Liquify.psd**, and you will see some watches on logs. The logs are the same image from a previous chapter, just that the hue was changed, and a filter of ink outlines was applied. We will want to distort the watches so they appear to be melted on the logs. The spherize filter will be used to bloat the image around the middle of the log, using a constrictor lasso mask.

Content on DVD

Use the **Lasso tool to draw a selection mask similar the shape of the middle log**, surrounding the area the first watch overlaps the log. It is important that you do not go larger than the log, because the center of the spherize bubble is in the center of your selection, and the bubble extends to the edges of your selection. We do not want a harsh transition so choose **Select >> Feather >> 16.** Feathering

the selection will make a big difference, and if you did it without the feather your watch will look more like broken glass rather than a melt.

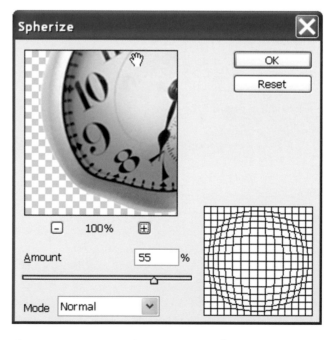

Choose **Filter** >> **Distort** >> **Spherize** >> **55** and you will see the feather helps give the melted look for your watch. Now make a new lasso selection, similar to the previous, except around the bottom log and watch overlap. Perform a spherize of –50 to make the watch converge to a small puddle in the center. Those familiar with liquify might be saying that is a good tool to use, and we will cover that next. The difference is that spherize was more evenly controlled.

LIQUIFY

Liquify is a distortion interface using brushes to warp, twirl, bloat, and pucker an image. Version 7 of Photoshop made liquify more useful by allowing you to see the underlying layers, using them as templates. Version 8 of Photoshop did some improvements to the usability of the masking features, which is similar to QuickMask mode.

Draw a selection rectangle around the entire large watch and choose **Filter >> Liquify**. The selection not only helps center the preview, but also makes liquify work much faster as it does not have to process any of the pixels outside the marching ants. Feel free to **play around with the tools. When done, hold down Alt [Option] and click on the Reset button** (which replaces the Cancel button). Follow these settings to set up liquify, so we can see the background image, and not have the previous image interfere. Click on the **Show Backdrop, set Use to logs, Mode to behind, and Opacity to 100%.**

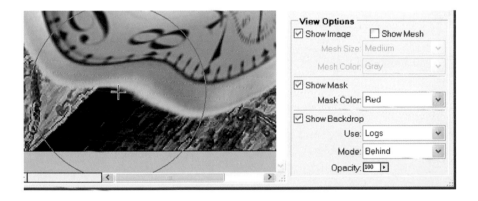

Use the first tool – which is the **Forward Warp – to push the middle of the watch into the log**. This tool is great for slimming hips, and is probably the most used tool in the set. You could try using the Bulge tool to bulge the center out even more. The secret to using the Bulge tool is to make the brush really big and just tap it slightly over an area you wish to bulge. Using the **Alt [Option]** key makes all the tools work in reverse. The Twirl Clockwise tool will go counter-clockwise if you use **Alt [Option]**, and you can make the Pucker tool into the Bloat tool by simply holding down **Alt [Option]**. Switch to the Mirror tool and just pull the top of the watch down slightly so that it hugs the log closer.

Liquify the small watch on your own, and only utilize the Turbulence tool. To make constrictor masks, paint with the freeze mask tool (F), which looks like a paintbrush. The areas in red will not be affected by any Liquify tools. There are five mask option buttons that can be useful for calculating a freeze area. They work with the transparency of your layer, or an existing layer mask. If you painted too much, you can use the eraser which is called the Thaw Mask tool, or click None to start from the beginning. After you have liquefied the left half of your watch, you can click the Invert All button to liquify the right half. When done distorting, use **the Dodge and Burn tools to change the lighting** near the edges of the watches to help them match the shadows and highlights of the logs.

16
TRANSPARENCY
AND BLENDING

*B*lack in a layer mask is completely transparent; solid white in a layer mask makes

a layer completely opaque. Using either 100% or 0% black will either show or hide a

layer. This chapter concerns the interaction of layer masks containing values between

1% and 99%. Painting black with a value of 50% on a layer mask combines the layer

at exactly half strength with the underlying layers. The other way to get layers to inter-

act with each other is to change the blending mode for a layer to something else besides

normal. Now that you are very familiar with layer masks, we will create a mask that

will make glass interact realistically with underlying layers.

TRANSPARENT GLASS

Open **Chapter 16/TropicalMartini.tif**, which has a layer of a tropical scene, and a
layer for a green drink. The drink does not appear to belong in this scenery,
because you cannot see through the glass. You could take the master opacity down
of the entire layer, but then you would see through the cherry. The martini glass
itself contains the information we need for the mask. We will use one of the RGB

Content on DVD

channels of the martini for our layer mask. Hit **Ctrl 1 [Command 1] to see the red channel** of the document. **Turn visibility off for the "Tropical Scene" layer** to see the martini glass only. The red channel could be a good candidate, but the cherry and drink gray values are nearly the same color. We need a channel that has an edge for the cherry so we can make it opaque, and the drink semi-opaque. Don't worry about having the exact gray value for the green drink, as we have curves that can adjust that later. **Hit Ctrl 2 [Command 2] to solo the green channel;** this looks better as the cherry has a contrasting edge with the drink. The details of the glass rim and the shadow at the top of the green drink are preserved. **Ctrl A [Command A], Ctrl C [Command C]** to select all and copy the red channel data as gray values to the clipboard. **Make a new layer mask for the Martini layer**, by clicking on the add layer mask icon while the Martini layer is active in the layers palette. **Alt [Option] click the layer mask** for the martini layer and **Ctrl V [Command V]** to force paste the data into the layer mask. This will not work if you just select the layer mask, you must see the layer mask to paste into it. **Click on the Martini layer thumbnail**, to show your results. Very good, except the data is not centered, so we will nudge it into place. Usually this will center, but this layer is missing the pixels outside of the martini. With the **selection edges still active, click on the layer mask**, to make that the target of the nudging. Use the **cursor keys to nudge it into place** and **Ctrl + [Command +]** to zoom into a 100% view to be more accurate. Keep your eyes on the cherry stem, as it is a good candidate for registering the mask.

The cherry is almost transparent and the glass is too opaque, but this is easily fixed. With the layer mask still the targeted layer item, **Ctrl A [Command A]** (to include the entire background), then **Ctrl I [Command I]** to invert or make a negative of the data. To finalize the mask is not difficult, but be careful to paint only in the mask and not the image. Until you get familiar with this process it is better to **Alt [Option] click the layer mask thumbnail**, so you can see what you are working on and reduce error. Hit **Shift O, until you get the Dodge tool**, which looks like a magnifying glass. Change the **option bar setting to Highlights**, the 20% default is a good value. On the mask, **rub the Dodge tool over the cherry area**, and like magic it will take the light grays only and lighten them to white. Now click back on the layer swatch for the martini so you can see your result in color. The drink looks pale, and we can fix that also using dodge, but be careful and click on the layer mask swatch to make that active. There is a very thin black line which confirms that the layer mask is active—look for the black line as it is a very important point (one day we hope that Adobe can make this line red, and thicker). Now **change your Dodge tool to Shadows**, because having the correct range makes the Dodge tool work much better. **Dodge the green liquid mask area**, and it will begin to bring the green drink back. The bottom of the glass could use the Burn tool to make it more transparent. Practice using your Shift O to quickly switch between tools, and changing your option bar settings from highlight to shadow, and your result should look as realistic as ours. We also created a reflection layer you can turn on, for some additional realism.

You may notice a path that is in the file. The path was used to construct the darkening of the layer mask where there is a single pane of glass. The glass should be more transparent through a single rim than through two rims of glass.

GRADIENT TOOL MASKS

Hit (**d**) to get default colors and (**g**) to switch to the gradient tool. Let's take a closer look at the important options for the gradient tool. In the Options bar there is actually a big difference if you click on the swatch (blue circle #1), or the arrow after the swatch (blue circle #2). Clicking on #1 gives you the options needed to create a new custom gradient of your own. We will click on #2 and make sure that we have the first gradient preset for foreground to background; if you hold the mouse over the swatch long enough, the name will appear in a yellow "post-it" note.

Open **Blending.tif**, which is a document of our model Angelique in three layers. **Turn visibility on for each layer, from the bottom up.** If you ever open a file someone else created, this is a good way to become familiar with how it was built. Notice that the center layer overlaps the other two layers. Add a layer mask to the center layer by **clicking the center layer thumbnail, and then click the Layers palette to add a layer mask icon**. We will next pour a gradient directly into the layer mask while our final image is visible.

Drag from red circle 1 to red circle 2 to draw a gradient going from white to black, masking off the left edge of the center photo. Experiment with different angles to get a good feeling for the gradient tool, and notice that each time it draws a new gradient. Next **change the blending mode to darken in the Options**

Content on DVD

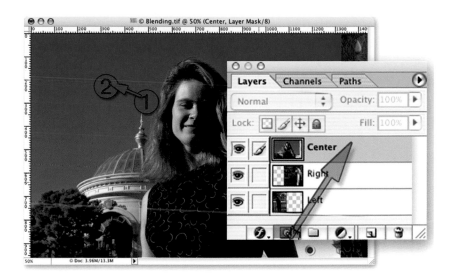

tool bar (blue circle #3). When you drag a gradient it will now only darken pixels. Configuring the gradient tool with blend modes can be useful when you are designing such artwork. Notice in the tool bar options that you can reverse (blue circle #4) the gradient in case you pulled in the wrong direction (it often happens to all of us), and would like to invert the gradient. With the gradient tool darken mode still enabled **draw a gradient on the right half, going from the center of the model outwards to the edge.** If you make a mistake use undo, but you can now see how useful the blending mode of darken is.

BRUSHING LAYER MASKS

To blend in the final touches switch to the paintbrush by hitting (**b**) and swap your foreground background colors by hitting (**x**) on the keyboard. You will want a **large soft brush of diameter 300 and hardness 0%.** Making sure you are still targeting the layer mask, **paint over what you wish to black out** on the layer mask. Use (**x**) to switch colors, and **paint with a white soft brush to reveal in the layer mask.**

You can do anything to a layer mask that you can do to a layer, even apply a curves or levels change to help your mask look good. In summary, the secret to getting soft transitions is to use the gradient tool or a very soft brush. You can afterwards do a motion blur on a layer mask to smooth out ever more spots. The Gaussian blur can help, but it leaves some rounding of the edges that you may have to fix manually. The Blur tool would be a great option, but it often has a very slow response.

CLIPPING GROUPS

You can spot a clipping group within a file, whenever the layer name has a downward hooking arrow in front of the layer. There might be more than one layer that

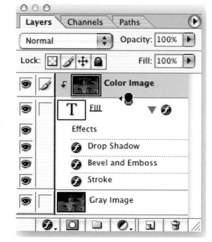

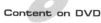

Content on DVD

has the arrow, but the important layer is below the arrows. That layers transparency is actually used for all the ones that have an arrow. Masks are powerful, but they act only on a single layer. Open **Chapter 16/ClippingGroup.tif**, where we will remove the existing clipping group, and show you how to create one.

You can use Layers >> Release clipping mask, but there is a more convenient method. **Hold down Alt [Option], and move the mouse between layers** until the cursor changes to overlapping circles joined by a left arrow. **Click between the layers to remove the clipping group**. To put the clipping group back just **hold down Alt [Option] and click again in between the "Color Image" layer and the "FIJI" layer and click to create a clipping group**. The "FIJI" type has layer effects applied to it; notice that the effect of bevel still applies itself to the color image of the Fijian dancers.

The only useful thing that a clipping group can do which a layer mask cannot, is the ability to use live type. Stay away from clipping groups, as soft or hard masks can do the job better being applied to layer sets. Layer masks are less confusing to follow for the next person or yourself who may pick up a file. Layer masks also have a very useful feature under the blending options, which we will discuss next. The blending option of "layer masks hides effects", can be enabled so that you can use a mask to constrict a drop shadow. This is done in the next screenshot where the word pattern overlay fades off softly without a drop shadow at the bottom.

LAYER BLENDING OPTIONS

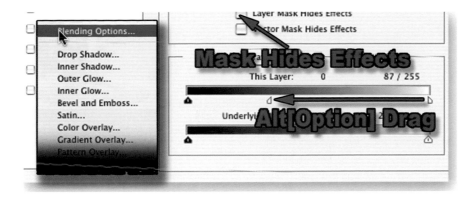

Open **Chapter 16/TropicalMartini.tif**, and we will again make the glass transparent. This time we will use a method that is not as accurate, but very quick. Quality is most important, but in video there are times when the image will not be seen for very long and the quantity of images masked can be more important. With the martini layer selected, click on the circle f in the Layers palette to change the default blending options for the layer. You will see two gradients at the bottom and one is for this layer ("Martini"), and the underlying layer ("Color Reflection"). On the gradient for this layer **hold down Alt [Option] and drag the left half of the white marker**, to split it towards the center, as pictured in the illustration. You will begin to see the highlights of the glass disappear, and the palm tree should show through the stem. Your drink will get desaturated, but this method is a lot faster for those intense deadlines in the video world.

Content on DVD

BLENDING MODES

Blending modes are so powerful and useful, that you will find yourself using them every day. We already introduced you to them in many interactive chapter examples. This section will therefore cover tricks for using them on layers and brushes. You do not need to understand what every blend mode does to take advantage of using them. There is a great keyboard command that cycles layer blending modes. Open **Chapter 16/Blending Modes.psd**, and you will see a document with two layers. **Select the move tool, click to target the "Blend Me" thumbnail in the layers palette, and use Shift − to cycle upwards and Shift + to cycle downwards.** If done correctly, the word "normal" in the layers palette will change to a different blending mode. This is a great key command as you can visually find the best blending mode you need. Be careful, as this keyboard command can also change the blending mode for painting tools if they are active. You may later find your tools acting very strange, such as a paintbrush that does not paint. Hit (**b**) to switch to the paintbrush, and **use the blending mode cycling key commands.** See how the mode in the toolbar option for the brush changed and not the layer

Content on DVD

blending mode. To get all tools back to normal choose **Window** >> **Tool Presets** >> **Flyout Menu** >> **Reset All Tools**. It takes years of working in Photoshop to understand and remember what each blending mode does. The following table will help you to explore and understand new ideas for using blending modes:

Dissolve	Transparent edges generate dust, similar to the result of a noise command. Brushes with soft edges will paint as if loaded with fairy dust.
Behind	Paints only on transparent pixels. Also available for custom shape tools, set to fill pixels in the tool options bar. Layer transparency must be unlocked.
Clear	An eraser only found on brushes. Useful for custom shape tools, set to fill pixels in the tool options bar.
Darken	Compares with the base color, and the result is the darker pixel.
Multiply	Combines with the base color, to darken by the amount in the layer or click of a brush. A favorite for creating shadows.
Color Burn	Darkens the base color to reflect the blend color. Increases contrast. White produces no result.
Linear Burn	Darkens the base color by decreasing brightness. White produces no result.
Lighten	Compares with the base color, and the result is the lighter pixel.
Screen	Multiplies inverse of blend and base colors. Result is always lighter. Black produces no change. White produces white. Similar to combining two movie projectors on one screen.
Color Dodge	Base color is brightened by decreasing contrast. Black produces no change.
Linear Dodge	Brightens the base color by increasing the brightness. Black produces no change.
Overlay	Base color is mixed with the blend color to increase saturation. The luminosity of the base color is undisturbed. Fully saturated base color produce no result.
Soft Light	Similar to shining a diffused spotlight on the image. Painting with black darkens and saturates, good for fixing washed out areas. Painting with white good for adding spectral highlights. Useful for getting a photography magazine look.
Hard Light	Works as soft light with multiply. Not very useful.
Vivid Light	Combines with base layer to either add or subtract contrast based on if pixel is above or below 50% gray.
Linear Light	Combines with base layer to either add or subtract brightness based on if pixel is above or below 50% gray.
Pin Light	Blend layer pixels lighter than 50% gray replace darker base colors. Blend layer pixels darker than 50% gray replace lighter base colors. Useful for making gradient map type effects. Similar to After Effects Colorama.
Difference	Subtracts the blend and base color depending on which has the greater brightness value. White inverts the base color values; Black produces no change. Nice effect if you duplicate the underlying layer, invert the pixels and apply difference.
Exclusion	Similar to Difference but lower in contrast.

Hue	Preserves base color luminance and saturation with the blend color hue.
Saturation	Preserves base color luminance and hue with the blend color saturation.
Color	Preserves base color luminance with the blend color hue and saturation. Useful for colorizing grayscale images.
Luminosity	Preserves hue and saturation of base color with the blend color luminance.

SECTION IV
BETTER IMAGES

17
COLOR CORRECTION

Before beginning this chapter, you should have color-calibrated your monitor recently. Chapter 2 provides a step-by-step walkthrough of how to color-calibrate your monitor. Photographers adjust their ISO, aperture, and exposure to get good images. Even after taking many pictures, it is difficult to get perfect results every time.

AUTO COLOR CORRECTION

There are three auto corrections in Photoshop (Levels, Color, Contrast), and their purpose is to balance your color and exposure. Open **Chapter 17/Auto Levels.tif**, and you will see an image that looks flat and lacks detail.

Content on DVD

Three Auto Methods

Visually, you can see the image is under-exposed, many people would use brightness and contrast to fix this. Never use brightness and contrast! Adobe has not even given it a keyboard command, because it is not a good option. Choose **Image >> Adjust Levels** and you will see a mountain-shaped graph for the input levels. This is a histogram for the average of RGB, and you can see that the right edge does not have peaks. Higher peaks represent more pixels for that color value on a

Original image needing correction.

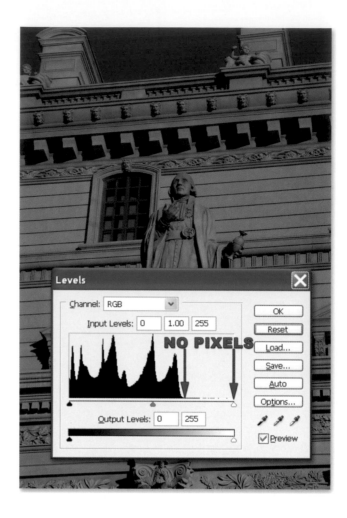

Levels & Curves options.

range of 0 to 255. The right edge is flat and has almost no pixels. Hit **Ctrl 1 [Command 1] to see the red channel** alone, and it looks similar to RGB. **Compare Ctrl 2 and 3 [Command 2 and 3]** and you will see that they progressively have less pixels for the green and blue channels.

Click the Options button. This is the options for the Auto button on this palette, and not the Auto Levels menu command. Experiment with the three Algorithms options, and Snap Neutral Midtones checkbox. You should find that the image improves the most using the middle option, which is the same as using the Image >> Adjust >> Auto Levels command. In fact, **hit Cancel twice** and we will use the keyboard command, which is quicker. **Hit Shift Ctrl L [Shift Command L] for Auto Levels.** Keyboard commands are the best way to do auto color corrections.

Final Auto Levels correction.

Which Auto Method to Use?

Now you might be excited and think you should use Auto Levels for all images. Well this is not true, and we will prove it by opening **Chapter 17/Bad Auto Levels.psd.** The image is just a flatbed scan of some red craft paper and with blue

Content on DVD

and green sharpie handwriting. **Try Auto Levels**, and you will see that the image looks awful, so **Undo**. In this case you will want to **do an Auto Contrast**. This leaves the relationship between RGB alone, and does not shift the color. Once you have color-corrected many images, you will be able to decide which auto methods to use, just by looking at the image. The simplest and quickest way until you get to that point is to try Auto Contrast first to balance your lightest and darkest points. Then try Auto Levels, if you think your image could be better.

Another important point about auto color correction is to crop your image first prior to color correcting. The reason is you could scan multiple items in your scanner, or have the edge of a negative in your scan. Your auto color correction methods calculate the correction based on all the pixels in your document or selected pixels. If you were to scan four photographs at once, first draw a rectangular frame around one of them and do your auto color correction, then do the other three. You also want to crop out the edges of transparency or any other material to get a better color correction, having the auto color correction only analyzes the image. Some people believe that auto methods are only meant for speed, and should not be used for good results. The auto methods give you spectacular results, but you need to know how to use them first before you can understand professional manual corrections. Use auto methods to get your overall image balance. Then, go into the manual methods to fix specific areas or middle tones only if necessary. Learn the following chart, and you will get better results using auto methods, and setting up your image for manual corrections.

Auto Contrast	Enhance Monochromatic Contrast	Alt Shift Ctrl L [Option Shift Command L]	Clips tonal range of RGB identically. The highlights became lighter and shadows darker, but the color relationship between RGB is maintained.
Auto Levels	Enhance Per Channel Contrast	Shift Ctrl L [Shift Command L]	Maximizes tonal range of each channel individually. Color casts may be removed or introduced.
Auto Color	Find Dark & Light Colors with snap neutral midtones enabled	Shift Ctrl B [Shift Command B]	Finds an average color then adjusts levels to neutralize the color, while minimizing clipping.

Difficult Images to Auto Correct

Content on DVD

Open **Chapter 17/Paris Wheel.psd** and **try the 3 auto color correction methods on the visible layer.** You will find little or no improvement, because of the reflection of the flash in two reflective glossy areas. The auto color helps by adding warmth back to the image, and that is a move in a good direction. What you should do is take out the reflections by cloning them out using the retouching tools discussed in Chapter 18. Then you should run Auto Levels after the overexposed highlights have been removed. **Turn the visibility on for the layer called**

"Cloned & Auto". This is the background layer with the two reflections cloned in, and an Auto Levels balanced image. **Turn on the next layer called "Black Center"** which is a layer to get rid of all the busy distractions going on, in the center of the wheel. The lesson to learn from this image is to clone out camera flash hotspots, because your auto contrast will work much better without them. The original image was not a good shot, but we made it usable, and even opened up the eyes. You can look over the hidden layers in the "Paris Wheel.psd" file to show you how we used the eyes from another image.

Flash hot spots interfere with auto correction.

No hot spots make better auto corrections.

MANUAL COLOR CORRECTION

You often have an image that is still too dark or light after auto correcting, and you can fix this with your RGB images by pulling the middle slider in the input levels – you never really have to touch the output levels. If after auto color correction your image has a color cast, pull the slider for an individual channel. If you have a red cast pull the middle red slider to the right or either the blue and green slider to the left. Auto color corrections are done to improve the entire image, whereas manual color corrections are done to improve a portion of the image.

Dodge, Burn Saturation

Yellowish fur.

Content on DVD

Open **Chapter 17/Polar Bear.psd**, and the image has good color except that the polar bear looks yellow. You can apply the auto methods to this image to see what happens, but you lose the reddish orange saturation of the rocks if you use methods other than auto contrast. Switch to the saturation tool by **hitting Shift (O) until you get the sponge, and set the option to desaturate**. Rub the tool over the polar bear and you will see his fur get cleaner. You can also make the fur brighter by hitting Shift (O) to switch to the Dodge tool and brightening the midtones.

SETTING THE WHITEPOINT

Content on DVD

Open **Chapter 17/DinnerMenu.psd**, which is a flatbed scan of a menu. The original menu has a white background, but even with the scanner auto correction we

Clean fur.

got a dingy, yellowish background. Auto corrections do not help, because there is a white halo around the type which is the whitest point of the scan. We can correct this easily, by choosing **Ctrl L [Command L]** and **selecting the third test tube**, which is to set the whitepoint. **Click on the yellowish background**, until you find the preview makes your image white. If you did not get white, then click on the options button in your levels palette, and then click on the highlight swatch and set that to perfect white.

Precise Manual Correction

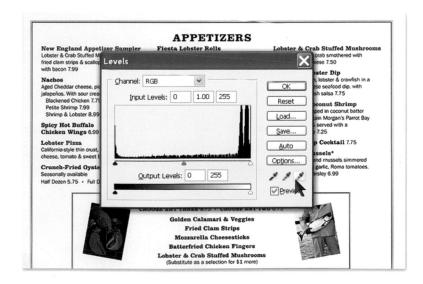

The right side has new white point set by levels.

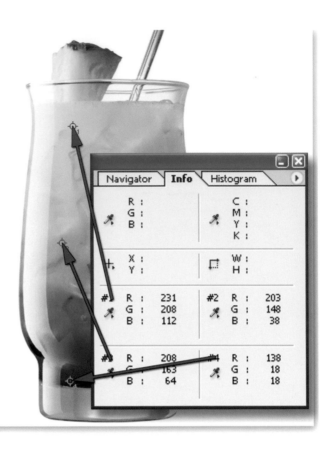

This section applies to print more than video, so it will be short. Open **Chapter 17/Pineapple Punch.psd**, and switch to the eyedropper tool using **Shift (I)**. **You will then notice four color sample targets** which are used for measuring color. Then choose **Image >> Adjust >> Curves**, and you can see the value for each target in the info palette. We use curves because it has a graph with multiple definable points. You also can simultaneously watch the info palette to bend your curves into the desired numbers. The info palette will have two numbers divided by a forward slash when you apply curves. The forward slash separates the before and after values. This method works much better in CMYK as it is easier for people to think in subtractive color theory. For example brightening up the $\frac{1}{4}$ tone yellow, means removing CMK inks, and adding yellow. To work with these color sample targets you will need to hit Shift (I) until you get the eyedropper with the target. You can then **click and drag to change position, or Alt [Option] click to delete one.**

SHADOW/HIGHLIGHT

Open **Chapter 17/Musky.psd**, which is an image where the color is washed out. We did everything we could using auto contrast, color, and levels. The foreground image has a very small color range and looks flat. It was taken with a tackle box

Content on DVD

Content on DVD

Before Shadow/Highlight.

camera on a summer day when there was a lot of light in the background, but the foreground was under-exposed. The problem was that the image was backlit and the detail in the midtones and shadows are flat and need more range. Photoshop CS added another great color correction filter, accessed by **choosing Image >> Adjust >> Shadow/Highlight**. The image immediately takes on default settings,

After Shadow/Highlight.

and although it opens up the shadows showing detail, this actually shows off more of the camera noise. **Take the shadow amount slider and move it down to 30** to bring back some of the dot. The default is 50%, which is set to compensate for backlit photos. Next, we will extend the range of the highlights by darkening them. We can do this by increasing the strength of correction based on a range based supplied by the tonal width. The radius is the amount of neighboring pixels that it will consider for determining what is the highlight in the image. So **increase the highlight amount to 13**, bringing back the blue sky. This also improves the blown-out highlight hair color towards a midtone. Usually both amount sliders are the two adjustments you will have to make, unless it is not correctly determining what is in the highlight or shadow. Radius is similar to fuzziness in the color range command. You can load the settings musky.shh if you would like to see what we used to improve the clouds, and bring back color to the skin and gloss to this Musky.

COLOR REPLACEMENT TOOL

Before any color correction.

Content on DVD

Open **Chapter 17/ColorReplacement.psd**, which is a very cyan-looking image which looks as though very little can be done to save it. In scuba diving the sunlight is filtered by the water, and the red and yellow colors become lost the deeper you go. Running Auto Levels on the image is a big help, and we adjusted the hue of the image by +13, to bring back some red into the cyan green water which dominates the shot. We then ran Shadow Highlight with about 10% in shadows and 20% in highlights, but the image still needs yellow in the regulator hose.

Hit **Shift** (**J**) until you switch to the Color Replacement Tool (a paintbrush with an eye), **hold down Alt [Option]** and **sample the best yellow hose color**. This gives a base color for the Color Replacement Tool to use, but we will improve the color. **Double-click the foreground color swatch** to edit. **Drag the hue slider down towards yellow**; this improves the color form of what is in the image, which was derived from an existing color in the image. **Click the S ratio button** to switch to saturation and **drag the slider upwards to saturate the color more**. With this brighter yellow color we can **paint over the hose, and it will turn to yellow**. The color we used is R245 B236 G85, and you will want a 75% hard brush. The soft edge will help in case you make a mistake and drift off the edge of the brush.

With yellow color replacement on hose.

RAW AND 16 BITS

Converting Raw Files

The raw format plug-in is one of the most exciting additions to Photoshop CS. Not all of us have digital cameras with raw format capability, but we have provided a file for you on the DVD. In the next few pages, you will learn about the benefits of having more than 8 bits of color information per RGB channel.

Open the file **Chapter 17/DSCF0620.RAF**. Photoshop recognizes this RAF file format as a raw file format, so it will use the raw plug in which gives you additional color controls not normally available in Photoshop. The image should be very dark, but if not then click on **Settings >> Camera Default**, so you see the image as it was actually shot. This is the original untouched raw image with no

Content on DVD

correction and exactly as recorded by the camera. You can see in the title of the window, valuable information about the shot.

Camera Model	Filename	ISO	Exposure	F stop	Zoom
Fuji FinePix S2	DSCF0620.RAF	200	1/45	4.0	53 mm

Original Raw image.

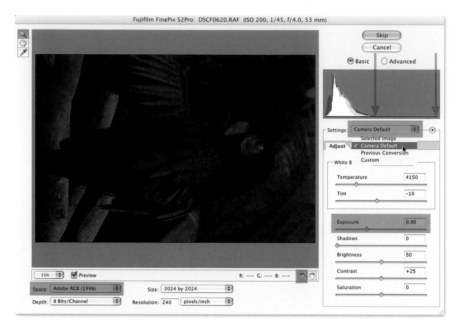

The image was taken without a flash, and the lighting conditions were not good. We went with ISO 200, a longer exposure, wider aperture; but there was not enough light in the room. Knowing the image was in RAW, it has a good chance of being saved.

Notice the mountains of RGBCMYKW that we call the histograms. The histogram is very dominant on the left of the image–but there is a nice hump to the mountains! **Move the Exposure slider to about 3.2**, until the histogram is spread evenly across the width. You will get an instant preview if the preview box is checked, and you should always keep that checked. Now **tab into the shadows box,** and **use the up cursor to change the shadow slider to 2.** Using the cursor is a nice way to fine adjust a very sensitive setting like shadows. You could also hold down Shift to adjust in larger increments when needed. Exposure and shadows are the two most important settings you will adjust in almost all images. You saved a beautiful parrot – or actually a Macaw to be correct!

The parrot needs to be rotated, and you can do this by **clicking the counter-clockwise circular arrow icon** on the bottom right of the parrot image. Look to the left and you will notice that space is Adobe RGB (1998) which is the color profile most digital SLRs shoot in, and that is a great color space with a wide gamut of colors. There are some cameras which can even do 48-bit per channel, and you can switch to ProPhoto RGB for those.

16-bit channel images are already huge, and you should make your images 8-bit before using them in your video editing application. Even a printing press cannot take advantage of anything greater than 8-bit, so why is 16-bit so great? Because the extra 8 bits of data has a detail for the color correction and contrast adjustment phase. Now you might notice that if you change your depth from 8- to 16-bits per channel that there is no change. That is just the setting for the resulting file, and not how much data is used in the process of the color correction in the raw mode. If you plan not to do any more color correction, then **keep the setting at 8-bit before clicking OK** so that you will not get a larger file than needed. If you want to unsharp mask or do more color correcting outside the raw plug in, convert the image from raw to 16-bit then. Next, you will want to choose what resolution to convert to. All but one of the resolution choices have either a + or − after, to symbolize that you will either be upsampling or downsampling. The Fuji S2, 3024 × 2024 does not have a + or −, and is the native CCD resolution or 6.12 mega pixels.

Converted Raw image.

Chromatic Aberration

This is a problem of a purple fringe of pixels more often seen in digital cameras. The purple pixels are actually caused by the lens not focusing different wavelengths of light onto the exact same focal point. An achromatic lens can solve this problem, but you should return your camera if this problem is seen in many of your pictures. Luckily, if you shoot in raw mode, there is a lens tab which can be used to remove the purple fringe of pixels. Open **Chapter 17/ ChromaticAberration.psd**, to examine what the problem looks like so that you can identify it in the future when looking at images.

Purple fringe of chromatic aberrated pixels.

Raw Plug-in Tips

Drag more than one raw image onto the Photoshop CS window, to color-correct each image, and open it into a Photoshop window. If at any point during the process you hit Escape or the Cancel button, you will stop the process where you were at. That stinks, as you will have to open the rest of the images again. A better solution is to hold down Shift, and the OK button will turn to a Skip button, so you can skip that image and color-correct the next. You could also hold down Alt [Option], when the OK button will turn into update. If you update the image, it will not open in Photoshop, but the position for the adjustment sliders will be saved for the next person who opens that image on your machine. Additionally, you may have noticed that holding down Alt [Option] changes your Cancel button to Reset, in case you wish to revert your settings to their original state.

If you plan to do some more work in Photoshop, do not go too high with sharpness in the raw plug. It is better to use an unsharp mask at the very end when you have finished retouching an image. Finally, be careful of saving your file in the Photoshop raw format, as we have experienced occasions when the image could not be opened at a later date, using the same machine. There is really no benefit to saving an image from Photoshop in the Raw format, as the psd format is cross platform. The Photoshop Raw format also does not save the unprocessed bits, as does your native camera raw format.

18
FIXING IMAGES

$\mathcal{R}$estoring and retouching images is a major fascination which motivated many people to learn Photoshop, and write books on those tools. We all were very excited the first time we used the clone tool to remove dust, and saw how easy it was. This chapter goes beyond the basics of learning those tools, and introduces you to new techniques not in other books. We start out slowly with a filter, and pick up the healing brush.

DUST & SCRATCHES

Preventing a Bad Scan

Use large positive transparencies, when scanning, prints and negatives do not hold as much detail as a film positive. Larger originals have more detail and smaller dust. Before scanning prints, use cheesecloth with medium pressure. Napkins or Kleenex are not recommended as they leave fibers. For film, use film cleaner to break down oily fingerprints, humidity, and dust. The final step is to blow off your originals with a can of compressed air, and to keep your scanner glass clean. Scratch the outside area of your film to help find the emulsion side if needed.

Place the scratched side touching your scanner glass. Be extra clean when enlarging scans, as even microscopic dirt begins to show.

Dust & Scratches Filter

A dirty scan.

Content on DVD

Open **Chapter 18/Dust_Spots.psd**. This image has dust lint, and plenty of dirt spots which were magnified in the scanning process. The black dirt is most obvious on the white plate. The dark areas have equal amounts of dust, but it is not easily seen. The dust and scratches filter reduces noise, but at the cost of losing detail and softening the image. The subject of resolution and why more pixels are always better was discussed in Chapter 3. Luckily, the person who scanned the image gave us twice the amount of pixels needed for video. The extra pixels will help give our dust and scratches filter better results. Use **Filter** >> **Noise** >> **Dust & Scratches** to remove the dirt. Increasing the radius will quickly make the image softer, but will remove more and larger pieces of dust. The threshold range of 0 to 255 is the amount of color difference needed before removing a pixel. Larger thresholds protect more pixels from being altered by the filter, and usually a low number is preferable for a threshold between 1 and 50. **Click and hold the filter Preview** to see the original image, then **release the mouse** to see the filtered preview, the Preview checkbox must be enabled. Most filters work this way, and you can click drag to preview another area. Being in 100% view provides the most accurate view of your result, especially for video.

With a radius above 2, much of the contrast is being lost. **Cancel** Dust & Scratches, and then **duplicate your layer**. With the new top selected **apply a Dust & Scratches Radius 2, Threshold 19** to the top layer and **click OK**. We duplicated the layer so that an original is underneath; this allows us to combine two versions of the image. In that way, we get our original layer contrast and the top layer removes the dust. This is best done with a layer mask, filling it with black, and painting over the layer mask in white to remove dust. To make things go quickly, switch to the eraser tool by **hitting (e)**, and **erase over the grapes to restore the beautiful spectral highlights** in the original layer we had prior to the dust filter. The eraser is a destructive and quick method. Later, we will teach you to use layer masks, which takes only two extra clicks to use once you master the interface.

HEALING BRUSH

There should still be one dust spot, between the two pieces of melon. It was left over from the biggest spot, and was not worth running the Dust & Scratches filter too high or we would lose too much detail. Switch to the Healing Brush using **Shift (J)** and **set it to 40 pixels 100% hardness**. This brush size is intentionally too big, but I want to show you the difference between using a soft and hard brush. **Alt [Option] click over the cantaloupe shadow area left of the black dot**, to define your source area. **Click to heal, and try removing the spot.** Because the brush was too hard and big, it used some neighboring orange pixels from the cantaloupe. **Undo this** and **try it again using a 40 pixel, 0% hard brush**, and it should be much easier for you to get rid of the spot. The Healing Brush matches the shading and color of the source and the destination pixels. The Rubber Stamp tool is similar, except that it eventually gives you a soft image if your brush edges are set too soft. A hard transition or artifact can be left behind if your brush is too hard. Use the Healing Brush often, but if and when it gives you a bad result, then switch to the clone stamp. On images with fine details, or edges of color transitions, you

Dust and lint is removed.

will want to use the clone stamp tool. The final image has the color adjusted, and the saturation brush was used over the melons.

Cloning Within a Constrained Selection

Pencil marks and smeared pastel chalk.

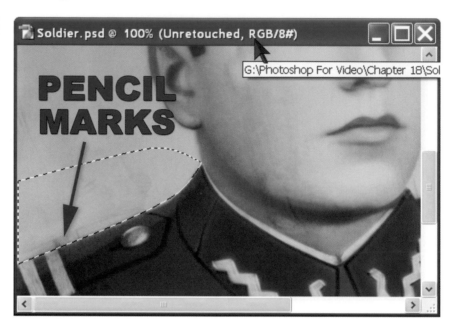

The next image covers difficult situations for the Healing Brush. Open **Chapter 18/Soldier.psd**, and you will see residual pencil marks above the shoulder. The photo artist made this image using a pencil to make holding lines, and pastel chalks to fill in areas. We will use similar digital methods, on an area above the shoulder shown by the path called "Pencil Marks". Try using the Healing Brush on the area, and you will see that it will be difficult to fix this area of the background next to the shoulder. Bring the **path palette** to the front and **Ctrl [Command] click on the path named "pencil marks"** to select the trouble area we want to fix. **Ctrl H [Command H]** to temporarily hide the marching ants. The edges are very important, and hiding them will make it easy to see what your result will be. Switch to the Clone Stamp tool by hitting (**s**) and use **Alt [Option] to define a source point** and **clone over the pencil marks** with a **40 pixel, 75% hard brush**. Notice that you will only replace pixels within your hidden selection area, and your brush will not go past the edge of the shoulder. The edge between the shoulder and background might show stair steps; this could have been avoided by feathering our selection before cloning. We will fix this another way by first choosing **Select >> Deselect** and hitting (**r**) to switch to the blur tool of about **9 pixels and 50% hard**. The blur tool looks like a drop of water, so just **rub it over the edges you wish to smooth** and the pixels will melt into each other. Using too large or hard a brush would make the area look soft. You can fix the rest of the image using the techniques you have learned in this chapter, or turn on the retouched layer if you wish to view the results instead.

CLONE STAMP

Removing background clutter draws more focus on your subject, making your videos have more impact. Photographers consider that when they are composing

Original Photograph by Johnny Sarena.

a shot, but with wildlife photography the animals do not cooperate. Open **Chapter 18/Shark.psd**, and we remove the small fish which got into this beautiful shark close-up. Most people grab the Healing Brush and try to get rid of the fish. The first time you use the Healing Brush on the big fish, it will leave the remnants of a black blob where the fish was. This eventually works, but it will take many brushstrokes to get an acceptable result. Clone stamp out the bigger fish, and then use the Healing Brush to smooth the transition. The Healing Brush has modes, but most are not useful, except Replace. Choose the **Healing Brush** and use the **Replace mode to replace the big fish with water**. The transitions are not smooth, just as if we used the clone stamp tool, but we will fix that with another quick pass. With the **Healing Brush hit Shift - (minus)** to switch the toolbar option mode to normal, **and paint out the residual blob** left by the Replace mode of the brush. The other fish was cloned out directly with the Healing Brush; this is because the black fish is surrounded on all four sides by blue water. The Healing Brush has trouble with edges, because there is no data for it to use to calculate. It also has a big area of black which dominates the final Healing Brush calculation.

Retouched image.

PATCH & COLOR REPLACE TOOL

Similar to the Healing Brush, the Patch tool does amazing calculations to smooth out source and destination pixels. Open **Chapter 18/Patch_ColorReplace.psd**, and we will remove the orange shirted guy from the image. The Patch tool can patch your selection or destination. In either method you make a selection, and

drag and drop it over your destination. This selection can be made with the Patch tool, or an existing selection.

Hit **Shift** (**J**), until you switch to the Patch tool, and **draw a rough selection around the guy**. Set your **toolbar option to Source** for the Patch tool, **and drag your selection to the left until it is under the left peak center, and drop it**. Did you see what happened! The Patch tool did an amazing job of patching your selection. There is an orange blob, where the guy used to be. You will fix that along with any artifacts like the thicker branch to the left of the orange blob. Imagine how many healing brushstrokes or clone stamps that would have taken.

Hit **Shift** (**J**), until you switch to the Color Replacement tool. This new tool improves and replaces and older method of using a paintbrush set to Color Mode. The best way to use this tool is not to set a color by double-clicking in your foreground swatch, but to sample a color from your existing image using the Color Replacement tool. **Alt** [**Option**] click on a **green area of the trees** to fill your Color Replacement tool with that color. Then, with a **brush radius of 100 pixels, brush over the orange** to get rid of it.

The Color Replacement tool is much more powerful than the old method of using a paintbrush set to Color Mode. The default color replacement toolbar options for Mode, Sampling, Limits, and Tolerance are what you will use most often. You can also use this tool to get rid of red eye. Another useful tip for this tool is if you want to shift the existing color of something. For underwater photography, we like to shift the water from green to blue. In that case sample the existing greenish water, double-click on the foreground swatch, and slide the hue towards blue. We get a better targeted result with the Color Replacement tool than shifting the hue on the entire image.

EXTENDING AN IMAGE

Float and Transform a Copy

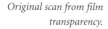

Content on DVD

Open **Chapter 19/Chicago_Pizza.psd**, an image from a scanned transparency. The photographer did not shoot the entire spatula, but we would like it to be shown in our video project. Switch to the rectangular marquee tool (**m**) **and draw a selection frame around the wooden part** of the spatula handle. **Hit Ctrl J**

[**Command J**] to float a selection to a new layer, and **hit Ctrl Left Bracket** [**Command Left Bracket**] to move the layer down in the stacking order of the layers palette. Switch to the move tool (**m**) and **move the layer up and left** making the handle appear longer. Hit **Ctrl T** [**Command T**] to transform this floating chunk of handle. **Enlarge 113% and reposition the floating wood handle** to match the angle of the edges in as few transforms as possible. Pay close attention to the distance between the metal rivets, to help get a matching transform, and zoom in to 200% to help.

Transforming layer to match original.

Cloning into a New Layer

There is a black edge of the original film transparency between our two layers. We could merge the two layers and just use the clone tool, but this book is about giving you new techniques. **Click the "Transparency Scan" layer thumbnail** and **click the new layer icon**; this creates a new layer above the selected layer. Hit (**S**) to switch to the Clone Stamp tool and **enable the Use All Layers tool bar option**. This will have the Clone Stamp tool use as all visible layers in your document as source pixels. We will want to clone, and choosing a good initial source point will help you clone the edge of the wood into the proper location. Zoom your **view to 200%**, and **Clone Stamp Brush set to about 30 pixels with 75% hardness** will help you get good results. Your do not want to make the brush any softer as your resulting image will be soft. Neither do you want your brush too hard, as it is difficult to get a smooth transition between images. **Hit Caps Lock and Alt [Option] click the cross-hair on the top edge of the wood**, to the bottom right of the area you want to retouch over. Caps Lock changes your cursor to a cross-hair, to target the exact pixel for your source point. **Clone Stamp the edge over**, and **repeat this process for the bottom edge**. You also want to **Clone Stamp the center highlight across the middle**. You can now **release Caps Lock** and **finish cloning the rest of the wood**. If you have some repeating grains of wood, or transitions that are not as smooth, switch to the Healing Brush and set it also to use layers. Finally, hit (**B**) to switch to the paintbrush and **Alt [Option] click on the black** to select it as your foreground color. Taking a sample is better, as there is a wide range of black color combinations that look the same, and you might notice a difference when you go to video. Then, **just paint on the top layer to round off the edge of the handle**. You will notice a white edge around the scan of the transparency, and also at the top right the remnants of a pizza pan from the photo shoot, which you can paint over. You can open the final image in your chapter folder and see that we added an adjustment layer to fill the rest of the background with black to get the final image.

Image courtesy of www. homeruninn.com.

19
PHOTO RETOUCHING

*C*hapter 18 took you through the process of restoring old and damaged photographs. The rewards of bringing an old picture back to life can range from money in your pocket to a teary-eyed surviving sister full of gratitude. The objective served by Chapter 18 was to restore a photograph to its original luster. Chapter 19 deals with optimizing a raw picture to achieve its highest aesthetic potential. This is a skill that can help to polish a video project using images for motion graphics. For example, taking a product shot with a 5 megapixel digital camera will give you enough resolution to zoom in nearly 400% and give you more control with motion than doing it with a video camera.

PEOPLE

The next time you are at the grocery store, take a walk down the magazine rack. Notice how everyone on the covers looks so beautiful that it defies reality. For what it's worth to your self-esteem, they just aren't that pretty. Every cover girl and super hunk that you see on the covers was processed through Photoshop. You may have heard the phrase "... it's all airbrushed." More accurately, it's all

distinct features, flattering lighting, strong composition, high-grade media, and Photoshop. Even though this book caters to the needs of video, the techniques in this chapter come into play whenever you want a beauty shot of a subject for inclusion with the video content or on the cover of a DVD.

Critical Analysis

Open **Chapter 19 >> Model 1** on the DVD. When you're about to retouch an image you have to begin with a critical analysis. No picture, model, camera, or scan is ever perfect, so you need to learn to look for certain criteria to meet your objectives. Each step we will be looking at may seem insignificant on its own, but when all the adjustments are seen to fruition, the end result is undeniably professional.

Content on DVD

We're off to a good start with this image already. It's lit fairly well; the green screen background is kind of even, and the model, Jennie, gives us good features to start with. However, there are a few issues we will need to concern ourselves with here. Her skin needs to be softened and evened out, including removing a couple of freckles and a birthmark on her forehead. The shadows to the left of her nose will need to be lightened. We will also tone down the green highlights in her hair from the background and bring out the brilliance of her irises.

Less is More

To get this photo ready for key display, we will go through the same process of color correction that is illustrated in Chapter 17. However, before we do any color correction, we want to use the Rubber Stamp tool and the Healing Brush tool to take out freckles and a scar. We recommend cloning and healing an image before color correction because color separation from levels and curves introduces more contrast in the image and makes using the Rubber Stamp tool and Healing Brush tool more of a challenge.

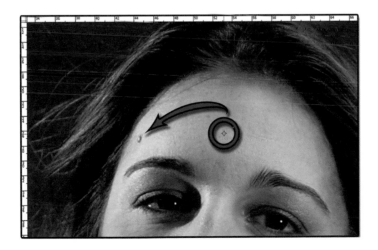

Using the Healing Brush, sample the middle of the forehead and apply a single click over the birthmark.

This particular image is best served by the Healing Brush, **J**. We'll start by using it to heal out the birthmark on her forehead. Hit **Ctrl Alt 0 [Command Option 0]** to view the image at 100%. Use the temporary Hand Tool to move the image around, **hold down the Space Bar**. You want to sample the area of her forehead in the middle, **Alt Click [Option Click]** to match the light and texture of the neighboring skin. Use a brush size about 30 pixels across with a hardness of about 25%. Make sure that the options bar is set for normal mode, select Sampled as the source, then click one time right over the birthmark and watch it disappear.

Next, we'll use the Healing Brush tool to heal out the minor wrinkles in the forehead. Sample from a clean spot on the forehead again and clean up the lines on the forehead with the aligned box checked in the options bar. Once the forehead is finished and we have a nice clean area of skin, we will sample the center of it, **Alt Click** [**Option Click**], and uncheck the aligned box in the options bar. When we heal the few freckles on her nose and cheek, the Healing Brush will begin each stroke from the center of the forehead. You may need to resize your brush as you go, so don't forget your shortcuts for resizing them that you learned in Chapter 1. You may also want to repeat this process on the neck and below the eyes.

Background Removal

We'll use a similar technique to the one used in Chapter 14 to separate Jennie from the background. Create a new layer. Hit **G** for the Paint Bucket tool and set the foreground color to white. Click inside the image to make a solid layer of white. Select the background layer and hit **Ctrl J** [**Command J**] to copy the layer then drag it to the top of the Layers palette. Create a new Hue/Saturation adjustment layer and bring the green saturation slider to 60%.

Select the copied layer. Create a Garbage Matte around the model with the Marquee tool, **M**, or the Lasso tool, **L**, and click **Add Layer Mask** on the bottom of the Layers palette. Go to **Select >> Color Range** and hold the **Shift** key down as you click and drag around a portion of the green screen. Bring the Fuzziness slider to around 100 and hit OK when you're done. The marching ants should indicate a fairly good selection with the exception of a little bit of the hair and jacket. Hit **Ctrl Shift I** [**Command Shift I**] to invert the selection and hit **Q** for the QuickMask. Use the Brush tool, **B**, to brush out the areas inside the model's space that we don't want selected, and hit **Q** again to exit the Quick Mask. Go to **Select >> Modify >> Contract** and enter 2 pixels. Hit **Ctrl Alt D** [**Command Option D**] to adjust the feathering of the selection by 2 pixels, and hit OK.

Select the copied layer of Jennie, and then turn off the Hue/Saturation adjustment layer. Click on the Layer Mask icon and use the Brush tool to mask out the rest of the green screen. After we have the green screen taken out, we might want to refine the edge around Jennie. Go to **Image >> Adjustments >> Brightness and Contrast**, and bring the contrast slider up beyond 0% to sharpen the edge. Transversely, you can soften the edge by going to **Filter >> Blur >> Gaussian Blur** and adjusting it to blur the mask. That's why you want to error on the side of caution when you modify the selection to contract by 1 or 2 pixels – it's much harder to contract a mask. As an alternative, we like using the Smudge tool, **R**, to refine the mask. To try it, select the mask (not the layer itself) and stroke in the direction of the hair. If you are trying to finesse a thin strand that's blowing in the wind, set the strength in the options bar to around 20% and follow the curve of the hair.

Color Correction

We'll begin the color correction phase by taking care of any spill over green around Jennie's jacket and hair. It's good to do this before the overall color adjustments, so we don't take samples from colors we don't want. We want to work with the most color depth we can get, so select **Image >> Mode >> 16 Bit**. There are two ways we like to remove chroma spill. The direct approach is to use the Replace Color tool, **J**. It gives you many of the options of a brush and it allows you to change only the areas you want, instead of the entire image. Just **Alt [Option] Click** on area of the hair or jacket that you want to replace with, and stroke along the trouble areas. If you are working with a composite that has already been color-corrected, my favorite method is to use a Selective Color adjustment layer. It's important to remember which positive colors balance the negative colors (see Chapter 2), because the four sliders used to enter values are expressed as CMYK values. This is a more advanced adjustment and it requires a practiced eye, but with time you may come to love working with selective color for fine adjustments.

After the green spill has been tweaked out, it's time to do the normal color correcting that we would do on any image. For a more comprehensive description of this process, refer to Chapter 17. When the standard adjustments have been made, we can start to make color adjustments intended for beautification purposes. Open a curves adjustment layer, hit OK for now, and make sure it is right above Jennie's layer. Hit **Ctrl G [Command G]** to group the two layers. This will make any changes done to the curves adjustment layer affect only the layer below it.

These areas will be used to define the highlight, mid tone, and shadow parameters for this image.

We want to bring out Jennie's flesh tones from the rest of the image. Click **I** for the Eyedropper tool. In the options bar, set the sample size to 5 × 5 average. Double-click the curves adjustment layer. We need to make three key selections. Begin by **Ctrl [Command] Clicking** a highlighted area on the forehead that looks like the brightest point on the model. Repeat that step for the darkest area – most likely found in the hair near the neck. Finally, find an area on the cheek that is evenly lit (not too bright or too dark) and **Ctrl Alt Shift [Command Option Shift] Click** the area. At this point, we've actually made five very important selections with only three clicks.

In the Curves window, select the dark marker and use the **Down** arrow key to bring the output value down between 5 and 10. Select the highlight marker and use the Up arrow key to bring the output value up between 245 and 250. The contrast of the image has been intensified for a dramatic look.

Use the newly created selections in the Curves window to define the luminance and color tone.

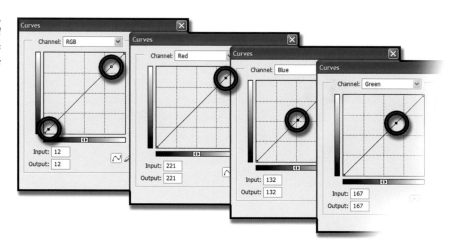

Next, we'll warm up the skin tones just slightly. Cycle through the different colors by holding down **Ctrl [Command]** while you hit **1**, **2**, and **3** for red, green and blue, respectively. Hit **Ctrl 1 [Command 1]** to bring up the red channel, and notice that the new mark selected is totally black, indicating that it is selected. Use the **Up** arrow key to raise the value in single steps about three times. You could hold down the **Shift** key to jump in increments of 10 if it served you. Bring the values for the green and blue channels down in the opposite direction by the same amount using the **Down** arrow key, and click OK. Jennie's skin should start to take on a nice warm tone by now, but you can dial the curves to suit your own taste.

Finishing Touches

We had Jennie use very little make-up. This image will benefit if we can soften a few of her features around her forehead, nose, chin, and cheek. Select Jennie's layer and copy it, **Ctrl J [Command J]**. Go to **Filters** >> **Blur** >> **Gaussian Blur**, bring the slider to about 4 or 5 pixels, and hit OK. Click on the Mask icon on the bottom of the Layers palette, then hit **Ctrl I [Command I]** to invert the mask. Make the foreground color white by hitting **D** then **X**. Select the Brush tool and make the tip size about 100 pixels with a nice soft edge around 50%. Bring the opacity down to 40% and the flow to 100%.

You are now ready to apply some virtual make-up to your model's face. Just like real make-up, it can be flattering or it can be garish. We're going for a flattering effect, so we've turned the opacity down and softened the edge of the brush so we can apply the virtual make up judiciously. As you apply the brush strokes, you're actually painting away the mask of the blurred layer. If you want to tone down the mask to reduce the blur effect, hit **Ctrl [Command] M** for the Curves window and drag the highlight marker down as you watch the amount of blur showing through to lessen. What you're doing with curves is bringing the white levels of the mask down, taking down the opacity. The benefit to using layer masks for this step is that it allows us to modify our work at any point, even after saving. If we used the Blur tool on the model layer, we would be locked into those changes when we saved.

EXTERIORS

Over the past few years, we have worked on dozens of commercial spots where the script called for an exterior shot at the end. Often, clients will try to pick up business by advertising during the winter months after Christmas. The challenge we are faced with is making the exterior shots look good. The crew brings back decent footage, but winters in the Midwest just aren't pretty. There's slush, salt, dead trees, and cracked pavements. We always beg for them to take the art department's

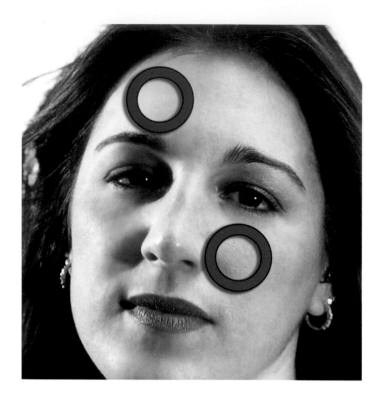

2 megapixel digital camera for stills, but they hate working with it. So we'll wind up having to work with an exported frame of video which yields fewer pixels and usually blows out the sky in order to properly expose the building. This section will illustrate how to make the most of an exterior photo.

Setting Yourself up for Success

If you have the means, give yourself a fighting chance by acquiring the photo with an SLR film camera or 4 megapixel camera. Higher megapixel cameras are encouraged, but when video is the distribution medium, even a 2 megapixel camera offers more than twice the definition of a video frame to work with. A camera that allows you to have full manual control is preferable if you know how to get the most out of its settings. If you want a deeper depth of field, the ability to close your iris and take the aperture from f2.8 to f11 will make quite a difference. Use a tripod. Even a $19.95 model from your local camera store will hold your camera still better than you can. Tripods become especially important when your shutter speed is set bellow 1/120th of a second.

If your camera allows for bracketing or multi-burst shooting, take advantage of it. Bracketing settings can take several shots within a couple of seconds using different exposures for each time it snaps a shot. Having the camera take one shot at the proper exposure, one shot slightly overexposed and one shot slightly underexposed will give you three layers to work with in Photoshop. Don't bother trying this without a tripod or on moving subjects. Also, keep in mind what time of day you are going to be shooting. In the U.S., taking the picture of a storefront that faces South at 7 p.m. in July could produce a lovely image. However, you'll have a very difficult time shooting a storefront that faces North at 4 p.m. in the beginning of January, just because of where the sun will be.

Finally, the best production is only as good as its pre production. Having a layout of what an exterior will look like in the end, including any graphics or compositing, will save you many curse words in the editing suite.

WORKING WITH THE IMAGE

Sometimes even a good photograph needs a face-lift to help make the sale.

Open **Chapter 19 >> Sportsplex** on the DVD. The figure above shows a before and after example of the Orland Park Sportsplex. This image has already been through basic levels correction, so we'll start by taking out some unsightly items in the picture. Use the Rubber Stamp tool, **S**, to take out the phone wires in the background sky. Be sure to use a brush with a soft edge, and sample close to wire so there will be little difference in texture, luminance, and color.

Content on DVD

The pavement is in need of repair, so we will just replace it with some of our own. Hit **Ctrl Shift N [Command Shift N]** to create a new layer. Fill the layer with black using the Paint Bucket tool, **G**. Go to **Filters >> Sketch >> Reticulation** and enter 9 for the Density, 24 for the Foreground Level, and 5 for the Background Level before you hit OK. You should now have a decent virtual black top to work with. Hit **F** for the Full Screen view. Hit **Ctrl T [Command T]** for the Free Transform Tool. Drag the black top layer down to line it up so that the top is just above the real street. Hold down **Ctrl [Command]** and drag the lower corners

Don't feel committed to keep the original parking lot if it doesn't look good.

out from the center. Then drag the lower center up until it starts to look like as though it is on the same plane as the real street. Hold down the **Space Bar** for the Hand Tool and **Ctrl** – or + [**Command** – or +] if you need to move the image around and resize it to see what you are doing. When you're finished, hit **Enter** [**Return**].

Double-click on the Background layer in the Layers palette and hit **Enter** [**Return**]; this will turn it into an ordinary layer. Drag the bottom layer to the top so it covers the virtual black top. Click the Create Layer mask and use the Brush tool, **B**, with black as the foreground to paint out the old street and reveal the new layer below. Make sure the brush has a soft edge with 1% spacing. For best results, work with the image at 100% scale, **Ctrl Alt 0** [**Command Alt 0**].

We'll replace the sky in a similar fashion as the street. Select the Magic Wand tool, **W**, and set the options bar to add to selection, 32 levels of tolerance, anti-aliased, and contiguous selecting. Click in the sky until it's entirely selected. Go to **Select** >> **Modify** >> **Expand**, enter 1 pixel, and hit OK. **Hit Ctrl Alt D [Command Option D]** to feather the selection and enter 1 pixel before you hit OK. Create a new layer, **Ctrl Shift N [Command Shift N]**. Hit **D** for the default colors. Go to **Filters** >> **Render** >> **Clouds**, and you will now have these really ugly clouds against a black sky. Change the blending mode of the clouds layer to Soft Light.

The last thing you need to do is create a Levels Adjustment layer for your final corrections, and add any text.

SECTION V

CREATIVE PROJECTS

20

CREATING CUSTOM BACKGROUNDS

*M*y friends and I all wore black tuxedos to our senior prom, while some of our

dates wore black dresses. When our photographs were taken, we stood in front of a

green screen. When we got our pictures from the photographer, they all contained a

background that looked like the cockpit of the Millennium Falcon during take-off into

hyperspace. As garish and funny as it was to my friends and me, we couldn't see our

tuxedos or the girls' dresses because the backgrounds were 90% black. We literally

looked like floating heads in hyperspace. If the photographer would have had only one

or two alternative backgrounds to choose from when needed, he would have received

far fewer complaints from angry parents.

There are a few issues to consider and some guidelines to follow when creating your

own backgrounds:

❖ The background can be used to subtly communicate a supportive
   message.

❖ If used in video, the background should not contain harsh contrast or extremely fine lines.

❖ The background is never as important as the subject.

❖ The background should complement the subject.

This chapter will guide you through the steps to build various backgrounds and show

you ways to create original canvases for your own development.

HELPFUL FILTERS

The Filter Gallery

Content on DVD

One of the most shockingly useful enhancements given to Photoshop CS/8 is the brand new Filter Gallery. Open **Chapter 20 >> Background** on the DVD. This is a Photoshop document with a circular gradient applied to the background layer and a model with the blue screen already taken out. Some people might consider this to be an adequate background for certain situations, but we want to bring our background up to a higher level of quality and texture.

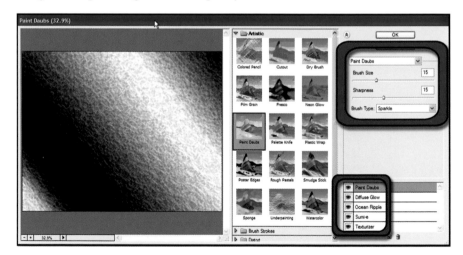

Select the background layer and go to **Filter >> Filter Gallery**. You will get a window that looks something like the figure above. The gallery contains most – but not all – of the filters found in the Filters menu under their respective categories. The center of the window is the browser where the filters are segregated into sub-menus of Artistic, Brush Strokes, Distort, Sketch, Stylize, and Texture. You can minimize the browser, allowing more room for the image preview, by clicking the double up arrows just to the top right. Even with the browser minimized, you can select a filter from the drop window. The drop window will not give you a graphic icon indicating its effect, but their names are a good indication, and that's all the warning Photoshop ever gave us in the previous seven versions.

Below the drop window, you have access to all the same controls to the selected filter as you would have in any other version of Photoshop. There are some great filters for creating backgrounds, but the real power of the Filter Gallery is not fully realized until you begin to combine layers. Below the filter controls is the Effect Layers window. At the bottom of the window, click the New Effect Layer icon. If you minimized the Filter Gallery earlier, expand it by reclicking the double arrows. Whichever effect is selected in the Effects Layers window is the effect that will be replaced the next time you click a new filter in the browser. You can add another filter by **Alt Clicking** [**Option Clicking**] another filter in the browser. The order of the effects will vary the overall image when restructured. You can change the order of effects by simply dragging them in whatever order you want. Apply the Underpainting and Craquelure filters in the Artistic folder using the **Alt** [**Option**] **click** shortcut. Change the order of the two effects, and notice how their order in the hierarchy changes the outcome of the image. Just like the Layers palette, you can solo an effect by **Alt Clicking** [**Option Clicking**] the eyeball icon on the left. Repeating this step will bring back the other effects. The only feature we wish Adobe would have included is the ability to save custom filters. However, if you ever want to save the perfect filter combination that you've just spent the last 20 minutes creating, you can record a new action in the Actions palette and simply hit **Ctrl F** [**Command F**] and the same settings will be saved. For a more detailed tour of how to build your own actions, go back to Chapter 9.

Gaussian Blur

We use Gaussian Blur on about 75% of all the backgrounds we create. The two figures above are examples of simulating depth of field changes. The two images have different shots of the model, but use the same background. The medium shot uses the entire background with a Gaussian Blur filter set at 2 pixels. The close-up used the Gaussian Blur at 9 pixels and scaled up proportionately with the Free Transform command, **Ctrl T [Command T]**.

Clouds

We don't think there is a software package on the market that can create clouds as beautiful as the real thing. However, at least these packages can make clouds that actually are more useful than just realistic-looking clouds. When you apply **Filter >> Clouds** to a layer, Photoshop uses the foreground and background colors to make clouds and a sky. One way to set the colors would be to select them in the Tools palette, but there is a more interactive way. Make a new document, **Ctrl N [Command N]** using the video preset of your choice. Hit **D** for the default black and white colors and apply **Filter >> Clouds**. What you get is what you get.

There are no adjustments for you to make in an effect palette. So when you have a black sky and white clouds, hit **Ctrl U [Command U]** to bring up the Hue/Saturation adjustment.

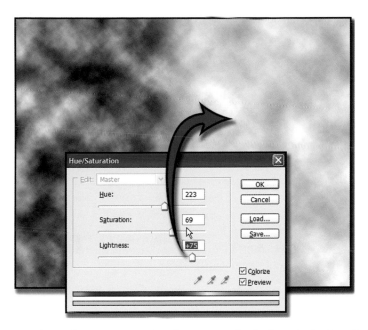

When you have the Hue/Saturation box open, check the colorize box, bring up the saturation to about 35%, and slide the hue over to blue. Adjust the brightness to set the time of day that works for you.

Lighting Effects

Open a new document with a white background. Apply **Filter >> Texturizer** to the background layer using the Canvas texture at 88% scaling, a relief setting of 4,

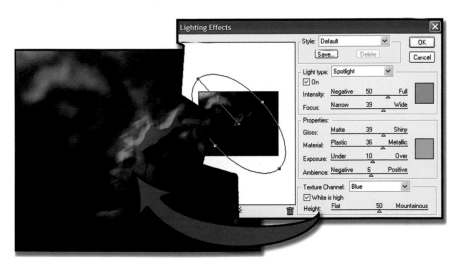

set the light to come from the top left, and then hit OK. Now apply **Filter >> Render >> Lighting Effect**.

The Lighting Effect window gives you plenty to work with, except for an adequately sized preview window. For now, we'll focus on controlling the light direction and placement. You can bring the light source to the upper left corner by dragging the dot in the corner from which it emits. Notice how the intensity grows when brought closer to the center, and diminishes when taken further away. You can also adjust the spread by pulling the side buttons in and out from the center. Moving the center will move the entire affected area. If your light is horribly bright, slide the ambiance down towards the negative end until you get a good spread of light. In the texture channel, select the red channel and bring the bottom slider to 60. Then hit OK.

For some nice touches to finish this background off, try applying **Filter >> Gaussian Blur** at 1 pixel. After you hit OK, hit **Ctrl Shift F [Command Shift F]** to open the Fade Effect box. You can only apply this command immediately after you apply the filter itself. Try setting the opacity to 88%, use the Multiply blending mode, and hit **OK**. Finally, click the Create New Adjustment Layer at the bottom of the Layers palette and apply a Hue/Saturation adjustment. Check the Colorize box and find a good tone for your new background.

HELPFUL TOOLS AND PALETTES

The Paint Brush

Chapter 8 provides a tutorial on how to create a virtual hill of leaves with a few strokes of your mouse. You can take that one step further and paint a layer of leaves over a solid color and give the leaves layer a color dodge blending mode to create more of a specific mood.

The Gradient Tool

The Gradient tool was described in detail in Chapter 6. Open a new document and try this Gradient tool trick. While you could technically get away with drawing a single gradient stroke, try setting the mode in the options bar to difference, select the Copper preset in the gradient editor, select the Angle Gradient option, and draw four gradient strokes. Bring each stroke from a different corner, and watch how the colors interact. If you have 10 seconds to spare, keep dragging more strokes with different gradient patterns, but keep the colors and blending mode the same. In 10 seconds, you might end up with something like that in the figure below.

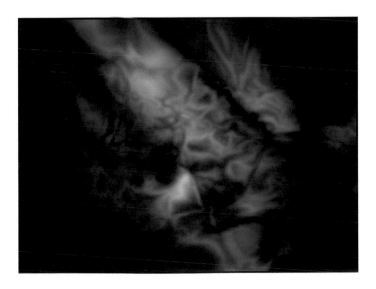

Remembering the role of a background, you may want to mute the image with a little Gaussian blur. A nice final touch would be to make a curves adjustment layer, bring down the brightness half way, pull the center of the line down slightly for a deeper gamma, and hit **OK**. Paint a black hole in the center of the adjustment layer's mask with a soft 300 pixel brush, and it might start to look even closer to the example.

Layer Styles for Backgrounds

One of the fastest ways to get a textured background is to use the Styles palette. Open a new document with a white background. Open the palette, **Window >> Styles**. Double-click the background layer and hit **Enter [Return]** to make it a regular layer. In the Styles palette, click the upper right arrow and select Abstract styles. You will be given six styles to choose from. All you have to do is simply click on any of them to instantly apply the style to the background. You can even double-click the effect icon in the Layers palette to further customize the style.

Actions for Backgrounds

Last, but not least, you can always open the Actions palette, **Window >> Actions**, click on the arrow in the upper left to open the Textures actions, and take your pick. There are over 25 options to choose from, and Cold Lava is a personal favorite of mine. If you tried the Gradient Tool background technique, take two more steps with it using Actions. Play the Cold Lava action and you will have a new layer with a black and white kind of swirly canvas. Change its blending mode to Color Burn over the previous background you created and you will have a lavishly textured backdrop.

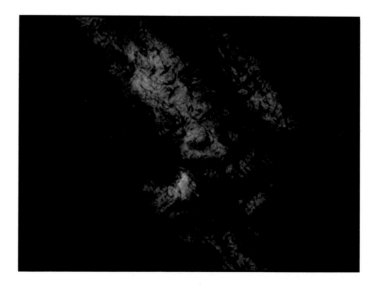

LOWER 3RD BANNERS

Lower 3rd banners are used everywhere in video, from talk shows, news broadcasts, and magazine shows to documentaries, reality shows, and even wedding videos. Lower 3rd banners do more than just identify who's talking, what they do, and whom they do it for – they offer a way to further brand your program. A well-developed program will have consistent art design that spans from the open and closing sequences to the commercial break bumpers and lower 3rd banners.

Custom Shapes with the Shape Tool

Mike Gondek is an ace when it comes to working with vector art, and provides an excellent review of how to create vector art in Chapter 7, as well as what vector art actually is. Be sure to reread Chapter 7 to get a firm grasp of the Shape tool, but this section will illustrate the simplest of ways to take advantage of this very flexible tool.

Open a new document with one of the video presets with a white background that uses square pixels. We will use this document for the rest of the chapter. Enter **Ctrl I [Command I]** to invert the white background to black. Hit **U** for the Shape tool and select the rectangle shape with the shape layer setting in the options bar. Use any color but black so you can see what you are drawing. Hit **F** to use the full screen view. You'll want to be able to work outside of the canvas. Drag the Shapes tool along the document to cover the lower third portion of the image. Select the Direct Selection tool, **A**, and slightly **Ctrl Alt Shift [Command Option Shift]** drag the top two corners separately, converting them to curved corners. We're going for a very subtle curve on the top of the banner, as in the figure below.

Layer Styles for Banners

Chapter 6 takes you through Layer styles in thorough fashion. You can apply a layer style to a lower 3rd banner very easily, including clicking through the different styles in the Styles palette, **Window >> Styles**. The Rollover Button presets from the arrow button menu offer some fast and trendy one-click solutions. Be sure to follow the guidelines listed in the beginning of this chapter to avoid competing with the text for the attention of the viewer. So be careful when scanning through some of the Abstract Style presets, as they are too busy. The figure below has a layer style applied to it using an inner shadow, texture overlay, and gradient overlay with an overlay blending mode.

Transparency and Layer Masks

One final touch that we'll add to our banner will be transparency. We'll want to be able to refine the parameters of the banner, so make a copy, **Ctrl J [Command J]** and turn off the original layer while we work with the copy. Create a new layer, **Ctrl Shift N [Command Shift N]** and link it with the copy layer. Merge the two layers, **Ctrl E [Command E]** and add a layer mask, **Layer >> Add Layer Mask >> Reveal All**. Select the Gradient tool, **G**, and choose the black and white preset from the gradient editor. Make sure the options bar is set for a linear gradient, normal mode, and 100% opacity. Now if you drag the tool from the left to the right of the screen, you will see the stroke effect only the transparency of the banner.

After you have tweaked the transparency how you like and have entered your text (see Chapter 11 for an in-depth look at the Text tool), you need to define your alpha channel. Do this by turning off any layers except for the black background,

the lower 3rd banner with the layer mask, and the text. **Ctrl [Command] Click** the T icon for the text in the Layers palette, and the marching ants will dance around the text. **Ctrl Shift [Command Shift] Click** the lower 3rd banner layer icon, and the marching ants will now include both. Go to the Channels palette, **Window >> Channels**, and click the Save Selection As Channel icon, and a new channel named "Alpha 1" is added to the palette. Save your document, **Ctrl S [Command S]** as a PSD file and name it "Project Name" MASTER.PSD. Now save a copy of it, **Ctrl Shift S [Command Shift S]** as a Pict file. Be sure to check the Alpha Channels box and give it an appropriate name, such as the name of the person on the banner. We save my lower 3rd banners as PICTs because they have good compression quality, can contain an alpha channel, and they are a fraction of the file size of a PSD file.

21
MATTE PAINTINGS AND VIRTUAL SETS

This virtual set was created for The Homework Show using Photoshop and 3D Studio Max

$\mathcal{E}$*ver since the birth of celluloid, optical illusions and special effects have been parts of the filmmaker's repertoire. From Gone With The Wind and Citizen Kane to Star Wars and Lord of The Rings, matte paintings and virtual sets have either wowed us or sat in front of us without us ever knowing they were there. This chapter will briefly explain what each term means, and provide an example for you to follow along with.*

MATTE PAINTINGS

A matte painting is a fabricated environment that is intended to blend into a real set or exterior that has been recorded to film or video. This technique was popularized by *Star Wars* in 1977. One scene that used a matte painting was an overhead angle looking straight down on Obi Wan Kenobi sabotaging an electrical panel suspended high over a seemingly endless pit. The actor, floor and electrical panel were real, but the surrounding walls and bottomless pit were painted onto a glass plate with a hole in the center that framed the action. In the following example, we will be using two video clips, one digital photo, Photoshop, and a little help from After Effects to place an actor high atop a snow-covered mountain.

Planning Ahead

The key to special effects is in the planning. Rudimentary drawing skills are essential for communicating with others working on the shot, and especially for working out the logistics of coordinating your steps. If you don't have access to a talented storyboard artist, you can still get your idea across by using stick figures and crude sketches, such as in the figure below. Notice how the extreme wide shot has a box around the actor. This box is an important guideline for helping us to compose the shot in the field when acquiring the footage.

Planning your shots helps you to develop the idea as well as serving as a checklist to make sure you get everything done.

Composing the Shots

To sell the illusion that our actor is on a mountain top, both video clips need to have no extraneous noise in them, such as sidewalks, cars, and fire hydrants. We made sure to start with a medium shot of the actor walking into frame to show the viewer an idea of scale to refer to. The next video clip had to be far enough away to reveal the actor's entire body, even during movement. Additionally, the second shot needed to have enough clean area around the actor for us to blend into the matte painting or plate.

Work with a frame of video that gives you a good indication of how far the action will take place.

You don't have to go to Colorado to get a shot of a mountain.

The last image we need to capture is our mountain. We found our mountain in the parking lot of my local grocery store. The angle of the picture needs to be very similar to our video footage. If we shot our actor from a high vantage point looking down on them, we don't want to frame the "mountain" from down low looking up. Having the storyboard or a printout of a frame from the video will help to keep you on track if you try your own project. For illustrating purposes, we've decided to keep it sweet and simple by shooting both actor and mountain straight on. We also framed the mountain with the camera as close to the snow as possible while using as wide an angle as possible to maximize the depth of field. To get an even greater depth of field, we slowed down the shutter and closed the iris as much as we could while maintaining proper exposure.

Painting the Matte

Content on DVD

Open **Chapter 21 >> Snow Mountain** on the DVD. This is a Photoshop document with three layers labeled "Video" and "Snow Mountain". The top layer is an exported still frame of video where the actor extended their arms out the furthest. This layer is mostly used for a reference. We'll borrow some surrounding snow to make a smooth seam for our matte. The second layer is the mountain of snow. The Video layer has a resolution of 720×534 and the original snow mountain has a resolution of 2560×1920. The Snow Mountain image was doubled in size to give an ever larger illusion. The Video layer is already placed where we ultimately want it to go for the final effect.

View the document at 100%, **Ctrl Alt 0 [Command Option 0]**. Use the Marquee tool, **(M)**, to draw a selection around the actors that leaves out the trees, traffic, sky, and microphone. Create a layer mask by hitting the Add Layer Mask icon on the bottom of the Layers palette. Drag the newly created mask into the trash can and select **Apply** when Photoshop asks you what to do.

Using a combination of the Clone Stamp tool, (**S**), the Healing Brush, (**J**), and Layer Masks, we will blend the edges of the two layers together and create a hole for the video to play through later in After Effects. Clone in a little extra snow around the edge of the video layer with the Clone Stamp tool. Use the Healing Brush to even out the transitions between strokes if necessary. Click the Create Layer Mask icon on the bottom of the Layers palette and use a large, soft-edged brush to feather and blend the seams between the two layers.

Blend portions of the video layer outward into the background.

The final step we'll take in Photoshop will be to create the final mask. Link the Video and Matte layers and hit **Ctrl E** [**Command E**] to merge them together. Select the Rectangle Marquee tool and drag a selection that is inside the video layer, but allowing plenty of room for the actor to not be touched. Go to **Selection >> Modify >> Feather or Ctrl Alt D** [**Command Option D**] and enter a value of 10 pixels. Click the Add Layer Mask icon for the set and **Ctrl Click** [**Command Click**] the layer mask to create a selection. In the Channels palette, click Save Selection As Channel icon to create the alpha channel. Switch off the Video layer, save the document onto your hard drive as a PSD file, **Ctrl Shift S** [**Command Shift S**], and it's ready for compositing.

Compositing

You can finish this exercise within your video editing application if you don't have After Effects. The difference is that you might not be able to apply an adequate virtual camera zoom out move like After Effects would allow.

If you have access to After Effects, open a new project, **Ctrl N** [**Command N**] and **File >> Import >> File** the video clip Long Shot. For best results, copy the file, **Chapter 21 >> Long Shot** from the DVD to your hard drive. Then import, **Ctrl I** [**Command I**], the PSD file that you just saved to your hard drive from the previous section. Before you hit OPEN to accept the footage, select **Composition** in the **Import As** menu. Importing as a composition will bring the image in as a

Content on DVD

whole composition with all layers intact as well as separate layers in a labeled folder. Drag the Long Shot file and drop it in the New Comp icon at the bottom of the Project window. This creates a composition with the exact dimensions, frame rate, duration, and pixel aspect ratio automatically. Twirl open the folder containing the PSD file and drag and drop the Video and Matte layers into the newly created comp in the Project window.

The elements are now centered in the timeline for the composition. Make sure that the order of the layers in the timeline are Matte, Video, and Long Shot from top to bottom respectively. Click the Video layer and hit **T** for the opacity setting and enter a value of 40%. **Ctrl Click [Command Click]** the Matte layer so that the top two layers are selected. The Matte layer is larger than the canvas, so drag the layers around in the Comp window until the whole of the Matte is over the Long Shot layer and the Video layer matches up closely. Once you get them lined up, turn off the Video layer with the eye icon on the timeline.

Next, we have to tether the two visible layers together, so if you have After Effects version 5.0 or higher, you can simply click the Parent bar in the timeline for the Long Shot layer to link with the Matte layer. Now you only have to create keyframes for one layer and the other will go along for the ride. If you have an earlier version of After Effects, you will need to select both layers and enter in keyframes at the same time.

Bring the Current Time Indicator to about 1 second in the timeline. Hit **S**, then **Ctrl P [Command P]** to bring up the Scale and Position properties. Click the stop-watches for each property, and your first keyframes are set. Bring the Current Time Indicator to 2 seconds. Now enter a 25% scale value for the Matte layer and place it squarely in the center of the composition. The keyframes are now all created.

For the finishing touches on this animation, drag a selection around all four keyframes and **Right Click [Command Click]** to bring up the keyframe assistant menu. Select Easy Ease to put a curve on the velocity of the animation and softening the movement. Click the Motion Blur checkboxes for both layers and turn the Motion Blur switch at the top of the timeline. You can preview your work before you do the final render by hitting **Ctrl Number Pad 0 [Command Number Pad 0]**.

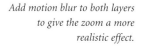

Add motion blur to both layers to give the zoom a more realistic effect.

VIRTUAL SETS

A virtual set is basically a background, but it's intended to look like a real (or not so real) set or environment. With the proliferation of 3D applications and blue/green screen keying techniques, the lines between reality and fabrication are constantly being blurred. This section of the chapter will take you through the steps of creating a pseudo realistic-looking room for an actor to be keyed or superimposed over.

The kitchen background was created entirely in Photoshop by Jessica Yach.

Different Styles of Virtual Sets

If you were working on a commercial ad for a carpeting company, one approach you could take might be to show piles and warehouses of carpet samples and carpet rolls behind a spokesperson. To show a tiled background of nine different carpet colors behind a spokesperson would simply be using a background. To use a still of a warehouse as the background in a way that makes a spokesperson appear to be on location at the warehouse is using a virtual set. A virtual set can also be a film or video background.

Sometimes, reality is not what will serve the purpose best. For a children's show on WFBT in Chicago, the art department at Weigel Broadcasting creates a new virtual set each week for a new character portrayed by the host, George Blaise. The show focuses on a different story book each week and creates a fictional character with a humorous twist for teaching lessons. Each character has a different theme and requires a unique virtual set to complement them. These sets are created in Photoshop with the intension looking very cartoonish for the entertainment of kids.

Sometimes, a virtual set is fashioned to look like a cartoon rather than a realistic appearance.

Creating the Virtual Set

Content on DVD

To give a creative example of how to apply a virtual set, we'll use the carpet company ad scenario mentioned earlier in this chapter. **Open Chapter 21 >> Carpet** on the DVD. This is a Photoshop document with two layers containing our model and a picture of a living room with carpet.

This ad used a living room for its virtual set instead of a carpet warehouse. The idea is to sell a benefit instead of a product.

A common way that local commercials are edited is to put a spokesperson facing the camera squarely, with flat product shots keyed behind, or shown in a picture-in-picture effect. That style looks very dry, boxy, and boring. What's worse is that this kind of image illustrates no benefit to its viewer because most people don't put swatches of carpet on their walls. The living room example, however, has a stronger sense of composition, depth, and offers a very clear benefit to a viewer looking for a new carpet. We will build three virtual sets to import into a video editing application from the carpet document.

When these images were taken, the living room was shot with a digital still camera with its widest angle of view, and the height from the ground was documented. The video of our spokesperson was shot in front of a green screen, with the camera supported at the same height as the still camera. Having the digital camera on hand to see the living room on the LCD screen helped to match the tilt angle. A second digital still was taken of another floor with different carpet using the same tilt angle and height.

Compositing

The still of our spokesperson was taken from an exported frame of video. We won't be using this layer for our final images, only as a reference. Solo the layer named living room, and **Alt Click [Option Click]** the eye icon in the Layers palette. Use the Magnetic Lasso tool, **L**, to draw a selection around the perimeter of the carpet. Feather the selection by 1 pixel, **Ctrl Alt D [Command Option D]**. Click the Create New Adjustment Layer icon on the bottom of the Layers palette and select Hue Saturation. Check the Colorize box and bring the Hue slider over until the carpet turns a shade of blue, and then hit OK. The curves adjustment layer already has a mask built into it and only affects the carpet because of the selection we made with the Magnetic Lasso tool. Save two separate Pict files, **Ctrl Shift S [Command Shift S]**. One file should have the adjustment layer on, and the other should have it turned off. Repeat this process for a third carpet sample and save it.

Bring the three new virtual sets you just created into your video editing application or compositor application of choice. Import **Chapter 21 >> Spokesperson** on the DVD into the program as well, and place it on the second video layer in a timeline. Avid will convert the media into OMFI data on your hard drive, but Premiere and Final Cut Pro will want to work with the original files, so you may need to copy it to your hard drive. Evenly distribute the three virtual sets beneath on video layer one spanning the duration of the video clip. Apply a softly edged wipe transition between each virtual set. Now all that is left is to remove the blue-screen from our video layer and the effect is complete – three carpet samples in the same room within 5 seconds.

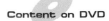

Content on DVD

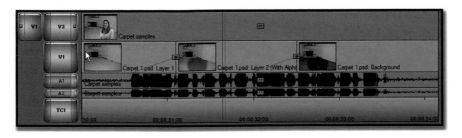

Apply a wipe between the three new images and key the spokesperson on top.

The final effect simply illustrates the benefit of having carpet samples in your home, where it would be installed.

As you become more experienced with the concept of virtual sets, you may start to notice when color temperature and luminance levels may differ between the background and foreground. Matching the background using the curves techniques described in Chapters 18, 19, and 24 is one answer to that issue. Another advanced situation is building a virtual set to be zoomed and panned in unison with a video foreground. In that scenario, the motion tracker in the professional version of After Effects is at the start of the solution. These issues are a little too advanced for this chapter, but you may be compelled some day to incorporate them in a future project.

22

ILLUSTRATIVE EFFECTS

HALFTONE PATTERN

Making Gradated Halftone Dots

*In lithographic printing, dots are used to reproduce an image onto paper. Look with a magnifying glass at your favorite magazine, you can see these dots. Combing the skills we learned from adjustment layers and layer masks, we will take you through the process of creating halftone patterns, you can use for artwork. Open **Chapter 22/HalftoneRadial.tif,** which is a radial gradient in an adjustment layer. Choose **Layer >> Rasterize >> Fill Content** on the gradient adjustment layer to make it into a standard layer of pixels. The next filter we are about to run will not work on an adjustment layer, the image is in grayscale mode which affects the result of the halftone filter.*

Content on DVD

Color Halftone

Max. Radius: 12 (Pixels)   OK

Screen Angles (Degrees):   Reset

Channel 1: 108   Default

Channel 2: 162

Channel 3: 90

Channel 4: 45

Choose Filter >> Pixelate >> Color Halftone >> Radius 20 and click OK. Your result will be solid black dots, which vary in size, over a white background. The size of the black dot depends on how dark the original pixels were, and the radius value. The radius value is the size of the pixel if the original color was black. We always have the preference for our painting cursors to be in actual brush size, and this helps to guess what size your halftone dot will be from this filter. The actual result is about 6 pixels larger. The radius is the most important value you set with the color halftone filter. **Select all** the dots, and **copy** this to your clipboard. **Choose Image >> Mode >> RGB**, and **fill your layer with green pixels. Alt [Option] click on your layer mask** and **paste**. If you click on the swatch for your artwork, you will have white dots on a green background. Actually, the dots are transparent and the white background behind is showing. We will make artwork of green dots, with a purple stroke. **Click on the layer mask** and hit **Ctrl I [Command I]** to invert the layer mask pixels. **Click on the circle f** icon in the layers palette, and **apply a stroke effect of purple** onto this layer. These halftone patterns of dots actually make good background violators for product shots or price points.

Adding a Product Shot and Contracting a Layer Mask Edge

Content on DVD

Open CookieBar.psd and you will see some artwork which has a layer mask. The layer mask is pretty good except for the top, which has a row of white pixels which need to be removed. Set your **view to 200%** and you should see the hairline of white pixels. We will fix the layer mask by using a constrictor mask, and expanding it 1 pixel, and painting in the layer mask to remove the hairline border of white pixels. **Ctrl [Command] click on the layer mask** to select the cookie bar, **Select >> Inverse** to invert your selection to the background. Choose **Select >> Modify >> Expand 1**, to expand your selection 1 pixel. Our constrictor mask is looking good, and we need to hide it and paint in our layer mask. **Hit Ctrl H [Command H]** and **click on the layer mask** and **paint with black to remove the white hairline.** Often you will want to feather your constrictor selection in such a case to avoid stair steps, but do not feather too much or your edge will look too soft. Hit **Ctrl [Command]**, to temporarily switch to your move tool, **drag and drop your cookie bar to the Green Halftone dots**. Before you reposition or move around the tollhouse bar choose **Select >> Deselect** so that you move both the artwork and the mask together. We used the cookie bar shape, and expanded our selection and filled it with black. You can Gaussian blur this to get your gradient. You will want to flatten your gradient against a white background, or else the color halftone filter will not return any result. Color halftone also has an interesting effect on color images.

Open **Chapter 22/RobinWilliams.psd**, and turn on the "color halftone" layer to see the result of a color halftone effect on a CMYK image.

Content on DVD

INTERLACE SHIFT

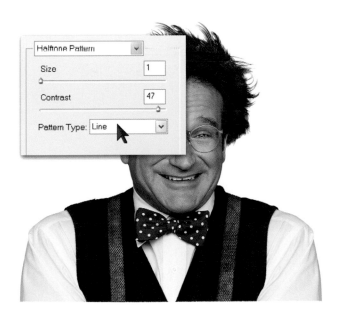

There are some good filters available to make an image look like it is on TV. We can make our own effect using Photoshop to darken alternating lines and shift the pixels over horizontally. Open **Chapter 22/Interlace Shift.psd**, and you will see a document with two identical layers. **Click the "Duplicate" layer mask** to make it active and run **Filter >> Sketch >> Halftone Pattern >> Size: 2 >> Pattern Type: Line**. Use the **Select all command**, and then **copy** the black lines to your clipboard. **Click on the "Duplicate" layer thumbnail**, to switch from the mask to the artwork, and **use the right cursor** to nudge everything to the right. The final step is to **paste your clipboard**, which creates a new layer of black lines, **and set that layer to multiply**. The final image below was then put into an image of a TV set, and some shadows and highlights were added around the tube to give it a rounded dimension.

PEARL IRIDESCENCE

Original Photo by Gregg Deacon.

Open **Chapter 22/Iridescence.psd** to see what the finished effect looks like. **Delete all the layers except background**, and we are ready to start. **Select the background layer and hit Ctrl J [Command J]** to float a copy into another layer. We are going to use this copy to interact with the underlying layer, so **change the layer palette blending mode to Color Dodge**. Now to give the waves a color we are going to solarize the image using an extreme curves setting. Hit **Ctrl M [Command M] and load the Pearl.acv curve**. The image now has the iridescence of a pearl, but does not look as smooth because of some of the noise. We can reduce this noise using **Filter >> Noise >> Dust & Scratches 20**. We can go with such a high setting for Dust & Scratches, because the layer on top has a blending mode that is used for color more than holding the luminosity definition. Video is in RGB and has better blues and saturated colors than the printed CMYK version in this book. For a final touch, we added a glow coming from the eyeball using the lens flare filter. The lens flare filter does not have a preview you can zoom in on, so **create a new layer filled with black** and the **blending mode to lighten. Choose Filter >> Render >> Lens Flare** and use the default settings. It is much easier to move the layer until the lens flare is over the center of the eyeball.

Content on DVD

FAIRY DUST

Photo from
www.msAngelique.com.

Add sparkle to your images digitally, by sprinkling some digital fairy dust. Open **Chapter 22/Fairy Dust.psd** and bring your brushes palette to front. From the **brushes flyout menu >> load brushes >> Chapter 22/fairy dust.abr**. Switch to your brush tool by tapping (**b**) on your keyboard and **right click [Ctrl Click]** and **choose the brush called fairy duster**. This brush has settings enabled which

Content on DVD

make it paint differently than most brushes you have in Photoshop. The shape of the brush will change size and angle randomly because of the jitter amounts applied to them. The brush has scattering set to the maximum of 1000%, which will make the brush scatter paint drops like a spray can. The color dynamic has a little jitter for the hue, you can change this to the brightness instead. The last setting under other dynamics is flow jitter which really for this brush gives some variety to the opacity. **Choose the layer called fairy dust and paint into it with a white foreground color and a 10 pixel brush**. A layer effect of glow gives a yellowish glow to what is painted on your layer. You can toggle the visibility eyeball for the glow effect to see just what the brush does alone.

Now we can change the lighting to look ethereal by using a blending mode and a layer which is blurred. **Duplicate the background layer** by dragging the name over the new layer icon in the layers palette. **Change the blending mode of the background copy layer to Overlay and run Filter >> Gaussian Blur >> 4** to soften the layer. We took the opacity of the background copy layer down to 75% and with the eraser set to 50% reduced the hot spot on the model's face.

Fairy dust with ethereal lighting.

COLOR SCRATCHBOARD

Open **Chapter 22/Color Scratchboard.psd**, and we will transform the image into an illustration. The style we will simulate is when an artist painted a canvas with vibrant colors, and then covered it with an emulsion of India ink. Later, the artist would use a tool to scratch off the emulsion in the shape of an illustration. **Duplicate the background layer and run Filter >> Stylize >> Find Edges**. We also need these data in our clipboard for a mask, so **copy the Find Edges result**.

We need some India ink, so **create a new solid Color Adjustment layer of Black**. Target the layer mask by **Alt Click [Option Click] on the layer mask** and **paste your clipboard**. To see your resulting artwork, you **need to exit viewing the mask and Alt Click [Option Click]** on the layer thumbnail, to view the artwork. It looks good, but how about opening up some more color? We can do this by opening up the highlights and midtones in the mask. Select the layer mask swatch, hit **Ctrl L [Command L]**, and pull the **black input slider to about the middle**. The midtone slider will follow half the distance, which is what we want. The black solid color layer shows the find edges layer underneath. **Choose the middle Find Edges layer** and saturate it by hitting **Ctrl U [Command U]** and pulling saturation all the way up to **100%**. A similar effect could have been done by just running the Filter >> Stylize >> Glowing Edges, but this exercise teaches you how to use your image as a layer mask to create effects. Experiment with more filters and blending modes, and you will be making your own custom effects rather than being limited to default Photoshop filters.

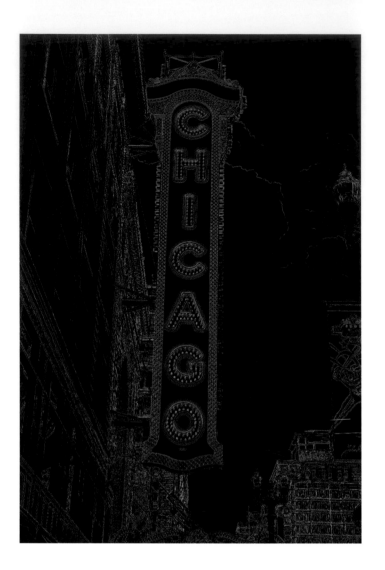

23
GRADIENT
TRANSITIONS

*I*n film and video, different clips or scenes are connected by transitions. Anytime you use a simple cut between two shots, you have a transition from one shot to the next. A very common editing technique is to use a dissolve as a transition that fades between the two shots over time. Ten-frame dissolves are common in commercial ads. Feature films and prime-time dramas often use dissolves that last over 5 seconds. Transitions are also used to start and finish a given program by fading from and to black.

The most important fundamental to keep in mind with transitions is that every transition must communicate something to support the content. A cut can communicate terror when a wide shot of a villain shooting a hero cuts to a close-up of the hero's love interest reacting to the action. A dissolve is used between two shots to communicate a relationship between the two, to convey the passage of time, to give the impression of great distance, or to "soften" the feel of the transition.

Today, we can buy video editing software applications for less than a couple of hundred dollars that give us the ability to choose between hundreds of wild, goofy, and often useless transitions. Many of these superfluous transitions communicate nothing beyond "hey, look at this transition!"

In order to utilize creative eye-catching dissolves that support a given message, many editors and graphic designers work with Gradient Map transitions. They offer more flexibility and different options for fading between clips. This chapter will explain what they are, how they work, how to create them, and finally, how to use them.

UNDERSTANDING HOW THEY WORK

When creating a gradient map dissolve, the transition will look at the luminance levels of a designated image or movie file and fade from clip A to clip B starting with the darkest areas of the image and finishing with the brightest. The gradient map can be any image, graphic, video clip, or animation. However, for getting the best results and for purposes of this chapter, we'll focus on using a graphic image that we will create in Photoshop.

BUILDING GRADIENT MAPS

Gradient Tool

Open a new document with a video preset, **Ctrl N [Command N]** and hit **G** for the Gradient Tool. We're only going to use shades of gray, so for now, select the default black and white gradient preset in the options bar. If you use the standard gradient style and drag your tool across the document, you will have a map for a soft-edged wipe transition. A radial setting will give you a soft circular wipe. If you select the angle style in the options bar and create your gradient, you will have a map for a soft-edged counterclockwise wipe, as shown in the figure below.

Noise For Maps

In Chapter 20, we went over several ways of making backgrounds, from generat-ing clouds to exploring the filter gallery. Remembering that a gradient map can be

any image, any background you can come up with using the techniques brought to light in Chapter 20 can be used as a map for an organic-looking dissolve.

Open a new document. Fill the background with black using the Paint Bucket Tool, **G**, and go to **Filter >> Noise >> Add Noise**. Set the filter for 70% Gaussian distribution, check the monochromatic box, and hit OK. You should now have a bunch of white speckles. Go to **Filter >> Blur >> Motion Blur**, enter a 45 degree angle blur at a 52 pixel distance, and hit OK. Our speckles have now taken on a brushed metal texture. You'll notice, however, that the outer edges are brighter than the center. These edges are outside of the action-safe region, so our dissolve won't fully benefit from this gradient map yet. Hit **C** for the Crop Tool. In the options bar, enter a width of "720 px" and "540 px" and resolution of 72 pixels per inch. Now drag the Crop tool inside the image, leaving out the brighter edges, and hit **Enter** [**Return**]. The final step to do before saving this image is to apply Auto Levels, **Ctrl Shift L** [**Command Shift L**] and it's ready to be used as a gradient map.

Designing Gradient Maps

By now, you should be catching on to the principle of creating a gradient map. Open **Chapter 23 >> Gradient Map** on the DVD. This is a Photoshop document

Content on DVD

The dissolve begins with the dark areas and finishes with the white areas.

with four layers. The bottom layer is the last frame of the outgoing clip used in a sequence. The second layer is the first frame of the incoming clip that we're going to be fading into. The top two layers have been left blank.

Select the "gradient 1" layer in the Layers palette. Activate the Gradient Tool, (**G**), and use a radial black and white gradient. In the options bar, go into the gradient editor and change the white to a gray value of 127 using the brightness slider. Drag the tool from the center of the document to the outer edge. If your center is gray instead of black, check the Reverse option in the options bar next to the opacity window and redraw the gradient. Select the "gradient 2" layer. This time, go into the gradient editor and change the gray color to white at 255 and the black color to gray at 128. When you make your gradient this time, we want the center to be white and the outside to be gray.

Turn off the visibility of the gradient layers and the "incoming" layer. We want to make a selection around the paper, hand and pen as in the figure below. Once you've made your selection, click the "gradient 2" layer in the Layers palette, and then click the Add Layer Mask icon. Click the link icon between the layer icon and mask icon. This will allow us to move the gradient and its mask independently of each other. Click the layer icon and turn the opacity of the "gradient 2" layer down to 50% (**5**), and move or resize it to cover only the area around the

Any creative way you can make a black and white image can be reflected by the final wipe dissolve.

paper, hand, and pen, **Ctrl T [Command T]**. Don't worry if you have to reshape it into an oval to cover the region you want. When you've got it where you want it, hit OK and turn the opacity back to 100%. Save this document as Hand Gradient Map.

Adding a Brightness & Contrast adjustment layer can help make working with the Magnetic Lasso fast and easy.

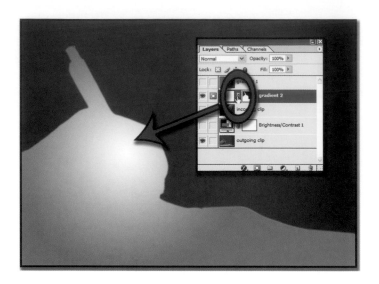

Move the gradient 2 layer to cover the majority of the hand, pen, and paper.

WORKING WITH GRADIENT MAPS

After Effects

It would be too slow and cumbersome to bring individual clips into After Effects just to perform a custom gradient wipe. Instead we'll create an animation in After Effects and use that animation to define the transition in Avid. Most other video applications, such as Media 100, Final Cut Pro, and Premiere can accomplish the same task. Open a new project in **After Effects**, **Ctrl N** [**Command N**], and import the Hand Gradient Map that we just made in the previous section. If asked, choose Merge Layers. Drag the Hand Gradient Map into the New Composition icon at the bottom of the Project window. Hit **Ctrl K** [**Command K**] for the Composition Settings window and change the duration to 3 seconds - "3:00", and hit OK.

This intermediate step in After Effects makes our work much easier than exporting the original video clips into the timeline, rendering the timeline, and importing the new video clip back into a video editing application.

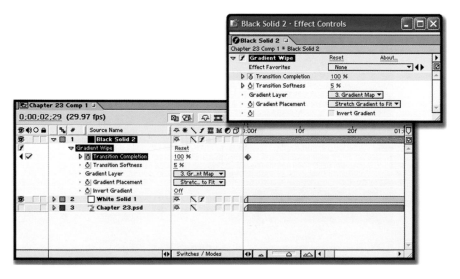

In the timeline, turn off layer 1 – we don't actually want to see it. Hit **Ctrl Y** [**Command Y**] to create a new solid layer. Make it the same size as the composition and set the color for white. Make another solid layer the same way and make it black. **Right Click** [**Command Click**] the Black Solid layer and select **Effect >> Transition >> Gradient Wipe**. In the Effect Controls window, set the transition softness to 5%, the gradient layer to Hand Gradient Map, hit **Home** on the keyboard, and turn on the stopwatch for transition completion. Hit **End** and enter 100% for transition complete. Hit **Zero** on the number pad to see a preview. As long as you have black fading to white, you can render this as a Quicktime Movie through the Render Queue, **Ctrl M** [**Command M**]. Save it as Matte Wipe.

Avid

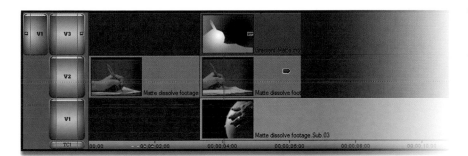

Setting up the timeline is very exacting, but surprisingly simple.

If you're using Avid, import the Matte Wipe you just made along with **Chapter 23 >> Clip 1 and Chapter 23 >> Clip 2**. Create a new timeline, **Ctrl Shift N** [**Command Shift N**] with three video layers. Place Clip 1 on video 2, Clip 2 on video 1, and the Matte Wipe on video 3. Place Clip 2 and Matte Wipe at the end of Clip 1. Make a freeze frame of Clip 1 and extend it through the 3-second duration of the Matte Wipe. Your timeline should look like the figure above.

In the Effect palette, go to **Key** >> **Matte Key** and drag it to the Matte Wipe clip in the timeline. When you play the timeline (you may have to render), you will have a custom transition using a gradient map.

Avid offers a very direct timeline-based approach to this effect. Other video editing applications such as Premiere and Final Cut Pro offer similar means to the same end. For example, in Premiere you don't even need to import the animated matte that we built in After Effects. You would place one of the clips on Video 2 or higher and manipulate the transparency settings in the Effect Controls palette. You would need to choose Image Matte and select the animated file as the matte source.

24

PHOTO MONTAGES

$\mathcal{P}$hoto montages are becoming very popular in the repertoire of service offerings

from many production companies and independent videographers. Weddings,

anniversaries, bar mitzvahs, reunions, and corporate parties are getting more *entertainment from a multimedia presentation of animated photos set to music and shown on a big screen during the event.*

The word 'montage' comes from the French word 'monter', which means to mount. There are several flavors of montage, but this chapter concerns itself with a cinematic technique of juxtaposing a succession of pictures for a thematic effect. This technique is akin to a slide show, but any slide show would be quite jealous of what we can achieve today on a desktop computer with a little help from the Adobe Digital Video Suite.

ORGANIZING LARGE PROJECTS

We once had a contract to provide videography services for a bar mitzvah. We were able to double the amount on the invoice by up-selling my client to include a photo montage to be projected on an eight-foot screen during the event. This client was very adamant about using every single photo she had given to me. There was a total of 144 images. Necessity being the mother of invention, we had to come up with a way to tackle this project in a way that would bring it in on time and still impress my client.

Strategy

A montage is not going to be the reason for an occasion, so don't make it too long. Our experience has led me to believe that 5 to 7 minutes is about the best duration for an audience of 50 people or more. Anything longer than 10 minutes will challenge their attention span, and anything shorter than 5 minutes will call into question whether it was worth it in the first place. When calculating the duration, count on around 4 seconds of screen time, with 1 second for each in and out transition. The average then becomes 10 pictures each minute. So, if a client gives you 50 pictures, you're off to a good start. They will most likely want to have a music background, so make sure they give you enough music to work with. We'll want to keep the mood of the music in mind when we build the montage.

Organizing and Scanning

The first task is to organize the images. Set aside some time with the client to go over the images and separate them by theme, such as old family photos versus new baby pictures during an anniversary party. Organizing the pictures before bringing them into the computer is surprisingly helpful.

Next, we have to get the images into the computer. We use a combination of a flatbed scanner and a digital still camera. Using my camera allows me to get images into Photoshop faster than my scanner. We set up an easel to hold the pictures one at a time under soft, diffused, even lighting and we capture the pictures at 1280 × 960 pixels. We could bring them in as high as 2560 × 1920 pixels, but we usually don't need to zoom in on an image more than double, and my final destination is DVD, which is only 720 × 480 pixels.

If you will be using a scanner instead of a camera, try to line up the pictures as straight as you can while leaving at least a half-inch of space between them. Scan them in at a resolution between 150 dpi and 300 dpi. If you haven't looked at Chapter 9 (Speeding Up Photoshop), read the section on the new Crop & Straighten feature. This command will create new and separate files from different pictures contained within a single scan. Organize your files in the computer

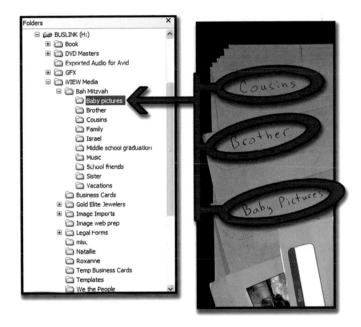

Keep your computer files and your paper files organized identically so you can find the original image quickly if necessary.

identically to the photographs according to whatever theme you are using by giving the photos and files identical numbers in identically named folders. Also, if you need to rescan an image for any reason, you will be able to find it quickly.

Photoshop

If any of the images need special attention beyond Auto Levels, do your corrections now. Don't get ahead of yourself, these pictures will be on screen for an average of 6 seconds, including 2 seconds of transition, so don't spend too much time perfecting them. We just want to make sure that they are discernible. Some minor cropping and rotation may also be in order at this point to correct for proper head room and look space.

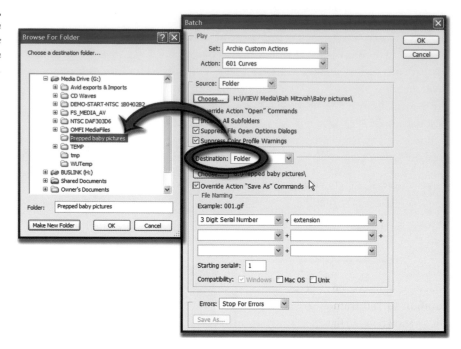

With any of the images open, create an action named "Montage Prep" applying Auto Levels, **Ctrl Shift L [Command Shift L]** followed by a regular Levels, **Ctrl L [Command L]** bringing the white output down to 235. This action will provide a quick color correction and bring the luminance down for DVD or VHS white levels. For a detailed demonstration of how to create an action, read the Actions section in Chapter 9, Speeding Up Photoshop.

Go to **File** >> **Automate** >> **Batch**. Select the Montage Prep action that you just created to play on the folder that contains all of the images you are working on in a particular theme. We're going to create new copies of all the images in new folders just in case Auto Levels doesn't have a favorable effect on a picture. Be sure to check "Suppress File Open Options Dialogs" and "Suppress Color Profile Warnings". For the destination, create a folder with the same name after a word

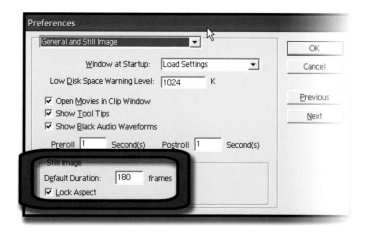

that signals it has been prepared, such as "prepped baby pictures" or "prepped brother". For the file naming, we want to be able to identify the images and to lay them out in order, so select 2 (or 3) Digit Serial Number + extension. Hit OK and let Photoshop do the work for now.

Premiere

Photo montages can be created with any video editing application, but we are using Premiere for this example because it can work with virtually any size an image that can be made. Premiere also works with the original file without having to convert it to a proprietary format like OMFI. If we worked on the Mac platform, Final Cut Pro would be a close second if we still intended to bring my timeline into After Effects via Automatic Duck. Final Cut Pro would be plenty of horsepower to finish many basic animated sequences that used zooms, pans, tilts, and flips.

After all the files have been saved to the new folder, we'll import the whole folder in Premiere. First, go to **Edit** >> **Preferences** and set the still image default duration to 180 frames, (or 150 for PAL projects,) check Lock Aspect and click OK, as shown in the figure above. These settings will make each still last for 6 seconds and keep the height and width proportional when resized to fit the video monitor. This is the whole reason for using Premiere. Avid and After Effects could easily

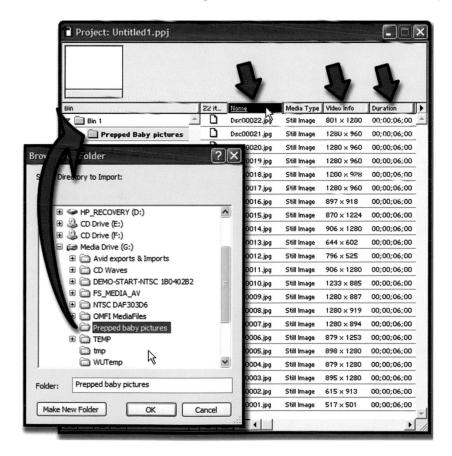

This illustration points out that all of the different images are numbered, descending, and all have different dimensions.

bring in all of the photos on their own, but Avid requires using a cumbersome plug-in for each clip to resize it properly, and After Effects doesn't resize each image to fit the monitor automatically.

Right Click [**Command Click**] in the Project window and select **Import >> Folder**. Navigate to the folder where you've saved your new optimized copies and hit OK. Back in the Project window, click the Name bar to reverse the order of the files. We actually want the order to go from the highest to lowest – just the opposite of the order we ultimately want. Select all of the clips in the bin by either dragging over them or hitting **Ctrl A** [**Command A**] and dragging them to the Video 1 layer in the timeline. The order of the clips should be the opposite order we want as they descend from highest to lowest. Save this project within the same master folder of your montage.

If you're familiar with Premiere's Automate to Timeline command, refrain from using it if you plan to bring the timeline into After Effects. If this command is used to disseminate the images, the application will alternate the images between Video 1A and Video 1B, allowing you to place any transition between them. It's great if you're going to finish the project in premiere – you can even determine the transition and transition's duration automatically. After using the Automate to Timeline command, importing that timeline into After Effects will separate the Video 1A images from the Video 1B images into two different halves in its own timeline. For the purposes of this particular exercise, we don't want to do that.

After Effects

One of the best advantages of using the Adobe family of products is their interoperability. There are two levels of After Effects that Adobe makes available – Standard

When the Premiere project is imported into After Effects, the order of the images are the same in the timeline, but ascend in number in the source column.

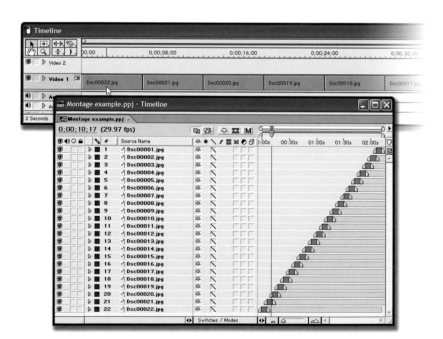

and Professional (formerly Production Bundle). All of the steps listed in this chapter for After Effects only require the standard version of the program. We can bring in the Premiere project as a composition by hitting **Ctrl I [Command I]** and selecting the project. Once the Premiere project has been imported, double-click it in the Project window to open the timeline and comp window. The timeline has all of our images laid out for us just as they were in Premiere – in the wrong order.

Select all of the layers, **Ctrl A [Command A]**. Hit **Home**, then ([), to bring all the layers to the start of the timeline. **Right Click [Command Click]** any one of them. In the floating menu, go to **Keyframe Assistant >> Sequence Layers**. Check the Overlap option, set the duration for 1:00, and choose a transition to cross dissolve front and back layers. Hit OK.

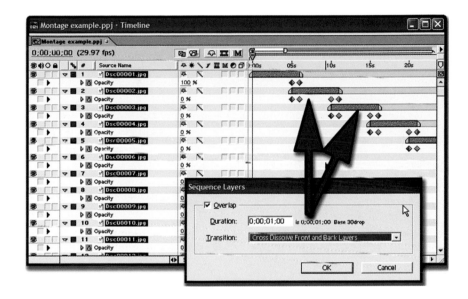

After Effects can resequence the layers with an arbitrary transition that you can define.

At this point, you have a sequence of images laid out in the same order as your client's folder. Each image has a duration of 6 seconds, and there is a 1 second dissolve between each image. Every image has been resized to fit within the boundaries of your video format's resolution. The rest is completely up to you. Depending on your skill level and/or your sense of adventure, you're options can be as open as the blue sky. Scale, rotate, flip, flop, and whatever else you can think of. You could emulate a similar motion graphics sequence found on VH-1's *Behind the Music* and *Driven* or *60 Minutes* by starting out on a wide shot of the photo and zoom into a close up of a face.

If you have After Effects version 5.0 or higher, you can lay out the images in 3D space with lights carefully placed, and fly a camera through a maze of your clients photos. Even if all you ever intended to do in the first place was to just dissolve a motionless full-frame picture into the next full-frame picture, After Effects is likely to be able to render out this sequence faster than Premiere could, especially if you have version 6.0.

There are many insights we could give on how to animate layers and what kinds of movements would work best, but that's a topic for another chapter or perhaps another book. In the meantime, remember to complement and feature the content, not the animation. Bold and fast movements may work well for a 8th Grade graduation montage, but may not have a positive effect on a memorial montage at a funeral.

MERGING A PANORAMA

A panorama is another kind of montage, and is a still representation of what a video camera might see as it pans from one direction to another. A panorama can offer high-resolution, large-format prints, a 360-degree Quicktime VR movie, or can be animated in video for various effects. Kodak would have you believe that a cheap disposable camera can give you beautiful panoramas with a single picture, when all that is being done is cropping and enlarging, as illustrated in the figure below. While it is possible to come up with an interesting composition and printing dimension, a true panorama is engaging and very dramatic. Just look at Mike's

When an image is merely cropped, resulting in a wide aspect ratio, it is not a panorama.

This is a huge 360-degree angle panorama that Mike made from nine separate images.

panorama from the island of Fiji. There are more examples (good and bad) of panoramas on the DVD for you to critique and learn from. Some of the DVD examples are even tiltoramas.

Setting Up for Success

We'll get to the Photomerge function in Photoshop in a moment, but no merging or stitching program is perfect. Some level of artistry and skill needs to occur. The best panoramas are planned out ahead of time.

What to Do:	Why You Do It:
Use a tripod.	The pictures will need to be as precise as possible in order to be organized properly.
Use a tripod with a level.	If you have one, use a level to keep the horizon from shifting. It will be especially noticeable in a panorama.
Overlap your images by 20% to 50%.	The lens will distort more heavily at the edges. You can compensate by using more images with less movement between then.
Use the rear nodal point of the lens.	If your tripod will allow it, slide the mounting plate to where the middle of the camera lens is at the center of the pivot point when panning.
Use manual exposure.	Don't trust the camera to think for you. Get an average meter reading spanning the whole area and use it for the whole pan, or you will have too much variance between your pictures.
Use an appropriate style of lens.	A wide-angle lens will yield a large amount of barrel distortion for large panoramas, but may serve you with merging only two or three images. Telephoto lenses will produce less distortion and will give you easier images to work with, but may not be as dramatic as you would hope for.

The New Photoshop Photo Merge

Open **Chapter 24 >> Panoramic 1** and **Chapter 24 >> Panoramic 2** on the DVD. We're going to take one step to get these two images ready for merging. You can see how the sky is slightly brighter in Panoramic 2 when compared to Panoramic 1. We want to get them closer to each other so that we have a smooth transition when we merge them together. In Panorama 1, select the Eyedropper Tool, **I**, and

Content on DVD

Use the Eyedropper tool to get an exact Red, Green and Blue color value for a portion of sky shared by both photos.

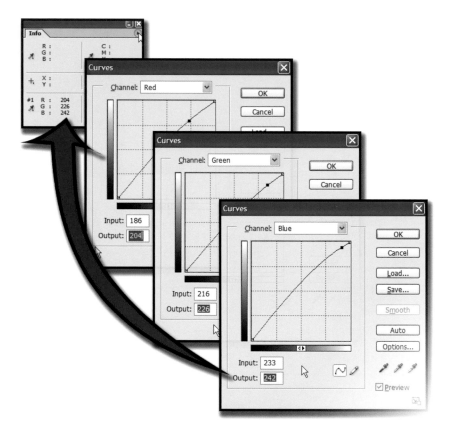

Use Curves to match colors between two images.

open the Info palette, **Window >> Info**. Hold the Eyedropper over a part of the sky just above the left corner in front of the building. The corner is in both images, so it should be a good reference point. Write down the Red, Green, and Blue values in the Info palette. Now go back to Panorama 2 and adjust the curves, **Ctrl M [Command M]**. With the curves window open, bring the eyedropper to

Photoshop has added a merging/stitching utility within the program.

the same point in the sky in Panorama 2 and **Ctrl Alt Shift Click** [**Command Option Shift Click**] to set marks on each color channel. We used this same technique in Chapter 19 to further separate some key points, but now we're going to bring each sample for the three channels to match the red, green, and blue values that you wrote down from Panorama 1. When you finish, hit OK.

Go to **File** >> **Automate** >> **Photomerge**. If you have any other images open, remove them from the dialog box and hit OK. Photoshop will automatically scan the images and lay them out for you how it thinks they should be organized, and blend the two together. You can still manipulate the individual pictures to finesse the results. The tools you have to work with in Photomerge are the Select Image Tool, **A**, Rotate Tool, **R**, Vanishing Point Tool, **V**, Zoom Tool, **Z**, and the Hand Tool, **H**. The space bar Temporary Hand Tool short cut works as well just as normal.

There is also a small Navigator window, which is very useful when working with several images. The Settings box toggles between Normal and Perspective

Checking "Cylindrical Mapping" helps to correct some of the keystoning of the composite when Photoshop compensates for perspective.

merging. Clicking the Perspective option will allow you to access the Vanishing Point Tool and choose which picture you want as your center of focus and determine how the merge will manipulate the image to compensate for barrel distortion. The Composition Settings box lets you apply Cylindrical Mapping and/or Advanced Blending. You have to choose Perspective in the Settings box before you can access the cylindrical mapping. For most panoramas, the cylindrical mapping option is a crucial element to get Photomerge to produce the best results. Advanced Blending may or may not have a favorable effect on the outcome, but if you're comfortable with using layer masks, we would suggest selecting Keep as Layers before hitting OK and blending the image the way you see fit.

Finishing Touches

This Photomerge was made from six different images, and resulted in a 120-degree angle panorama.

Even if the merge was perfect (it never is), you still have to blend with layer masks, color correct the image, and crop or clone the edges. Refer to Chapters 14, 17 and 18 for more information on layer masks, color correction and extending an image with the Clone Stamper Tool respectively.

When all is said and done, you may wonder what use you might have with a panorama for a video project. Here are just a few ideas:

❖ A panorama of the interior of a kitchen or living room could be animated during a remodeling commercial.

❖ An animated panorama is much more interesting than a static shot for an end page of a commercial.

❖ A panorama could be a nice touch on the front or back cover of a DVD/VHS.

❖ A 360-degree panorama can be used to simulate a huge camera trucking move around an actor, rather than a pan. For an example of this, open **Chapter 24 >> Spin** on the DVD.

Content on DVD

25
PSEUDO 3D
ANIMATION

Chapter 24 focuses on what most professionals are accustomed to being associated to the term photo montage. When done well, montages help to heighten the story on a television show about your favorite pop star, or to highlight a wedding reception. Lately, however, a more advanced visualization is just starting to emerge in places where traditional montages would be found. It's so new and fresh that there was no established term for it at the time this book is being written. We'll call it "Pseudo 3D".

In 2002, a documentary based on Robert Evans's autobiography 'The Kid Stays In The Picture', of the same name debuted at the Sundance international film festival. The materials used to make this film were limited to stock footage, archived film, and over 600 still images. Creative Director Jun Diaz developed a deceptively simple technique and style to immerse the audience in the world that is Robert Evans's life story.

The new creative ground that Diaz broke was creating 3D motion graphics from ordinary photographs by separating the subject of a photo from its background and animating them. The same tools and techniques used to achieve the film's effects are contained throughout this book. This chapter will take you through the strategy and workflow needed to accomplish this trend-setting style.

SELECTING THE RIGHT PHOTOS

The more complex an image that you select for this effect, the more difficult the work becomes. We will ultimately be selecting a subject/foreground, placing it on its own layer, and cloning out the empty space from the background. Knowing that, we need to exercise caution when looking at what we will have to clone. Cloning an empty space of generic background textures makes for an easier task than cloning a background of identifiable faces or print cut off by the subject. Not every picture will be a good candidate for this effect.

Very busy background and many holes to deal with.

Clean background and well defined borders are better to work with.

If you have the luxury of having multiple images to choose from, set yourself up for success and select the best candidate to work with.

It is important to look at the composition of the photo to determine your likelihood of success. When the foreground is cluttered with objects that cover portions of the subject, such as another person between the subject and camera, you need to evaluate whether or not you can include the foreground with the subject, if the foreground can be cloned out entirely, or if the picture is even worth the effort.

The fence would be very difficult to include with the effect, so cloning it out completely might be the best option for our purposes.

PREPARING THE PHOTO
FOR ANIMATION

Content on DVD

Open **Chapter 25 >> Pool Side** on the DVD. This is a photo taken in Tucson, Arizona. The area around our model's head and arms is all water, and will be easy enough to clone. Her hands are resting on the edge of the stones, so we'll make that a part of our foreground too. Normally, we would begin by doing our normal color correction, but this image is already optimized so we'll start by hitting **Ctrl J [Command J]** to make a copy of the background layer. Switch off the visibility of the background layer in the Layers palette and click the copy layer icon. Double-click the new layer's name and enter the new name of "foreground". Choose the Magic Lasso tool, **L**, and use it to draw a selection around the model and stone. We selected this particular photo for this exercise because there are nice clean lines to trace around for an easy mask. You may need to use the QuickMask, **Q**, to finish the bottom edge. (See Chapter 13 for more on the QuickMask.) Keep in mind that you can use any masking technique that you're comfortable with. Once you have your basic outline finished, click the Add Layer Mask icon at the bottom of the Layers palette and you should have a good starter mask. Use the same technique to select the water behind the arms and use a brush to mask it out.

When the foreground layer is done, turn off its visibility and turn the background on again. We now need to clone out our subject and rocks. Use the Clone Stamper tool, **S**, to take as much of her and the stone out of the picture as you can. (Refer to the section in Chapter 18 about Cloning to Extending an Image.) It's not necessary to remove the foreground completely – just enough to give us room to move them around later. Save this as a PSD file on your hard drive as Pool Side.PSD.

The water in this image is easily cloned over the foreground to make a new solid background of water.

ANIMATION

Fundamentals

After the foreground and background have been separated and prepared for animation, it's best to bring it into a bona fide compositing application such as After Effects, Combustion, or Commotion. However, basic animation can be achieved with most mid-to-high end video editing applications including Premiere Pro, Final Cut Pro, and Avid Xpress Pro/DV. Anytime you can bring a PSD file into a layers-aware application, you will save yourself a little bit of busy work. The figure below shows how Avid Xpress Pro prompts a user to indicate how a layered PSD file is to be handled, much the same way as After Effects offers different options. Both Avid and After Effects can create a sequence using the separated foreground and background on their own independent layers in exactly the same position as the original Photoshop document.

Many video editing applications and compositing programs allow you to import a layered Photoshop file as a preassembled sequence or timeline, retaining the same layer names and hierarchy.

Jun Diaz went into *The Kid Stays In The Picture* with a very clear strategy and philosophy about how they were going to communicate the story using animation. The key fundamental behind all of their special effects shots was to suggest motion and action, not to recreate it. One scene was a still of Evans in a car with an animated background slowly moving through the car window, suggesting that the car was in motion. Another series of stills were of Evans and a woman walking down a parking lot, with very subtle movements to suggest the direction in which they were walking. This demonstrated the power of the "less is more" belief. If Diaz and his team had tried to more closely imitate reality, the documentary would have taken on a similar aesthetic to *South Park*, the animated cartoon on Comedy Central.

After Effects 5.0 and Higher

Again, basic animation can be accomplished just fine in a program such as Final Cut Pro, Edition, Premiere, Vegas Video, or Avid, but to really polish this effect, we'll finish it in After Effects. Import the Pool Side file from your hard drive into After Effects as a composition. We're not going to work with the composition, but it's the fastest way to bring in all the layers at once. In the Project window, click the New Comp icon and choose a video standard for the aspect ratio and pixel aspect ratio. Twirl open the Pool Side folder in the Project window and **Shift Click** both layers. When they're both highlighted, drag and drop them both in the timeline making sure that the foreground layer is on top. Hit **S** and bring the scale down until the edges of the images are around 10% outside of the canvas. Both layers should update together as long as they are both highlighted.

We want to leave room outside of the viewable area to account for camera movement in future steps.

As long as you have access to After Effect 5.0 or higher, you can create lights and cameras. Before we bring in a camera, select the foreground layer, **Number Pad 1**, and hit **P** to bring up the position track. Click the 3D checkbox in the Switches column for both layers, and drag the Z position for the foreground left to around −60. This will bring it forward, away from the background slightly. You might want to experiment by putting a greater distance between the foreground and background as a way to give a greater sense of depth in the animation. You may also want to nudge the foreground up slightly to get it closer to its original placement from your perspective. If necessary, change the scale of the foreground or background to compensate for the difference in appearance. Go to **Layer >> New >> Camera** and select a default 50 mm, then hit OK.

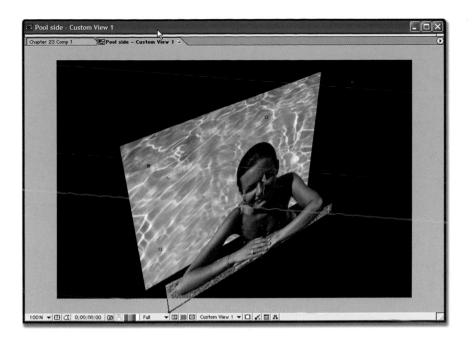

Ever since version 5.0, After Effects allows you to work in 3D space.

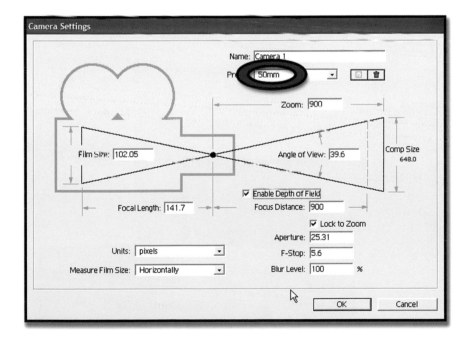

The camera settings are surprisingly sophisticated and comprehensive. Choose the 50 mm preset to keep barrel distortion or cropping to a minimum.

In the timeline, twirl down the camera's transform settings and click the Point of Interest and Position stop watches. Drag the two keyframes you just created to about 1:00 (1 second), **Right Click [Command Click]** on them, and choose **Keyframe Assistant >> Easy Ease.** This will soften the starting and stopping of the motion we're going to put into the camera.

Set keyframes for all of the camera's attributes to allow for intuitive animation.

Bring the Current Time Indicator to 5:00 in the timeline. Hit **C** for the Track Z Camera Tool in the floating Tool palette. If you hit **C** two more times, you will cycle through the Track XY Camera Tool and Orbit Camera Tool. Use a combination of these three tools to intuitively create movement for your camera by clicking and dragging inside the Comp window. A new set of keyframes will automatically be generated at the 5:00 mark, and will also have the Easy Ease curve applied to them.

To see a preview of your work thus far, hit **Number Pad 0**. If this is your first time experimenting with 3D camera moves, be careful. You may tend to over-do your moves because it's really quite fun. Exercise discretion – and remember that "less is more" should be your mantra. Exaggerated animation will scream at the viewer, but subtle animation will intrigue them and invite them into the world you create.

26
ENHANCED
FREEZE-FRAMES

ny video editing application can create a freeze-frame or a hold frame. When you add Photoshop to your workflow, your freeze-frames can be taken to a higher plane of creativity and impact. Freeze-frames are also known as Hold Frames. Their effect on video content gives the appearance of the video being paused. This is an effective tool for extending a clip for purposes of lengthening a dissolve transition, or to call attention during a voice over or the insertion of text. Recently, there has been a trendy new variation seen commonly on MTV, VH-1, FOX and most effectively on Bravo's 'Queer Eye for the Straight Guy', that is an offspring of freeze-frames and pseudo 3D. Pseudo 3D is discussed in detail in Chapter 25.

*An Enhanced Freeze-Frame plays like a normal freeze-frame at first. The video pauses, and the background wipes into a graphically created background, leaving the subject or person untouched. Some commercials and promos that have used this technique also add text, motion in the background, and a treatment on the subject. This chapter shows you how to make a very loud and fun statement using yet another fresh technique without an industry standard name. Open **Chapter 26 >> Freeze** to see an example of a freeze-frame versus an enhanced freeze-frame.*

Content on DVD

SELECTING THE RIGHT FRAME

Knowing when to freeze the video is a part of the skill of an editor. Staying aware of facial expressions, open and closed eyes, and basic composition are all taken into effect when choosing the frame to freeze/pause on. What makes a frame the "right" frame is also subject to personal preference, but having a method to your madness helps to define your style. Keen editors also try to find a "sweet spot" in the action or motion transpiring on screen. For example, if a freeze-frame were going to be used during a scene where one character punches another character, freezing before or too far after the point of impact would yield less tension than freezing on one or two frames beyond the point of impact.

To find the best candidate for an enhanced freeze-frame requires two added criteria. First, there needs to be as little motion blur as possible in the frame coming from the subject if it's possible. It's fine if the background is moving, such as through a moving car window, but the subject or person needs to be fairly defined – especially if the shot is a close-up. The other added quality that we're looking for is that there are little or no foreground objects to contend with, such as another actor's shoulder covering the intended target, as in frames B and C of the figure on this page.

TREATMENTS

In the previous chapter, the concept of pseudo 3D required a still image. Using an exported frame of video could serve as material for a pseudo 3D animation, but there is a catch. If you use a freeze-frame for your animation, you will see a jump cut, or an awkward transition from the edges around the subject that have been subjected to the Cloning Brush Tool. So, for the concept of an enhanced freeze-frame to work, we need to redefine the background and perhaps redefine the subject.

Open **Chapter 26 >> Enhanced Freeze-Frame** on the DVD. This is a frame of video exported from **Chapter 26 >> Freeze** at the timecode of 00:00:01:19 (1 second, 19 frames). We're going to get this image ready to bring into a video editing application. Start by making a selection around our model. The end result of this effect will be largely impressionistic, not realistic, so the selection doesn't need to be too exacting. The most important trait of the selection that we need is for it to be one to five pixels within the targeted area. Using a combination of the Magic Lasso, **L**, and the QuickMask, **Q**, will probably give a sufficient selection. Don't forget to refer to Chapter 13 for a healthy serving of selection tools.

After making your selection, hit **Ctrl J [Command J]** to copy it to a new layer. Create a new layer, **Ctrl Shift N [Command Shift N]** and place it below the selection layer. Double-click on the name of the new layer and appropriately name it "new foreground". Copy the new foreground layer and name it "old foreground". Create a new layer for a new background. Move this layer below the two foreground layers. (Chapter 20 is all about creating backgrounds if you want other ideas for making custom backgrounds.) For this example, we're going to fill the new layer with the background color, **Ctrl Delete [Command Delete]** and name it "new background". Go to **Window >> Styles** and access the arrow menu on the top right of the Styles palette to open the Buttons presets. Feel free to experiment with any style or background you like, but in the book, we'll be using the Abstract Fire style from the

In this clip, there are several candidates for a freeze-frame. A is too early. B and C occur very close to the point of impact but cover the actress's face. D holds on to much of the scene's energy and ends in a very dramatic stance with muscles flexed. E is too late, and has lost too much of the energy of the impact.

Content on DVD

The Styles palette can give you an instant background with a single click.

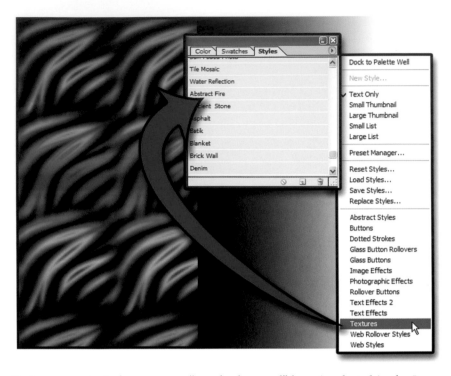

Textures presets. As long as your "new background" layer is selected in the Layers palette, all you need to do is click a style in the Styles palette to see an instant change.

Switch off the "old foreground" layer and select the "new foreground" layer. Go to **Filters** >> **Artistic** >> **Cutout** and enter the values from the following table:

Cutout Settings	
Number of Levels	4
Edge Simplicity	2
Edge Fidelity	1

While you're in the Filter Gallery, you can click the New Effect Filter icon and add a second filter to bring out another level of detail such as Artistic >> Plastic Wrap. Try adding it beneath the Cutout filter with these settings:

Plastic Wrap Settings	
Highlight Strength	15
Detail	9
Smoothness	7

There is an endless combination of treatments you could choose to apply, and this is only one suggestion.

As long as your video editing application of choice is capable of working with a layered Photoshop file, you're done. If not, you need to save each layer as a separate file with their own alpha channel. If you fit the latter description, Photoshop CS comes with a great new feature. Go to **File** >> **Scripts** >> **Export Layers To Files**

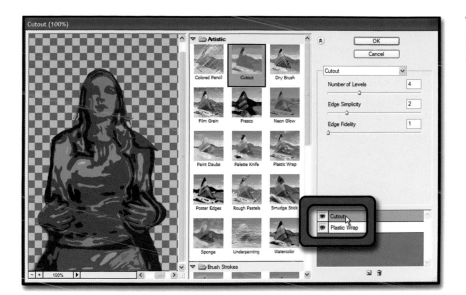

The order of the filters can drastically affect the outcome of the image.

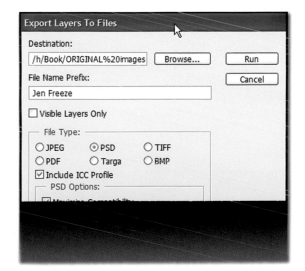

If your video editing application doesn't support the importing of a multi-layered Photoshop document, you can run a script to save each layer as it's own file. The resulting files will have the same dimensions, positioning, and their own alpha channels where applicable.

and select a folder destination and file format you want to use, then click Run. A few seconds later, Photoshop will tell you that everything exported fine.

FINISHING IN THE EDIT SUITE

I'll be using Avid Xpress Pro to finish this effect because when it imports a Photoshop file it can bring the layers in as a layered sequence. I already have a sequence built with the original clip, and the timeline marker is placed at TC 00:00:01:19 – the same frame that we exported for the exercise. Next, the Photoshop sequence needs to be loaded in the Source Monitor and splice-edited into the original clip for a duration of 3 seconds.

The layered Photoshop sequence can be splice-edited into the timeline at the same point of the original exported frame.

Splice the Photoshop layered sequence into the timeline at 01:19 in the clip. Ten frames into the enhanced freeze-frame is a good place to cut the top graphic, which is the New Foreground. The timeline should look something like the figure below. Set the New Foreground layer to fade in for six frames, and to fade out four frames. Fade the New Background in for 10 frames, and fade out for four frames. Starting right after the new foreground layer fades in, cut the Old Foreground clip. From that point create keyframes to animate the new foreground to scale up to 120% and move slightly to the right, making room for a text layer to be placed. The starting and ending keyframes should always remain the same. Create a keyframe in the effect editor 10 frames or so after it fades in to scale up to 120%.

After the Fade command, you only need to add one keyframe for the animation.

This is how Avid brings in the Photoshop document. The layers are in the same order as they were in Photoshop, and are a cinch to edit into the timeline.

Add whatever text you like and animate it in a complementary fashion to coincide with your enhanced freeze-frame.

27
FUN WITH
FILMSTRIPS

A Filmstrip (.flm) file can be generated from a video clip to be laid out like a strip of celluloid with timecode and frame number listed in Photoshop for a host of different uses.

*F*or years, Adobe has incorporated a rare and interesting digital format to be used between a few of their applications called the filmstrip. When this chapter refers to a "filmstrip", there is no celluloid involved beyond a metaphor. However, when a filmstrip is opened in Photoshop, it takes on the appearance of celluloid. This type of file is really a series of video frames laid out sequentially and numbered at the bottom of each frame as shown in the figure above. To generate a filmstrip, you need Adobe Premiere or After Effects. As long as you are able to create a filmstrip file, there are some very creative ways to take advantage of this unique format.

FILM GRAIN, HAIR, AND SCRATCHES

A very common treatment applied to video footage is film grain, hair, and scratches. Found in independent films, commercials, and music videos, an added sense of age, grit, and tension can be created with the use of filmstrips. There are plug-ins that can create this effect, but they can cost as much as Photoshop and may still require the professional version of After Effects. The technique covered in this section only requires the standard version of After Effects, Elastic Gasket for Avid, or any other video editing application that supports different transfer modes. Elastic Gasket is an AVX plug-in for Avid that allows use of After Effects plug-ins from within Avid.

A 1-second portion of NTSC DV video exported as a filmstrip file is just over 40 MB in size. Therefore, to create large filmstrips longer than 10 seconds may be a bit too bulky for most systems to work with. Even if you have hundreds of gigabytes allocated for your primary and secondary scratch disks, applying the simplest adjustment may take several minutes to update if the file's size is very large. This exercise is good for getting acquainted with filmstrips because we're only going to use a 1-second clip.

Using After Effects or Premiere, build a timeline with one second of white. Export the clip as a filmstrip. For example, in After Effects, you would build the 1-second timeline with a solid white layer and render the movie, **Ctrl M [Command M]**, with the same output as your intended project specifications (PAL or NTSC). If you don't have any of the programs mentioned, open **Chapter 27 >> Filmstrip Grain** on the DVD to follow along. When you have your filmstrip open in Photoshop, the Navigator palette, **Window >> Navigator**, and the temporary Hand Tool, **Hold Down Space Bar**, as well as the window resizing shortcuts (see Chapter 9), become increasingly vital in working with our file.

Content on DVD

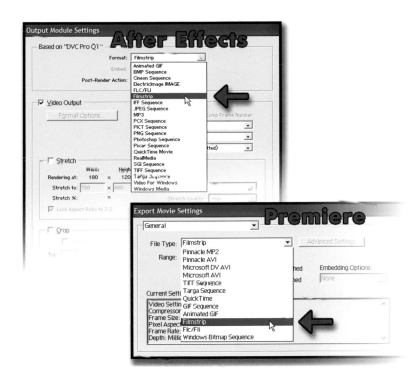

After Effects or Premiere are needed to generate a filmstrip file.

We want to stay aware of the sluggish performance that can characterize film-strip files, so we'll use a workaround to trick Photoshop into thinking that we have a normal-sized file. Use the Marquee Tool, **M**, to draw a selection around just one frame then go to **Filter >> Texture >> Grain** and enter the following settings:

GRAIN	
Intensity	75
Contrast	51
Grain Type	Regular

Hit OK when you're done. Then undo it, **Ctrl Z [Command Z]**, deselect your marquee, **Ctrl D [Command D]**, and apply the same filter to the whole filmstrip, **Ctrl F [Command F]**. Hit **Ctrl Shift U [Command Shift U]** to desaturate the grain.

The final touch we'll add to this file is a stray piece of hair. Select the Brush Tool, **B**, and make it about 5 pixels in diameter with black as the foreground color, **D**. Size the filmstrip so it fits on your desktop, **Ctrl Zero [Command Zero]**. Simply draw a line from the top to the bottom of the filmstrip. Don't try and make it a perfectly straight line either. A hair caught in a camera's gate would have a very manic motion to it, so putting a little shake in your stroke will help fill out the effect. When you're done, save the filmstrip to your hard drive.

The most flexible way to work with this filmstrip will be in After Effects. After you import it into the Project window, interpret the footage, **Ctrl F [Command F]** to loop it however many times you need to in order to cover your timeline and hit OK.

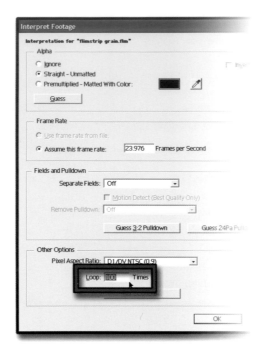

Place the filmstrip on the top layer of your timeline and go to **Layer** >> **Blending Mode** >> **Multiply**. Hit **Number Pad Zero** to see a RAM preview of your effect.

LIGHT SABERS

In 1977, *Star Wars* rocked the movie-going public with visuals we had never seen before. Although the look has since been refined, the original light saber effect was achieved by production artists painting the color of the weapon over the actual celluloid. For those of us in video, we certainly cannot paint directly onto the mylar in the cassette, but we can paint directly onto a Photoshop filmstrip. Not everyone is a *Star Wars* geek like us, but this is an excellent exercise to go through for achieving other goals such as rotoscoping. There are many variations of this effect being done by hobbyists and professionals alike, but the steps outlined in this section reflect the most direct and simplified path toward getting the look we want.

Open **Chapter 27 >> Light Saber.flm** on the DVD. This a raw footage, 3-second clip taken from *The F-Files: Fight The Urge*. It will give you practice at tracing over a moving image. Create a new layer, **Ctrl Shift N [Command Shift N]** and hit OK. Activate the Brush Tool, **B**, and set the foreground color to white. Make sure that the brush is set for 1% spacing, 20 to 40 pixels in diameter, normal blending mode, 100% opacity, and 100% flow. We need to draw all the strokes for one saber and repeat the process for the other two sabers on yet another two layers. Starting from the first frame, draw a straight line by clicking once over the tip of the blade then **Shift Click** at the base just above the handle. If you have enough screen space, work at 100–200% scale to help keep your strokes consistently placed over the blades. If you get impatient and lazy, the blade will appear to jitter around more than you probably want it to. Also, be careful not to paint beyond the borders of each frame as it will result in unwanted artifacts when played back.

Paint all 60 frames if you have the time. When you're done, go to **Filter >> Blur >> Gaussian Blur** and give it about 2.5 pixels worth of blur. Click **Add a Layer Style** at the bottom of the Layers palette and choose **Outer Glow**. Change the color to a shade of red (208, 55, 55, works well). Bring the size up to 28 pixels and hit OK. You should have a good idea of what it should look like. Repeat these steps

Content on DVD

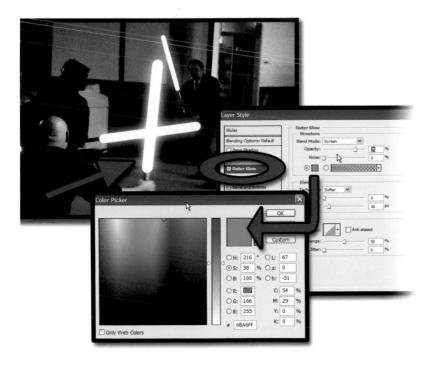

The secret to making the light sabers look white-hot is to use white instead of a color. The different colors are only suggested by the outer glows.

for the second saber on its own layer, but this time, set the outer glow color to blue (107, 166, 255,). In the figure above, we also used a third color, green for the final blade (108, 234, 43).

As an option, you can create another layer for a big blast of light when the sabers connect. Find the frame they hit, and paint a bright spot where they meet using a large soft-edged brush with a bright white for the color.

Add a white brush dab. Click once over each point of contact with a soft-edged, 100-pixel brush. When played back as video, it will show up as a pop from those hot weapons!

If we were to save and import the filmstrip into After Effects or Premiere at this point, we would lose the outer glows because they do not know how to interpret them. Perhaps someday Adobe will make Layer Styles uniform across their Digital Video Suite applications. In the meantime, we need to go to **Layer >> Flatten Image** and save the file to your hard drive. If you plan on compositing the colored blades separately from the underlining video, create a new layer and fill it with black, **Layer >> New Fill Layer >> Solid Color** and choose black. Place the black layer below the light saber layers but above the background layer. When you've finished, flatten the image. Save the file to your hard drive and it's ready to be imported into your video editing application of choice. If your application does not support filmstrips, you can bring it back into After Effects and render it out to an AVI or Quick Time file.

SEQUENTIAL IMAGES

Not every editor uses Premiere, and not every editor has access to After Effects. However, we don't know of a single video editing application that cannot generate a set of sequential images. Whatever format your video editing application supports – PICT, JPEG, PSD, TARGA, etc. – you know that Photoshop can work with it perfectly. With that understanding, any treatment that we can apply to a photograph can be turned into an action and applied to thousands of photographs automatically and played back as video. (See Chapter 9 for more on actions.)

Here's a bonus project. It's a less organic treatment found on the ground-breaking music video *Take On Me,* by A-Ha. If you were living under a rock in the mid-1980s or just not yet alive, the concept for *Take On Me* was to tell a fantasy love story between a lonely woman and a newspaper black-and-white cartoon character. All of the footage was shoot on film, but was later traced by pencil sketchers for any scenes that took place within the comic strip. This is arguably one of the greatest music videos ever made. To give a nod to the makers of that video, we're going to recreate a similar effect, in about 15 minutes.

From your video editing application, export about 10 seconds of video as a Photoshop sequence. If your application doesn't support a Photoshop sequence, any image sequence is fine. It's important that you create a new folder for these files you're about to build and keep nothing but this series of images in the folder.

Most video editing applications give you the flexibility of exporting video as a series of still images with a numerical order applied to them. Image taken from 'Come to the Light' by The Licks.

Open one of the images you just created. If you don't have any video footage to work with, you can open **Chapter 27 >> Sequential Images >> The Licks001** for the time being. Click **Create New Action** on the bottom of the Actions palette, **Window >> Actions**. Name this new action "pencil sketch", and hit OK. We're going to build a pencil sketching action in six moves.

Content on DVD

Custom Pencil Sketch Action		
	Step	Value
	Desaturate -	
1.	**Ctrl [Command] Shift U**	Automatic
2.	Layer Via Copy -**Ctrl [Command] J**	Automatic
3.	Invert top layer -**Ctrl [Command] I**	Automatic
4.	Set top layer to Color Dodge - **Alt [Option] Shift D**	Automatic
5.	Gaussian Blur top layer - **Filter >> Blur >> Gaussian Blur**	14 pixels *You may need to enter a different value depending on the image.
6.	Flatten Image -**Layer >> Flatten Image**	Automatic

Be sure to hit Stop in the Actions palette when you finish. Close the image, but do not save it because you don't want to run the same action on it twice. We just borrowed the file to build the action. The Gaussian Blur settings should be the only variable you might need to change on an individual basis concerning the contrast of a particular image and personal taste.

Go to **File >> Automate >> Batch,** and your "pencil sketch" action should be selected to play. Choose the folder you saved your images in and have Photoshop save and close the file when finished. If you didn't have your own video footage to work with, select **Chapter 27 >> Sequential Images** from the DVD and have Photoshop save them to a new folder on your hard drive. Hit OK in the Batch

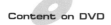
Content on DVD

Finish off the effect by changing the frame rate without affecting the duration of the clip.

window and grab yourself a cup of coffee while Photoshop takes over for a few minutes.

Once the files are finished and they've been imported back into your video editing application, the final touch we'll put on this is to give the illusion of a different frame rate. In Avid, create a motion effect with 100% duration and strobe every three frames. If After Effects is your weapon of choice, apply **Effect >> Time >> Posterize Time** with a frame rate of **12**.

This brings Section 5 – Creative Projects – to a close. We hope you've enjoyed them. They came from years of hard-won experience and experimenting. But the creative projects in this book only scratch the surface of what's out there. From here, you can create your own solutions to your own unique challenges and projects. It's been said that if you give someone a fish, you give him or her a meal, but if you teach them how to fish, they will never go hungry.

Happy fishing!!

SECTION VI
FINAL TIPS

28
TROUBLESHOOTING PHOTOSHOP

*P*hotoshop is a very solid application, and this chapter is here as an emergency

toolbox to keep your system running. With so many users on different systems, there

are bound to be problems.

FREQUENT ERRORS

These are some of the errors most often encountered:

- ❖ Application Error
- ❖ Application has quit because of illegal operand
- ❖ Illegal Instruction
- ❖ Photoshop caused a General Protection Fault in module [filename].
- ❖ Photoshop caused an Invalid Page Fault in module [filename]
- ❖ Segment load failure in [filename]
- ❖ The application 'unknown' has unexpectedly quit
- ❖ This program has performed an illegal operation and will be shut down. If the problem persists, contact the program vendor

❖ Type 1, Type 3, Type 11, Type 28

❖ Unable to initialize Photoshop because of a program error

❖ Unhandled exception detected. Application will be terminated.

❖ Unrecognized Handle Error

❖ Windows encountered a handling violation, no entry point found

There is not just one solution for each individual error, but this chapter helps you to troubleshoot and tune up your system: solving crashes, avoiding freezes, or improving a slow-performing system. Consistently occurring problems can usually be solved quite quickly. Sporadic or random occurring problems, usually take more time and effort to resolve. In both cases, the easy-to-understand steps below will help you narrow the possible causes.

RESET YOUR PREFERENCES

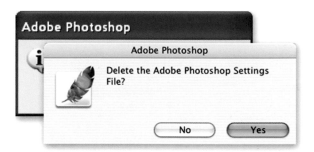

The most common resolution to Photoshop problems is deleting the settings files or preferences. Photoshop stores the location of windows in the preferences, so occasionally a window might appear off the screen and you cannot see it. Suppose you have a dual monitor set-up and you keep palettes on the second monitor. If the monitor gets disconnected, than Photoshop might still want to display them on the second monitor.

If Photoshop crashes after opening files, reset the prefs. Someone may have changed your scratch disk space or color management settings. There was a big problem with Colorsync 3.01 that would crash Photoshop if the file was embedded with a default CMYK profile.

Whenever Photoshop acts differently than your original install, reset the prefs. Nothing important gets lost, except what you changed about the application since it was first installed. To reset your prefs, boot Photoshop and immediately hold down **Shift Ctrl Alt [Shift Option Command]**, and a window will prompt you whether to delete your prefs.

HARD DRIVE MAINTENANCE

Should your hard drive be damaged or near capacity, Photoshop will not function properly. People are surprised when I show them their drive was full or their cache location was set to the wrong drive. The cache is hard drive space Photoshop processes that are stored in the background. A good estimate of about five times your file size, is what Photoshop reserves for storing data such as copies of your file for the undo command to work. Deleting or archiving some files can quickly fix the problem.

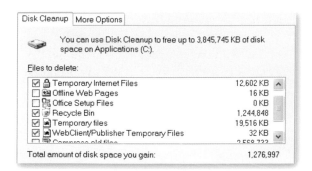

On the PC you can right click on your drive >> Choose Properties >> Disk Cleanup, to quickly free up some space. A similar problem occurs when there is a corrupt sector on the hard disk that needs to be repaired. Photoshop uses blank hard disk space for virtual memory, and when it runs into that bad part of the disk your application can crash when opening a file.

In Photoshop and video editing, a lot of data is written to your drive. Problems with your drive can cause Photoshop to not boot, or to freeze during the opening of files. Common problems occur with Master Directory Blocks, Volume Information blocks, cross links, and misallocated free space. Luckily there are utilities that fix most of those problems, except the dreaded leaf node errors. Mac users have a free utility in Application >> Utilities >> Hard Disk Utility. PC users can right click on a drive >> Properties >> Tools Tab >> Error Checking. The PC error checker is not as thorough as the free Mac Disk Utility, but the PC can additionally run Checkdisk by choosing Start >> Run >> CHKDSK C:/F. You can change the letter C to whichever drive you would like to check. The/F will fix the errors rather than just scan for them. The Mac Disk Utility overall fixes more problems, but the PC is pretty good at avoiding them in the first place.

Norton has utilities for either the Mac or PC platform. On the PC you should run both the Norton Disk Doctor and Norton WinDoctor. On the Mac you only need to run Norton Disk Doctor. The Norton WinDoctor is the important one to run more often. If you have major or severe errors running WinDoctor or Mac Disk Doctor, run them again until they run clean. A machine with major or severe errors is a time bomb which will eventually lose data. One bad thing about Norton for either platform is the extra installations that do not work as well. On the PC, disable the Protected Recycle Bin, by right clicking Trash >> Properties >> Norton Protection >> Disable. On the Mac disable Filesaver, by choosing it in the utilities and turn it to Off. A few people might disagree with us here, but we checked on which background processes crashed and froze machines, and they were both guilty.

Run Norton Speedisk to defragment your drive so the data is organized better. Data is read and written to a drive in similar manner to a record player needle. Not only does defragmenting make the needle jump around less, but the process also occasionally has found disk drive problems. The easiest way to keep your disk drive defragmented is by installing a drive for which the only purpose is to be used as a cache. Set the Photoshop preference for scratch disk to use this empty drive. Keep your applications and operating system on another drive, and your working project files on a third. This organization allows each of the three drives to work on its own item, and the temporary processes are written to the cache drive. When all the applications are closed down, the cache drive is empty, and therefore automatically defragmented.

FLUSH CACHE

If you ever try to save a document or run a filter and get an error saying there is not enough memory to save, purge your cache by choosing Edit >> Purge >> All. In video, your files are not as large so this may not help as much, unless you have high-resolution data in the clipboard or are working on a photo montage.

FILE BROWSER

If your machine is running slowly, and you have the photoshop file browser up, then close it. Double-click on an image in the file browser, it will open the image up. In the background though, thumbnails will be generating using the file browser. This is great when you need to continue browsing for more images, but close the file browser when done. If your computer freezes in the file browser, every time you enter a certain folder, purge the cache for the file browser. Choose File Browser >> File >> Purge Entire Cache.

FONTS

Often, a font can be damaged and can cause Photoshop to crash, or that font does not appear in the list of available type. Do a Find File for "adobefnt.lst" and delete the files. These files regenerate themselves and you will not do anything to harm your system, by removing them.

You might have loaded two of the same fonts, with different names, or perhaps the sector of the disk went bad where the font is stored. For this reason you want to close any fonts you are not using and see if this resolves your Photoshop problem.

NETWORKS, APPLICATIONS, PLUG-INS, AND PRINTER

If Photoshop is crashing or running slowly, try disconnecting from any network and rebooting Photoshop. The best way to fix any Photoshop problem is to find the source. Disconnecting your machine from the network eliminates more variables. Solving a technical problem many times is a process of elimination. Reducing the variables will help to solve the equation, and eliminate wrong guesses, thus saving you time. Perhaps your cache was set to a network drive, or a network font was loaded, or maybe you are running Photoshop from a server rather than your hard disk, as you thought.

Run Photoshop while there are no applications are running, as it might conflict, or you may be running in the last section of available RAM which overheats and becomes corrupted. Disable any third party plug-ins.

UPDATE YOUR OPERATING SYSTEM

On the PC, go to **www.windowsupdate.com**, and follow the prompts to update your windows operating system (OS). On Mac OS X choose the system preference called Software Update, and click Update Now. You can set check for updates to weekly, but on a laptop, turn it off. The Photoshop team at Adobe does a great job of releasing software that is compatible, but check their site for update patches, especially soon after your OS had an update. You can also go to **www.versiontracker.com** to search for updates to your plug-ins, and font management utility.

PRINTING

When documents do not print, make a new blank document, draw a simple shape such as a square, and test to see if that prints. You may have a complex path, corrupted font causing the problem. If the document is still not printing, there is probably nothing wrong with your file, but your printer, printer driver or operating system may be at fault. Reset your printer by toggling the power, then try printing the document again. If you have another machine, try printing the file from there. If the document prints, then go back to the original machine and reboot it. If the document still does not print, then look into your printer driver and preferences. In most system configurations, you can trash your printing driver and preferences and it will generate a new one which is not corrupted. If sending the document has no effect on the LCD or lights on your printer, then you may have a document stuck in background processing. Look into the help for your operating system to see how you can delete a document which is continuously spooling in the background.

RAM AND VIDEO CARD

Go to the website of your vendor and see if there is an update for your video card driver, especially if you have just updated your OS recently. Alternately, put a different card in your machine. Video card problems are mostly related to Photoshop not drawing all the pixels when changing views, but they can cause freezes or crashes when booting applications.

Computers do not like dust on the inside as it conducts static electricity. Shut down your computer, unplug it from the electricity supply, and discharge any static electricity from your body by touching something large and metal such as the power supply. Use a can of compressed air on the ram, processor, video card and cooling fan. You should hear a funny 'zip' sound when cleaning the fan as the blades will spin fast.

RAM is a more difficult one to troubleshoot, and it does not go bad often. The occasions we found a bad RAM chip, was after some recent office construction work when the cooling fan had sucked in all the dust and caused the chips to over-heat and fail, or after a lightning strike. We have also found a few machines to be running PC100 RAM when they should have had PC133, which causes sporadic crashes. Most RAM chips come with a little label nowadays, but you can add a really small one to help you remember what you put into your machine when upgrading. Use a utility to check your RAM check such as Micromat Techtool for the Mac. If you do not have a RAM checking utility, you will have to remove RAM chips individually, until you find which one is not working by a process of elimination. Finally, run an Apple system profiler or similar PC hardware profiler to check that all the RAM is recognized properly.

VIRUS AND POP-UPS

The PC has many more viruses than the Mac. Symantec makes Norton Anti Virus. Both Mac and PC versions are very good, and the virus definitions are updated regularly. On both platforms there is a live update, which you should run and manually check when your virus definitions were last updated. We set ours to check for updated definitions twice a week at night.

If you are on the Windows operating system connected to the internet, you will eventually find a page or e-mail that will attempt to hack into your registry. Most times, they will try to change your web browser to add a toolbar and pop-ups. They often monitor what sites you are surfing, or try to steal the software registration information on your computer. Get rid of registry hacks, cookies by using Lavasoft's Ad Aware and Spybot. Both get rid of items that monitor your computer and slow it down, and eat up drive space. These are available at:

http://spybot-spyware.com/
http://www.lavasoftusa.com/

MAC OS X

Log in as root or another user. If Photoshop works fine, than you know that you do not have to reinstall, and have narrowed down your possibilities. In that case you can delete the File Username >> Library >> Preferences >> Adobe Photoshop CS Settings. You also can check the permissions set on Photoshop. Select the Photoshop application and choose Command I to see the information. Twirl down ownership and Permissions, and you should have read and write access.

Mac OS X is a great OS, but the extra added security layers of UNIX can become corrupted, or set wrong after installing. If your application begins to boot but then quits, run the repair disk permissions from the disk utility. If you get any message such as a default file is missing or damaged, that means part of your installed Photoshop is damaged. You can Ctrl click on your application and choose >> Show Package Contents. This will reveal the individual package components of Photoshop on the Mac. You should replace the files from a back-up, or reinstall Photoshop.

PC WINDOWS

Before installing software, make system restore points. You can find this under Start >> All Programs >> Accessories >> System Tools >> System Restore. If you create a restore point when the system is working, you can return to that if any new software conflicts. System restore automatically makes crucial restore points, but the ones you make manually seem to work better.

If your application background has a different color than gray, then the problem might not in Photoshop, but your Control Panel >> Display >> Appearance tab >> Advanced >> Item: Application Background. Check to see if any other applications have the bad background color.

GET FREE HELP ONLINE

The Creative COW (Community of the World) website is staffed by some of the world's leading experts in digital video. Your posts are answered by forum leaders, and you also have the knowledge base of many other experts visiting the forums. When posting on these forums you get better response with clear, but concise, posts. Do provide enough details about the symptoms you encounter though, and fill out the user profile so that readers of your post know what system you are using. If you have questions about this book, you can post there also as the authors frequently visit the COW, to stay up to date:

www.creativecow.net.

Adobe also has forums, and a searchable database can help you solve many problems: **www.adobe.com/support/forums/main.html.**

Once you learn to troubleshoot Photoshop, you can eventually solve almost any problem, either on your own or with a little help from the massive Photoshop community. We hope that this chapter has taught you how to resolve some problems yourself, and that a lot of machines will be running better as a result of the information provided in this book.

29

EXTENDING PHOTOSHOP

*A*s much as Photoshop has to offer, there are hundreds of ways to increase the power, speed, creativity, and functionality of the application. Plug-ins are developed by independent parties to expand the capabilities of Photoshop. Go to adobe.com/plugins to see the most comprehensive listing of plug-ins.

To see what others are contributing to the Photoshop community, Adobe devotes a large portion of its website to serve as a creative hub for their customers to share everything from tutorials, templates and actions to brushes, patterns and styles.

PLUG-INS

Photoshop is an enormous program. On its 8th version, it has been used, tested, and refined by thousands of talented professionals working in dozens of different disciplines. Yet Photoshop still doesn't meet everyone's needs, or satisfy everyone's creative palette. However, Photoshop has always been one of the most collaborative application to work with third-party developers. An army of artists and programmers working for many different companies make a career out of designing utility

applications that can sit inside of Photoshop and offer you tools to automate difficult tasks and extend your creative arsenal.

A few plug-ins that we've used over the last few years are *Kai's Power Tools, Blade Pro, Eye Candy,* and *Xenofex.* These four plug-ins offer tools to enhance the creative muscle of Photoshop. However, to simply apply one of their filters to an image and call it art is very short-sighted. Using them to complement and support your images is how to get the most out of them.

In a six-year-old version of Kai's Power Tools 5 there is a filter called Blurrr. You might wonder what the relevance would be inside a program like Photoshop that already has eight different blur filters. The answer lies in the sophistication of the interface, level of nuance, and finesse found within the plug-in. If you were building a composite and wanted to simulate a camera's depth of field, the Gaussian Blur filter in Photoshop might work just fine, but the Blurrr filter creates more accurate blurring characteristics associated with lenses, such as ghosting in hard contrast areas and bokeh (blown-out highlights). Photoshop CS has added a great Lens Blur filter to the blur collection, but Kai's Camera Optics settings are easier to work with and give a much faster preview.

A surprisingly useful filter is Xenofex's Television. This gives seven different attributes to adjust for creating distortions associated with a worn-out television tube picture. Putting this kind of filter on an entire image makes little sense. Using the same filter on just a portion of an image within a television monitor, however, could be quite compelling.

Some of the stranger filters offered by third-party developers don't offer any apparent advantages beyond making a bunch of squiggly lines and a lot of noise.

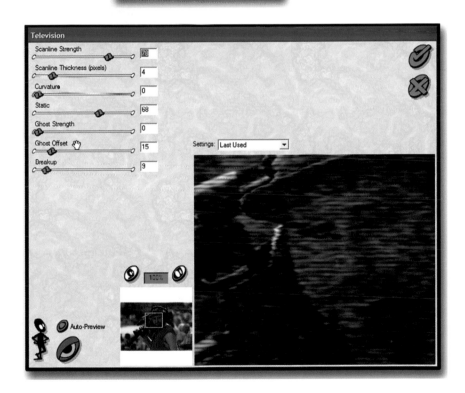

The concept behind these kinds of filters is that they will be used to texturize and blend an image or composite together, rather than to generate instant bubble gum art. Kai's Power Tools 5 has a filter called Frax Flame that does nothing more than generate different patterns and swirls of colors. If you make the noise that this filter creates the focus of an image, you would pass up the real potential of what it can do by simply blending a path for an eye to follow over an image.

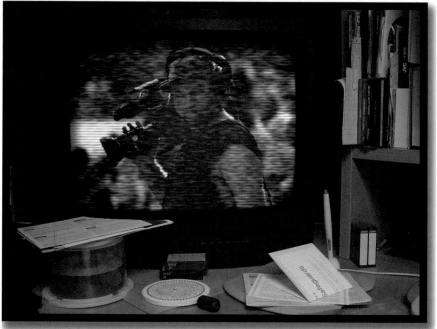

ADOBE STUDIO EXCHANGE

Adobe is a very supportive company to its customers. Beyond offering the usual driver updates and frequently asked questions web pages, Adobe Studio Exchange,

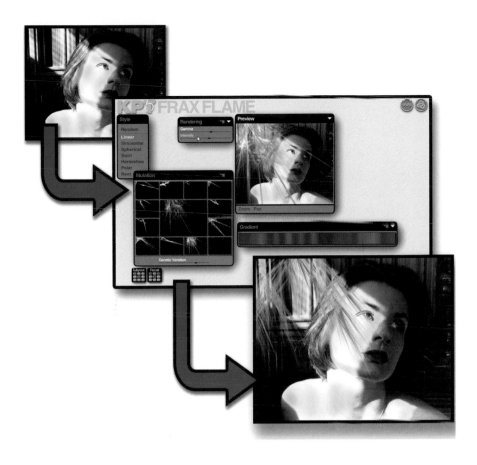

http://share.studio.adobe.com/ is common ground for a community of thousands of Adobe customers.

In the Photoshop section alone, there are categories for Actions, Brushes, Custom Shapes, Displacement Maps, Filters, Gradients, Patterns, Plug-Ins, Scripts, Styles, Templates, and Tutorials. There are literally thousands of submissions to go through. They are all categorized, described, illustrated, and rated on a five-star scale. You can even read posts from people who have downloaded submissions to get a better idea if it would benefit yourself.

Somewhere between the 2000 plus Photoshop actions found in the Studio Exchange is one of my favorites from Adi Carlo, called deelo's Pencil Sketch. The "A-Ha, *Take On Me*" creative project described in Chapter 27 is based on a variation of Adi's action that we downloaded in a split second for free. Thanks Adi – great job!

As video professionals, we are often disappointed by the cynicism and lack of courtesy found in many of the message boards on the web that support video editing applications and camera-related issues. Whenever we find ourselves browsing through 3D and artistically driven portals such as Adobe Studio Exchange, 3D Buzz, and 3D Cafe, we are reminded of what it truly means to be a professional. If a submission is done by an amateur or is less than stellar, people will clearly let them know, but will do so in a way that points them in the right direction and encourages them to bring their skills up to a higher level. Support is

The purpose of this website is to allow users of Adobe products (not just Photoshop) to share their wisdom and custom tools.

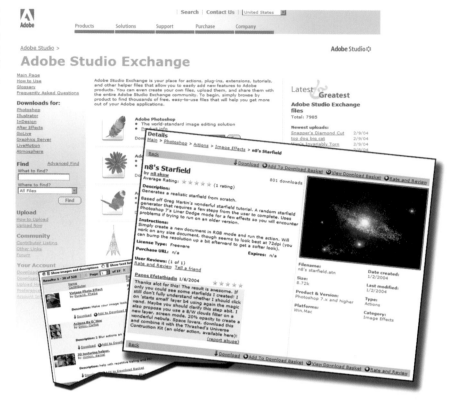

deelo's Pencil Sketch is one of thousands of actions free to be downloaded from Adobe Studio Exchange.

still given by the community. When a submission is found useful by others, there is a remarkable display of gratitude and kudos. It takes very little skill to insult and belittle another person's work, but great artists and great professionals have a way of making others feel great. Free cheers to Adobe for maintaining a hub for facilitating creativity and collaboration, and many regards to the participants of the Adobe Studio Exchange for making it the wonderful resource that it is!

30
ILLUSTRATOR FOR VIDEO

*P*hotoshop is an amazing program and tool for creating artwork for video. The next Adobe program for creating artwork you will want to master is Illustrator. You can bitmap vector artwork created in Adobe Illustrator for video by pasting it into Photoshop, or by using the export command in Illustrator. Since we only have one chapter to write about Illustrator, will try to push your skills into new realms, skipping the basics.

WARPING IMAGES

Photoshop can liquify an image, but for more precise distortion use Adobe Illustrator. The interface in Illustrator is called envelope distort, and it is very similar to the warp text interface in Photoshop. Most people know that it can be used to distort a vector object, but if you embed a placed image you can do this to a bitmapped object. **Open in Illustrator Chapter 30/Michelob_Ultra.psd** and you will give this bottle an hourglass figure. The Open command in Illustrator in this situation creates a new Illustrator file using the same name as the image you open, and embeds the image in the center with crop marks. You will get a prompt as whether to **preserve the layers, choose either option** as there only is one layer.

Content on DVD

You can click on the Links palette and confirm that the image is embedded, because of the icon after the file name. Hit (**V**) to choose the select tool, and then **click on the bottle** to select the image. With the image selected, choose **Object** >> **Envelope Distort** >> **Make with Warp**, and test out the different options by checking the preview box. The squeeze option is close to what we need, but we will cancel and make our own hourglass shape. Choose **Object** >> **Lock** to temporarily lock the image of the bottle so that we do not accidentally select it. Do a **Ctrl Y [Command Y]** to see the outline preview of the object, then hit **choose Object** >> **Crop Area** >> **Release**. This releases the crop marks and gives you a rectangle, exactly the same size as the bounding box of the bottle. We will be using a command of Make with Top Object to distort the image, and it is important to start with a rectangle exactly the same size as the image so your distortion moves will be controlled. If you were to use the rectangle now to make an envelope distort, Illustrator would apply something called the 2/3rd rule to the Bezier handles. This is important to understand, because after we apply the envelope you will want to tweak it if any area is too distorted or needs more distortion. To get no distortion for an area, you want the Bezier handles to both each cover 1/3rd the distance of the line for a total of 2/3rds.

The 2/3 rule of Bezier handles for smooth curves and distortions.

Hit (**L**) and **draw an ellipse for an area to subtract the left hip** of the bottle. **Alt Shift [Option Shift] drag an ellipse copy to the right** over the right hip. Select all to **select the three unlocked object**s, and bring the pathfinder palette to the front. Click on the **pathfinder** palette button of **Alt [Option] Subtract** to subtract the two ellipses from the rectangle. Use the convert anchor point tool to smooth out the corners to get a shape as the red line in the following image.

Choose **Object** >> **Unlock All** to unlock the bottle image, then **Select all** and run **Object** >> **Envelope Distort** >> **Make with Top Object**. Edit the points to get more of the result you desire. This tweaking of points can be a difficult part of project, but reference the 2/3rds rule of Bezier curves and you will get more realistic results.

ADVANCED STROKES

Content on DVD

Open **Chapter 30/Michelob_Ultra2.ai in Illustrator**. The distortion on the bottle looks good, so we set some type with a basic fill and stroke. You can see from the

magnified letter, that the stroke adds thickness to the center of the line. To get the stroke to go outwards do this in the Appearance palette. Hit (**V**) to get the selection tool, watch the Appearance palette, and **select the type**. Hit (**T**) to get the type tool, watch the Appearance palette, and **select the type**. Notice that the Appearance palette changes from type to characters, depending on how you select the object. The Appearance palette is a very powerful tool to master in Illustrator. The important thing to remember is watch the name of the first attribute in the palette. That attribute can be set to characters, type, groups or even an entire layer.

Type looks bad when stroke does not go outwards.

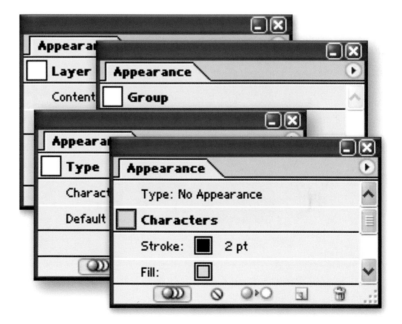

The mighty appearance palette can assign attributes to type in 4 different selections methods.

When selected as characters, you can see a 2-point blue stroke on top of a fill. If you put the fill on top of the stroke, it would stroke outwards 1 point. You can do this but not to an appearance attribute of characters, but type. The best thing to do is to **drag the fill and stoke to the Appearance palette trash can icon.** This sets the stroke and fill to none, similar to if you had chosen Appearance palette >> flyout menu >> clear Appearance. Switch to the **selection**

tool and then from the **Appearance palette flyout menu** >> **Add New Stroke**. This adds both a stroke and a fill, but to the appearance attribute of type not character. Make the **Stroke Dark Blue 4 points**, and the **fill Silver**, using the colors defined in the swatch palette for you. Drag and drop the swatches over the appearance palette attributes to assign colors. It may look as though we are back to where we were before, but if you have never done this before then you will see what you have been missing since Illustrator 9. **Drag the Appearance stroke attribute below the fill attribute**, and this will make your type stroke properly.

When it comes to the Appearance palette, we have only just begun. You will add multiple strokes to the type. Drag the Appearance palette stroke twice onto the grayed out page, to **make two more duplicate strokes**. Then **color the strokes on the bottom of the palette 10 point gold and 14 point dark blue**. The final image shown had a text warp and soft drop shadow applied.

CATERPILLAR

Illustrator makes creating mathematical artwork easy. Open **Chapter 30/caterpillar.ai** in Illustrator and **select the red gradient circle.** You are going to create the caterpillar effect and learn the power of repetition using the transform filter. The transform filter has such a simple looking name and control, that it is underestimated for what it can do. Apply **Effect** >> **Distort & Transform** >> **Transform**. The most powerful part of Transform is that it can make copies, so **input 19 copies, -10 horizontal, -89 vertical and click Preview.** You will have a straight line of 19 gradient circles. We would like the circles to get smaller, so change horizontal and vertical to 80%. Since transform is a live effect, **click OK** to confirm that. Look

Content on DVD

at your **Appearance palette and double-click the Transform attribute**. Change the **rotation to -15, click OK**, and you should have the same shape as in the grayscale caterpillar. With the red circle selected, hit **Ctrl Y [Command Y]** to prove this effect is live and you will only see the outline of two circles. Hit **Ctrl Y [Command Y]** again to go back to preview mode, and with the red circle still selected **click on the fill attribute in the Appearance palette**. This is important, as the next step will not work if you left the Transform attribute selected. Change the **Transparency Palette Mode to lighten**, and you will get interaction between the fills. The simple grayscale caterpillar to the right displays more effectively the visual effect of the gradient balls being squished against another. That is an amazing result of the lighten mode, and you can **edit the Gradient palette** and **drag to remove the three middle colors of the sensual red gradient**. There is so much more you can do, but these are just the building blocks for projects of your own. **Double-click the Transform attribute again, and enable reflect x & y, and change the Rubik's cube to the top left position**. Reflect and Center of Transformation work well together. You can set up a layer this way so everything you draw is reflected, and create a tessellation. It would have been amazing to see what an artist such as M.C. Escher would have done with Illustrator if he was still alive.

SPIROGRAPH 1

Content on DVD

Learning tools to create symmetrical geometry will help you gain illustration skills, and the ability to create and endless amount of patterns. Open **Chapter 30/Spirograph1.ai** in Illustrator and **select the red circle**. Hit **(R)** to change to the rotate tool and **Alt [Option] click on the spot where the two guides intersect**. The rotate window will appear, and we will **input 20 degrees and click Copy**. This will give us one copy rotated 20 degrees from the center of the point that we Alt [Option] clicked. Hit **Ctrl D [Command D] 16 more times**, so that we have a total of 18 circles × 20 degrees for 360 degrees. If we had a fill of none, then we would have simulated a Spirograph, which has dazzled children and adults alike. Instead with all the circles selected bring up your Pathfinder palette and **click on the Pathfinder Exclude button**.

SPIROGRAPH 2

Content on DVD

Open **Chapter 30/Spirograph2.ai** in Illustrator, and we will make a shape follow a spline. The Illustrator file already has a basic circle, along with a basic blend between two dark blue spheres. Both the blue spheres have a transparency mode of hard light, but blending modes do not work between live blends. To get the blue spheres to follow the shape of the black circle, we will use a command called Replace Spline. To make the Replace Spline command available, you need to select a Blend and a Spline. So **Ctrl A [Command A]** to select all and choose the command **Object >> Blend >> Replace Spline**. The spheres are following the shape of the new spline now, but the starting and ending points are not the same???

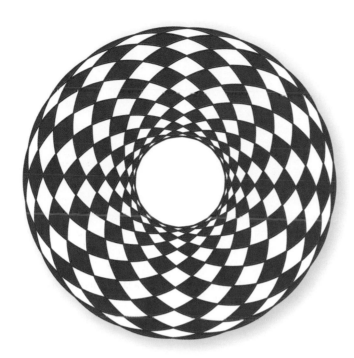

Created using transform again.

To correct this, hit (**c**) and switch to the Scissors tools, and **rub the** Scissors tool **anywhere over the spline**. The Scissors tool cuts the spline and gives us an overlapping end and start point for that vector path. We need more circles, so choose **Object >> Blend Options >> and set it to 28**. The blending mode still does not work, but we can help Illustrator by removing two things, the blend and the group. **Select >> All**, then choose **Object >> Expand**, and then choose **Object >> Ungroup**.

We have a great-looking 30 circles arranged in a circle, but how about having some green circles in the middle? Select all the circles, then choose Object >> Transform Each >> Horizontal & Vertical 40% >> click Copy. This will put a smaller copy of blue spheres on the original spheres. With the circles selected, change the colors of gradients to green, and set transparency mode to normal. The final image was created by selecting all and scaling a copy at 60%. You may have noticed one problem with the green circles, and how they overlap at the point they meet. That was fixed using one of the circles as a transparency mask in the Transparency palette. You cannot do this with a regular mask, as you would lose the stroke. Open **Chapter 30/Spirograph2_Final.ai** to see the final image, and how an extra part was created to fix the overlap of the green circles.

Content on DVD

CORKSCREW SPIRAL

We are going to end this with a simple but useful example for video. Have you ever wanted to animate type along a spiral, but had a hard time drawing one? Illustrator has a spiral tool hidden behind the line tool. You could keep drawing new spirals with the tool and **Alt [Option]** click with each time and try new

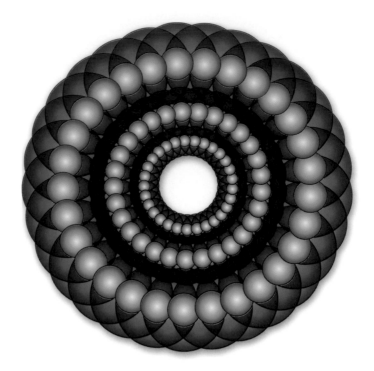

settings until you get it right. The best way to draw a spiral using the live interactive keyboard commands:

Change Decay	Control [Command] Drag
Add or Delete winds	Up or down arrow
Move Spiral	Spacebar

COPYING ILLUSTRATOR PATHS INTO APPLICATIONS

To get a vector path from Illustrator into Photoshop, you need to change **Edit >> Preferences >> File Handling & Clipboard >> Clipboard >> AICB**. You will lose

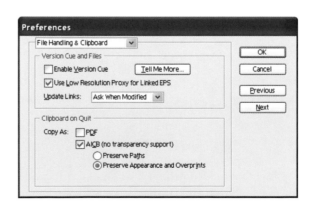

the transparency support of PDF, but you can now paste a vector path into a mask in After Effects, or use it as a path for a lightning strike to follow by pasting in the position attribute for the lightning endpoint.

The interactive examples above are not meant to teach you a single creative technique for using Illustrator in video. They are instead meant to build your toolset to explore the new territories that bring endless possibilities in Illustrator. There are so many more Illustrator for Video techniques to write about, from extruding type, lathing objects, generating wire frames, making graphs, selecting glyphs or even transforming direction handles. Illustrator is a great program, and is very fast when working with vector objects. You can choose between different end caps of strokes, make live blends, or even generate a graph. Those are the things at which Illustrator is better than Photoshop. Learning both programs and using this book will help you to build an arsenal of skills to create almost any graphic that you can imagine.

INDEX